MAKING

AMERICA

CORPORATE

OLIVIER ZUNZ

MAKING AMERICA CORPORATE 1870 - 1920

THE UNIVERSITY OF CHICAGO PRESS
Chicago and London

OLIVIER ZUNZ is professor of history at the University of Virginia. He is the author of *The Changing Face of Inequality: Urbanization, Industrial Development, and Immigrants in Detroit, 1880–1920,* also published by the University of Chicago Press.

THE UNIVERSITY OF CHICAGO PRESS, CHICAGO 60637
THE UNIVERSITY OF CHICAGO PRESS, LTD., LONDON
© 1990 by The University of Chicago
All rights reserved. Published 1990
Printed in the United States of America
99 98 97 96 95 94 93 92 91 90   54321

Library of Congress Cataloging-in-Publication Data

Zunz, Olivier.
    Making America corporate, 1870–1920 / Olivier Zunz.
        p.   cm.
    Includes bibliographical references.
    ISBN 0-226-99459-7 (alk. paper)
    1. Big business—United States—History.   2. Corporations—United
States—History.   I. Title.
HD2785.Z86   1990
338.7′4′097309034—dc20   90-31028
                                                                        CIP

♾The paper used in this publication meets the minimum requirements of the American National Standard for Information Sciences—Permanence of Paper for Printed Library Materials, ANSI Z39.48-1984.

To Christine—with love

CONTENTS

ACKNOWLEDGMENTS

I have accumulated many debts in the eight years that have elapsed since I embarked on this project. I would like to thank the National Endowment for the Humanities, the John Simon Guggenheim Memorial Foundation, the Hagley Museum and Library, and the University of Virginia for fellowships and research funds without which I could not have written this book.

Most of the evidence collected here can be consulted in nine archives and libraries. I wish to express my heartfelt appreciation to the staff of the Alderman Library at the University of Virginia, the Ford Archives, the Ford Industrial Archives, the Hagley Museum and Library, the historical archive of International Harvester Company (now Navistar International Transportation Corp.), the Metropolitan Insurance Company Archives, the Nebraska State Historical Society, the Newberry Library, and the State Historical Society of Wisconsin for their efficient help.

I have benefited from many opportunities to present my work in progress. First at the Ecole des hautes études en sciences sociales in Paris, where I have had the privilege of teaching the American history seminar every May since 1985. I thank Jean Heffer and the members of the seminar for their warm hospitality at the Ecole. I have also presented drafts of sections of this book at the Freie Universität in Berlin, the Mellon Foundation seminar at Brown University, the Chicago Historical Society urban history seminar, the University of Chicago social history workshop, the Center for Theory in the Humanities of the University of Colorado, the Columbia University seminar on the city, the Hagley Museum and Library, the business history seminar at the Harvard University Graduate School of Business Administration, the 1985 International Congress of Historical Sciences in Stuttgart, the Johns Hopkins University, a symposium on the social history of business at the Université de Lyon II, an NEH Summer Seminar for College Teachers I taught at Virginia, a conference on comparative history at Northwestern University, two annual meetings of the Organization of American Historians, the Université de Paris IV–Sorbonne, the committee on New York City of the Social Science Research Council, the Washington Area Economic History Seminar, and the Woodrow Wilson International Center for Scholars.

Roberta Senechal has been an outstanding research assistant and critic during her years of graduate study at Virginia. I am also grateful to Lottie McCauley and the secretarial staff of the history department for their unfailing performance.

Friends, colleagues, and students have been extraordinarily supportive. My greatest debt is to Charles Feigenoff, an accomplished editor who has challenged my reasoning every step of the way. Edward Ayers, Lenard Berlanstein, John K. Brown, Bernard Carlson, Kathleen Conzen, Ran Halévi, William H. Harbaugh, David A. Hounshell, Stephen Innes, Joseph F. Kett, Enno Kraehe, Maurice Kriegel, Kenneth Kusmer, Melvyn Leffler, Glenn Porter, Keith Revell, William B. Taylor, Ronald Walters, François Weil, and Richard Wilson have commented on parts or the entire manuscript. The errors of fact or judgment that remain are clearly mine.

Christine and our teenaged children, Emmanuel and Sophie, have helped me more than they know.

Charlottesville, Virginia
Fall 1989

INTRODUCTION

The growth of corporate power so profoundly and so rapidly transformed late nineteenth-century American society and culture that it aroused anew a characteristic American anxiety: the fear that dubious ethical standards, excessive profits, and rising inequality were threatening national values. Muckrakers and progressive reformers who wrote for a growing middle-class audience first held "robber barons" and then abstract corporate entities responsible for cozening the American public.[1] Small entrepreneurs who scrambled for survival, labor leaders who contended for workers' rights, social workers who doubted cultural homogenization, reformers who sought to regulate big business, scientific-minded observers who championed budget studies and the use of social statistics, all joined in the outburst of commentary and protest provoked by the corporations' unprecedented power to change American life. To the old nineteenth-century dualisms of rich and poor, doomed and saved, they collectively added new dichotomies of bigness and smallness, hierarchy and independence, homogeneity and diversity.

By the middle of the twentieth century, the corporate reorganization of American society was a fait accompli. In 1948, the corporate sector held almost 60 percent of national income-producing wealth; the largest 200 employers in that sector accounted for one of every five private nonagricultural workers.[2] By the 1950s, corporations had become part of the daily life of ordinary Americans, and Americans had grown used to them.[3] From the White House, Dwight Eisenhower, himself an exemplar of the organizational revolution, saw "big business, labor, professions and government officials" working together "in the calmness of a nonpartisan atmosphere."[4] Abundance, that great deflector of conflict, was elected to the pantheon of traits that define national character.[5] And corporate America became inextricably linked with the idea of postwar prosperity.

For those in doubt, the question was no longer—as it had been in the progressive era—what would America become once reshaped by the new corporate structures? It had become, how can one cope with life in a corporate setting? Some powerful voices still pointed to the destructive effects of corporate culture. They expressed old concerns about the immorality of excessive profits and the loss of the producer ethos. But they concentrated on a new source of malaise:

1

the weight of bureaucratic structures and the resulting loss of individual autonomy.

The American public was both entertained and sobered when Arthur Miller's *Death of a Salesman* was staged on Broadway in 1949. Through the voices of his characters, Miller reflected not only on a personal drama between a father and a son but also on the way modern business culture had refashioned middle-class life. Listen to Biff's despair and dreams of freedom and nature: "It's a measly manner of existence. To get on that subway on the hot mornings in summer. To devote your whole life to keeping stock, or making phone calls, or selling or buying. To suffer fifty weeks of the year for the sake of a two-week vacation, when all you really desire is to be outdoors, with your shirt off."[6]

Only two years later, another, this time more direct, critique of corporate capitalism appeared. In 1951, C. Wright Mills, breaking away from both the grand theory and the abstract empiricism that had overtaken the social sciences of his day (but also compounding Tocqueville and Marx in a mixture uniquely his own), enunciated his view of the stifling effect of bureaucracies on American life in his landmark book, *White Collar*. Mills described a set of characteristics, in his own words "more typically 'American' than the frontier character probably ever was." Mills's vision of the cultural and social process underway was highly pessimistic, for he saw social change depriving the American of his most essential attribute, his independence. As he put it, "American history of the last century seems to be a series of mishaps for the independent man." Mills's social criticism reflected his view of a "self-balancing society" where decentralization and fair competition stimulate free individuals to produce. For Mills, good competition could not be merely an "impersonal mechanism regulating the economy of capitalism" but instead "a means of producing free individuals, a testing field for heroes." In the course of the preceding century, however, independence and production (through craftsmanship or entrepreneurship) had given way to alienation and exploitation.

For Mills, salesmanship exemplified the malaise of his time. "In the new society," Mills argued, "selling is a pervasive activity, unlimited in scope and ruthless in its choice of technique and manner." In Mills's view, corporate capitalism, engaged as it was in such activities, created a sick society. "Among white-collar people, the malaise is deep rooted; for the absence of any order of belief has left them morally defenseless as individuals and politically impotent as a group. . . .

Newly created in a harsh time of creation, white-collar man has no culture to lean upon except the contents of a mass society that has shaken him and seeks to manipulate him to its alien ends."[7]

Following Thorstein Veblen's caustic critique of leisure (1899) and his analyses of the growing distance separating "those who worked without profit from those who profited without working,"[8] as well as Robert and Helen Lynd's discovery of a new "culture in which everything hinges on money"[9] in the Muncie, Indiana, of the twenties, Mills's analysis of white-collar workers remains a landmark in American social criticism.

Such criticism is essential in marking the moral dimensions of economic and social problems but, in itself, provides little guidance for the study of motivation and commitment, as Richard Hofstadter, the distinguished historian from Columbia, pointed out to his sociologist colleague. Mills had solicited Hofstadter's advice about how to respond to a critical review. Hofstadter's reply provided no solace:

> My primary *feeling* . . . is that this book is an excessively pro-jective book, in the psychological meaning of the word. . . . You detest white-collar people too much, altogether too much, perhaps because in some intense way you identify with them. There is a lot of human ugliness in the book—which is, I note, caught up in the jacket description of the book as a "merciless portrayal" of a whole class. There are some people and perhaps even some classes in society that may call for merciless treatment, but why be so merciless with all these little people? If their situation is characteristically as bad as you say it is—which I doubt—then in a book which candidly seeks to express emotion as well as to analyze, why no pity, no warmth? Why condemn—to paraphrase Burke—a whole class? . . . You have somehow managed to get into your portrait of the white-collar man a great deal of your personal nightmare, writing about him as though he must feel as you would feel if you were in his position. . . .
>
> Look at your introduction: the words you apply to the white collar man: living out in slow misery his yearning for the quick climb, pushed by forces, pulled, acted upon but does not act, never talks back, never takes a stand, in a fran-tic hurry, paralyzed with fear, morally defenseless, impotent as a group, open to the focused onslaught of manufactured loyalties, turns to his leisure frenziedly, bored at work, rest-

less at play, standardized loser, must practice prompt repression of resentment and aggression, etc. . . .

What I miss in your work is not the quality of mind, which you have in riotous abundance, but some human qualities, the absence of which is beginning to show *precisely because* you are trying to write humanistically meaningful books.[10]

Hofstadter presented a corrective of his own. He argued that corporate capitalism had not necessarily transformed middle-class life into an unending search for sales; he also suggested that people were not as easily manipulated as Mills (or Miller) believed, and that they were normally willing actors and participants in what they did, even within constraining structures of wealth and power.

In the following pages, I shall build on Hofstadter's insight by exploring the lives of those corporate managers and employees who staffed the corporations during the organizational revolution of the late nineteenth and early twentieth century. This multilayered transformation was not simply imposed from the top down by a corporate elite exploiting a growing labor force of immigrants, a growing army of white-collar workers, and a growing number of salaried managers. Rather, corporate goals were simultaneously adopted and devised by an aspiring new salaried class that grew with the corporations themselves and that helped transform the larger middle-class. Far from being the mere foot-soldiers of the elite, members of this new employee class interpreted the job of industrializing the land as their mission and, to a large extent, succeeded in shaping the workplace in their own image. Their lives exemplified the historically successful meeting of a large and ambitious project—the building of a continental economy—and an active social class.

In undertaking this study, however, I am writing a different history of corporate capitalism than either Hofstadter or postwar social historians envisioned. Few historians of the fifties and sixties, regardless of their ideological inclinations, were ready for the kinds of insights Hofstadter displayed in his private correspondence before his untimely death. When influential new left historians inquired into the larger political economy of capitalism, they—like Mills—appropriated the criticisms raised by muckrakers and Progressive reformers. Big business, they argued, threatened the traditional bases of American society. These historians saw financial speculation driving the economy and the political system and paternalism dominating social relations, and they emphasized these threats. These historians saw the efforts of the liberal state to regulate business and promote safety and social justice undone by the manipulative strategies of business leaders.[11]

Economic historians, in turn—influenced as they were by post-war Keynesian economics—did not focus attention on the business world, concerning themselves primarily with econometric models that concentrated on aggregate measures of growth and overall performances of the economy and sidestepping such critical issues as the great merger movement.[12] The smaller group of scholars who concentrated on business history considered only indirectly the two major topics of this book: the distinctive culture and social milieu of the growing managerial class and the formation of a new white-collar culture. Thus, Thomas Cochran, who studied an executive elite, the presidents and vice-presidents of large railroad companies from 1845 to 1890, was led to argue that the executive altered his policies "only at the command of his superiors." Although top corporate officials desired to maintain friendly relations with everyone in the organization, "it is the opinions of the small group of . . . peers or superiors that prescribe [their] role." While Cochran's study is filled with insights that underscore Henry Adams's famous observation that his generation was "mortgaged to the railways, and no one knew it better than the generation itself," Cochran in effect neglected the actions of middle-class middle managers in developing corporate policy and in bringing about what he otherwise regards as the "basic social 'revolution' of the twentieth century," that is "the gradual assumption of power by the heads of administrative bureaucracies, either business or governmental."[13]

With the explosion of social history in the sixties and seventies, a new generation of historians—I among them—was eager to break away from homogeneity. Engaged in a great search for pluralism, social historians did not directly address the creation of a bureaucratic work culture either, for new studies of white-collar workers and related bureaucrats seemed out-of-place after Mills's analyses, supplemented by Harry Braverman's widely read theories on the "degradation" of work in the twentieth century.[14] From the vantage point of the war on poverty and a search for a "great society," corporate employees appeared passive prisoners in a system they did not attempt to change. On the other hand, immigrants and workers, who had developed alternate cultures of their own and used them to resist corporate capitalism, deserved our attention. We combined a yearning for social justice with a search for groups often on the periphery of society. Spurred by the belief that people are responsible for their history, we devoted our energy, talents, and the technical resources derived from the expanding social sciences to give voice to those heretofore left out of the historical record.

In the process, we were, without realizing it, engaged in our own exercise in reification. We described how single groups reacted to capitalism [15] without studying the great mass of rank-and-file capitalists who worked within the growing corporate organizations. Consequently, most references to the professional and managerial class written in the last thirty years have reinforced the preeminence of Mills's conclusions by applying his lens to the historical data. [16]

The nature of this debate in the United States has changed markedly, however, in the last ten years. During this time, progress has been made in filling the gaps in business history. Brushing aside traditional moral and judgmental imperatives of much business history, a school of thought has emerged around the work of Alfred D. Chandler, Jr. Chandler had been studying the organizational revolution which produced modern management for some time when his masterly synthesis, *The Visible Hand* (1977), finally broke through the well-guarded barriers of academic subdisciplines. [17] Chandler, linking the growth of giant companies to that of a new managerial class, moved away from the exclusive study of financial manipulators and corporate presidents and vice-presidents to concentrate on management in a larger sense. He examined such issues as the creation of middle-level managers, the nature of their responsibilities, the new techniques of accounting and statistical reporting they developed, and the professionalization of their loyalties. He concluded that the spectacular maneuvering of the financiers had little impact on the day-to-day operations of the corporations they controlled. Instead, the men who mattered most in the American economy were full-time, salaried, career managers. Thus "the American railroad enterprise," he suggested, "might more properly be considered a variation of managerial capitalism than an unalloyed expression of financial capitalism." [18] The situation of the middle-level executives was therefore different from that of the top executives. These men (and they were exclusively men) dealt with issues largely outside the purview or interest of boards of directors—the daily routine of management.

Chandler, however, told his story from an organizational standpoint, without social analysis. His focus is management, not managers, and the many valuable insights he provides on managers are demonstrations of the power of deductive reasoning. Nonetheless, the middle-level executive is not simply a stage in an organizational flow chart, but a specific person in specific social circumstances whose degree of independence and whose part in a larger "business" culture can be assessed. For empire building was dependent on bureaucracy building, and the ultimate success of bureaucratic rules depended on the imposition of new values, shared, and, to a large extent, created by this new managerial stratum. These values could be, and were, at odds with the commercial and financial practices of the board rooms. By pointing to structural changes in the economy caused by the activities of a new managerial class, Chandler implicitly challenged social historians to move beyond their focus on the proletariat and open their studies to other causes and consequences of large-scale economic change. This volume takes up that challenge.

Chandler's work on management has, in effect, opened the door for social historians to examine the role of middle-management in the rise of corporate America. At the same time, social historians have realized that restoring the collective identities of workers and immigrants can no longer be a substitute for larger schemes of historical explanation and that their attempt to grasp the human experience in its complexity had paradoxically produced studies of increasingly narrow focus. Nonetheless, if the pluralistic vision of the last twenty years gave a fragmented understanding of history and seemed to sacrifice the whole to the parts, it also brought about invaluable new insights on class formation, class consciousness, and the relations among ethnicity, class, and gender in American society.[19]

To take a few examples, we now understand why it is inaccurate to explain the failure of radicalism in late nineteenth century America simply by pointing to a pervading countercurrent—the faith in the redistributive power of unlimited growth. Rather, radicalism's intellectual aspirations were generated in so many competing cultural systems in the late nineteenth century that radicalism could not unify a growing working class.[20] We have learned that there is no such simple relationship between collective action and standard of living, between contentiousness and consumption. Furthermore, tenacious habits of thrift, motivated by an acute sense of future need, effectively prevented the American working-class from believing in the therapeutic ethos of consumerism until well into the twentieth century.[21] In his famous 1906 essay, *Why Is There No Socialism in the United States?* Werner Sombart pointed to the American worker's superior purchasing power and the remarkable openness of a society where a worker "mixes with everyone—in reality and not only in theory—as an equal." Sombart's argument no longer persuades and reads only as a reflection of its times.[22]

Among the various subfields of social history, the growth of women's history, especially, has led to a serious incursion by social and labor historians into the new world of office workers, which was created by large corporations and the federal government after the 1880s. Women entered the clerical workforce massively. To be sure, there was a world of difference between a Marie Louise Broadhead-Smith, a niece of Sophie du Pont who, without personal wealth, had to work as a clerk in Washington in the late nineteenth century, and the girls hired from working-class families who were trained to sell merchandise in department stores.[23] The wide gamut of social origins that these women epitomize only underscores the extent of the cultural and social transformation underway.

While the insights derived from social history have been telling, there is a need for a synthetic approach. This is particularly true of the study of corporate capitalism, as it altered profoundly and irreversibly such areas as family life, education, consumption, technical culture. The question that I pose in this book should prove broad enough to achieve such a synthesis: how did corporate capitalism succeed in creating a new work culture and an altogether new outlook on life? My challenge is to shape an answer that goes beyond the traditional economic and technological determinants of most business history and beyond the traditional concern with power, manipulation, and resistance of most social history. The lives of ordinary people have often been defined as a direct reaction to well-known institutions. I believe that the situation is much more complex. The diverse group of individuals who staffed the early corporation, not all of whom shared the same purpose, did not so much react to the corporation as they did design it. In doing so, they transformed their own lives.

Thus I link the question of corporate growth to the process of middle-class formation and re-formation. It has been customary, if not satisfactory, to refer to the complex occupational transformation of the late nineteenth century—the growth of professional associations, the systematization of knowledge in universities and the ensuing certification process—as part of the creation of a new middle-class, distinct from an old middle class of independent entrepreneurs.

C. Wright Mills did much to define this new middle class, with which a growing number of Americans had identified, as a mental rather than an occupational category. He chose occupations that not only epitomized the changing work culture but also coalesced into a larger whole. Even Hofstadter, who brilliantly detected Mills's flaws, adopted his sociologist colleague's basic definitions. Hofstadter interpreted the turn-of-the-century reform movement as a way for members of an *old* middle class, who sought to impose a degree of social justice in the face of mounting corporate power, to hold onto their status or to regain the influence they had already lost.[24] Robert Wiebe also adopted Mills's categories to reverse Hofstadter's formulation and argue that "the heart of progressivism was the ambition of the *new* middle class to fulfill its destiny through bureaucratic means."[25]

This book focuses on the corporate middle-level managers who made decisions, devised standardized ways of working, and adopted new living patterns that weakened the significance of geographical boundaries within regions and reduced the de facto cultural autonomy that had characterized many communities.[26] These managers played an important part in promoting a new work culture and, as an influential group, they carried the organizational revolution into key sectors of society long before competing versions of Taylorism and scientific management extended it to millions of workers. These middle-level people grew in number very rapidly and spread throughout the country. Members of the upper class were influential in building organizations and funding them, but they had little direct contact with the growing number of people they employed. Middle-level managers did. In their turn, white-collar employees, salesmen, and other lower-ranking representatives of growing corporations— although constantly in touch with managers—also contributed to the definition of their own codes of life and methods of conduct. Middle-level managers and white-collar workers were largely independent actors who brought about much social and cultural change. Only by finding out exactly what these bureaucrats did can we understand the bureaucratic ethos of the new middle class and its consequences not only for the progressive movement but also for the formation of the American middle class in the twentieth century.

The social history of American industrialization and the growth of corporate capitalism, therefore, must include a close study of these disparate but related groups of salaried workers, their relationships among themselves and with other segments of society. What follows should not be read as the history of a particular corporation or place but rather as an extended essay on social change based on case studies. In order to study the role of managerial groups in effecting the social change that marked the period, I approach the connection between business and society, not through broadly defined institutional or cultural history, but through collective biography constructed from the personnel records of five large corporations—the Chicago, Burlington, & Quincy Railroad; the E. I. Du Pont de Nemours Powder Company; the Ford Motor Company; the McCormick and, then, International Harvester Companies; and the Metropolitan Life Insurance Company. These large firms conducted business in all parts of the country and abroad, but most of their activities during this period were concentrated in the old industrial belt which stretched from the eastern seaports to the Great Lakes.

I have identified large sections of the selected corporations' employees—all the salaried personnel of the C. B. & Q. railroad (about 200 managers in the 1880s), all the C. B. & Q. office workers in Chicago in 1880 (more than 300 clerks), all the salaried personnel of Ford between 1908 and 1912 (about 1,200 people), all the salesmen at Du Pont (420 in 1917) and International Harvester (more than 500 in 1910), and smaller groups of employees at Metropolitan Life. I have built career profiles for many of them, and whenever possible, I have supplemented company records with information on the communities where corporate employees lived, using sources such as local newspapers, census records, the files of local genealogical societies, records of local associations, and private correspondence. These sources have enabled me to trace, in many instances, national origins, occupational backgrounds, residential arrangements, and attitudes toward family life.[27]

This book, then, examines the social characteristics and values of people who participated in the formation of corporate bureaucracies. It documents the ways managers and salaried workers created new perspectives and implemented them. By uncovering how the emergence and growth of salaried personnel on such a grand scale translated into life-styles (methods of computing, of buying, of building, of educating, and so on) which became America's dominant cultural form and which contributed to the homogenization of the different segments of American society, I posit a theory of change that does not assume consent or mask conflict behind functionalism. I seek to understand how, despite enormous social tensions that often erupted in some of the more violent class conflicts of the industrial world, organizational synthesis participated in a more homogeneous social order, capable of integrating people of various origins into a new American middle class.

ONE

LOST
AUTONOMY

As for me, my bed is made: I am against bigness and great-
ness in all their forms, and with the invisible molecular
moral forces that work from individual to individual, steal-
ing in through the crannies of the world like so many soft
rootlets, or like the capillary oozing of water, and yet rend-
ing the hardest monuments of man's pride, if you give them
time. The bigger the unit you deal with, the hollower, the
more brutal, the more mendacious is the life displayed. So I
am against all big organizations as such, national ones first
and foremost; against all big successes and big results; and
in favor of the eternal forces of truth which always work in
the individual and immediately unsuccessful way, under-
dogs always, till history comes, after they are long dead, and
puts them on the top.

William James, letter to Mrs. Henry Whitman, 1899

CHAPTER ONE

A s large business organizations of the late nineteenth century stitched regional networks together to create a national market, they altered both the form and meaning of local autonomy. Through vertical integration and mergers, authority and information were regrouped in fewer centers.[1] The towns that composed the industrial belt of the east and expanding midwest were caught up by the same economic trends and experienced an extraordinary rate of population turnover and exchange. Each place became more readily identified as part of a network of places and relied increasingly on the network's existence for its life.[2]

The local elites as well as the larger middle class were caught and recreated in this transformation. Early in the twentieth century, keen observers contended that corporate capitalism had split the educated middle class into two groups—the independent entrepreneurs and the salaried professionals. In 1903, the *Independent*, the old abolitionist magazine once run by Henry Ward Beecher, argued that William Graham Sumner's famous "forgotten man" had changed. He was no longer a man who conducted a modest business, an independent operator or a professional, for the ambitions of men like this "made the trust laugh." In the view of the *Independent*, the trusts were saying:

> We can show you quicker ways of accumulating capital than
> by putting savings in the bank . . . . Independent business
> enterprises conducted by individuals, are not up to date.
> Those of you who are wasting life as our competitors may
> sell out to us if you like. We will pay your salaries to work for
> us if we find you worthwhile. Or, you can go through bank-
> ruptcy if that suits you better. As for you professional gentle-
> men, the sooner you quit dreaming and talking about your
> ideals, the better off you will be. Your ideas are too loose,
> and you speak your mind too freely. If you want to make a
> living from now on you will have to preach, or practice law,
> or lecture, or conduct your newspapers to suit us. We don't
> think it necessary to buy out your good will, or to place you
> on our salary roll, but in one way or another you all will have
> to curb your tongues.

The *Independent* added, "This purpose of the trusts, already partly realized, is likely to be more fully achieved in the near future. The middle class is becoming a salaried class, and rapidly losing the economic and moral independence of former days."[3]

The division of the middle class into those who contributed to the building of corporate capitalism and those who clung to proven, and presumably more fulfilling, ways of doing business was a major problem of the day. Herbert Croly, although willing to concede that large corporations were performing a public service, struck much the same note in *The Promise of American Life* (1909). He questioned the corporations' preference for "well paid and well trained men, who could do one or two things remarkably well, and who did not pretend to much of anything else."[4] At stake was the loss of free-ranging, independent judgment as well as the loss of economic independence.

For these observers, the contrast with old ways was blatant. Only three decades earlier, local merchants, not distant manufacturers, still controlled the economy. It was the merchants who determined what products would be manufactured and what industrial ventures would be supported. The reasons for this dominance are well known. In the United States, a country to which industrialization came slowly, merchants controlled networks of exchange and access to money. They provided master craftsmen with capital to expand and marshalled demand for their products. Merchants also controlled the distribution of manufactured goods. Well into the second half of the nineteenth century, most manufactured products were still generic goods. As such, they required none of the special merchandising techniques that would dictate manufacturers' control of distribution. The merchants, who had contacts throughout a market that was diffuse and unconcentrated, simply added the products to their own distribution system. The manufacturer, by contrast, remained a man of "limited horizons," who knew business conditions only in his immediate geographic area.[5]

But as industrialization proceeded, merchants lost their preeminence. By the late nineteenth century, the roles of merchants and manufacturers were reversed, as manufacturers, looking for capital to expand and economies of scale, strained against the mercantile yoke and eventually broke it. Their influence was especially felt in goods such as agricultural machinery and sewing machines that "were technologically complex, expensive items requiring close and often extended contact between manufacturer and consumer or required elaborate, innovative marketing apparatus."[6] Producers in these fields replaced merchants as distributors of manufactured goods because they could do it at a lower unit cost and because independent wholesalers became increasingly unable or unwilling "to merchandise goods effectively."[7]

After 1880, these changes took place with increasing rapidity. A number of manufacturing establishments became large corporations, and, within twenty to thirty years, such large corporations controlled not only the railroads in which local merchants had once heavily invested but also many of the functional mercantile networks—especially the concentrated urban markets, where firms often established permanent salesforces. With vertical integration—both backward toward sources of production and forward toward the development of corporate salesforces—manufacturers became senior partners and often the employers of merchants who had heretofore dominated local economies. Furthermore, the new market for industrial securities prompted the development of investment banks and related financial services. These institutions ultimately eclipsed local merchants as a source of funds for new or expanding enterprises. Legal expertise also adapted to corporate requirements. Thus if we are to understand the extent of the transformation that resulted from the incorporation of America, we must begin by capturing the relationship between the mercantile economy as it still existed in the second half of the nineteenth century and the growing corporations.

The changing relationship between Pennsylvania hardware merchants and the Du Pont company—one of the large business firms I examine in detail in this book—illustrates this transformation. The story that emerges reflects the adaptability of Pennsylvania's local elites, who, in many instances, were able to ensure their own dominance well into the twentieth century by accepting the conditions of corporate hegemony. In many small towns, the local merchants thought of themselves as the "natural" leaders of their community. They dominated politics, influenced the institutions of social control, and gave the tone to local culture. Even as the growth of industrial corporations undermined the economic independence of small centers, this old middle class, to use C. Wright Mills's term, maintained the control of institutional and social networks.

Nonetheless, participation in the wider economy lessened their independence. The merchants' ability to maintain local influence and thus their own status became increasingly dependent on their relationship with the growing corporate economy. In some places, it took little time for powerful foreign economic agents to disrupt the existing balance.

Eventually, some outraged merchants took their complaints to courts and regulatory commissions. Newspapers followed the debates in all parts of the country as the critics of big corporations won some of the key decisions that led to the emergence of the regulatory state.

But before turning to the reactions against the corporations in the public arena, let us see what exactly took place in one region. A close look at Pennsylvania merchants and a foray into nineteenth-century mercantile culture provide a view of the local elites and the middle classes of American towns as they embraced and were absorbed by the corporate network.

PENNSYLVANIA MERCHANTS AND THE
E. I. DU PONT DE NEMOURS POWDER COMPANY

Pennsylvania was fertile ground for manufacturers and enterprising merchants of all kinds. The breadbasket of the original colonies, Pennsylvania also industrialized early. German and English immigrants developed iron deposits found across the colony and established textile mills. The dense network of small cities that had spread across the state by the end of the eighteenth century was drawn even tighter in the nineteenth as canals and railroads crisscrossed the region.[8] The primary reason for the development of this impressive transportation network was the presence, in seemingly inexhaustible quantities, of coal. Increasingly during and after the 1850s, coal was both a source of energy for transportation and a marketable commodity. With some 15,000 square miles of Pennsylvania bituminous coalfields, the railroads had a cheap, plentiful source of fuel. Pennsylvania's abundant anthracite deposits—practically all of the nation's supply was located in a 500-square-mile area in the northeast corner of the state—was shipped to the Middle Atlantic and New England States to heat homes, offices, and factories.[9]

The Pennsylvania hardware storeowners of the nineteenth century were the successors of the old general storekeepers, whose shops had been the center of rural transactions for several generations.[10] In most communities, the store was old and well established and, in some, had been in the same family for several generations. These hardware stores were heralded in local histories, not only as community landmarks but also as engines of local economic growth. For many hardware storeowners did more than supply construction materials, agricultural implements, and household goods to the neighboring region. Because hardware dealers were situated at the center of their towns' mercantile network, they often contributed heavily to related business ventures and acted as developers. With other merchants, they stood behind forms of economic innovation that brought unification and exchange. They invested in local railroads well before the age of the great railroad tycoons. In fact, their efforts made the subsequent reorganization of the railroads into large economic and financial units possible. As Henry Adams remarked, building a transportation network, although a "single fraction" of society's work, was so big as to require "capital, banks, mines, furnaces, shops, power-houses, technical knowledge, mechanical population, together with a steady remodelling of social and political habits, ideas and institutions to fit the new scale and suit the new conditions."[11] The investments of the Pennsylvania merchants were the first step in this multifaceted venture. The local transportation companies, builders, and banks that flourished during the period depended on the capital merchants provided. These merchants as a group tended to be boosters of their local economies, and they strove to make their towns hubs of economic activity.

Pennsylvania dry goods merchants naturally had contracts with the large regional manufacturers. They sold iron goods, steel sheets, builder's hardware, tools, coach trimmings, saddlery hardware, and such consumer goods as shoe findings and household furnishings manufactured elsewhere. Also included in their inventory was powder manufactured by the E. I. Du Pont de Nemours Powder Company. As Du Pont changed from a medium-sized, single-product manufacturing concern to a modern corporation, the relationship between Du Pont and these merchants changed, and their autonomy was lessened dramatically. These Pennsylvania merchants lived the transformations that the progressives, who believed as a matter of course in the moral superiority of smallness over bigness, would later condemn.

In the 1870s, Du Pont employed just over three hundred workers to manufacture blackpowder in four blackpowder mills along the Brandywine River. It also kept two other small mills running on Wapwallopen Creek, near Scranton, Pennsylvania, on the edge of the anthracite region. From these facilities, the du Ponts, who had expanded their factories to meet the demands of the Civil War, dominated the production of gunpowder and other explosives in the United States. The older du Ponts were manufacturers, not corporate managers. Although Joseph Schumpeter's description of the industrialist as a man who both risks his own fortune and runs his own show was meant to apply to the British industrialists of the Industrial Revolution, it fits the du Ponts and other Gilded Age manufacturers well.[12] Schumpeter's typical firm was a single-unit concern with one proprietor and two or three partners producing a single product line (there were two basic sites in the case of Du Pont). These entrepreneurs assumed many tasks that would be described in our day of salaried managers and capitalist investors as subordinate management functions. The partnership between Henry du Pont and his nephew, Lammot, which shaped the powder works of the 1870s, followed this pattern and functioned without a hitch until Henry's decision in 1880 to resist Lammot's plan that Du Pont manufacture high explosives or dynamite.[13]

Although the firm continued to prosper in the latter part of the nineteenth century, by 1902 it had seemingly fallen into difficulties. Its leadership was aging and had lost enthusiasm, and preliminary negotiations to sell it were held with a competitor. At this point, three du Pont cousins, Pierre, Coleman, and Alfred, took over. As Pierre and Coleman in particular were quick to realize, the older management was discouraged because it underestimated the firm's assets. The older du Ponts had eventually invested in the Repauno dynamite works in Gibbstown, New Jersey, that Lammot du Pont, Pierre's father, started in 1880, then in a very large blackpowder works in Mooar, Iowa, built in 1888, and finally in a pioneering smokeless powder plant at Carney's Point, New Jersey, built in 1891. By the time of the 1902 purchase of the Du Pont firm by the three younger cousins, the firm had a payroll of about 1,500 employees. Rather than sell, the new generation of du Ponts developed a new course that was to change entirely the company's way of doing business with local merchants.[14]

Until the reorganization of the early twentieth century, the du Ponts depended on merchants in their effort to maintain control of a national market. Old Henry busily corresponded with an extensive network of independent agents. These agents, who ran the gamut from small hardware dealers in rural and mining districts to prosperous merchants in industrial centers, sold the powder on their own account. There were a great many agents. Between 1876 and 1885, the company corresponded with 215 agents in thirty-four states. In important geographic locations such as Pennsylvania, the company listed no fewer than 56 agents in thirty-three towns and cities.[15]

A few agents were entrusted with so much business that their Du Pont work occupied much of their time. The largest of all Du Pont agents, Furman Kneeland, was not in Pennsylvania but in New York. Kneeland was instrumental, after the Civil War, in creating the Gunpowder Trade Association, the horizontal combination through which Du Pont, Laflin & Rand, Hazard, and a few other firms sought to control prices.[16] The next two most prolific agents were both in Pennsylvania: J. T. Jones in Philadelphia handled imports of raw material (soda) as well as sales, and Henry Belin oversaw Du Pont business in

CHAPTER ONE

Du Pont Agencies in Pennsylvania, 1876–1885

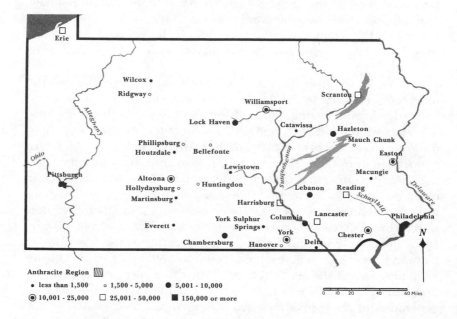

the heart of the Pennsylvania anthracite country. A majority of Du Pont's Pennsylvania agents in the 1880s, however, were businessmen who had still only a limited connection with the firm and who pursued many other interests: half of them exchanged fewer than 100 letters apiece with Wilmington during their tenure as agents.[17]

By examining these Pennsylvania merchants in their dual role as individual entrepreneurs and as representatives of a firm of growing national importance, we can begin to appreciate not only the workings of local forms of economic activities in relation to national ones but also the social position of merchants in their own communities. We can evaluate their level of independence on the eve of the corporate revolution and trace their eventual subordination to corporate power. It is in their complementary roles of entrepreneurs and agents that we see these men responding to the growing corporations.

SOUTHEASTERN PENNSYLVANIA

Merchants enjoyed a remarkable degree of influence and independence in the well-settled, agricultural and industrial areas of southeastern Pennsylvania. Indeed, in Du Pont's case, the most prominent members of local communities represented its interests, and Du Pont capitalized on an existing social and economic order. These merchants were not entrepreneurial heroes who fit C. Wright Mills's notion of the risk-taking individual before the rise of corporations, that is, independent entrepreneurs formed by healthy competition. Such heroes only exist in an invented past. Rather, they were the inheritors of precorporate forms of local wealth and power. Through the 1880s most of them managed to use their connections with growing corporations to reinforce their local status.

The Stichters of Reading and the Smalls of York were representative of the influential hardware merchants in this wealthy, agricultural sector where, by the late nineteenth century, German and English settlers had merged into integrated local elites. They were typical of a larger yet restricted group of local merchants—about one hundred strong in a town of over 40,000 inhabitants—who collectively ran their community and whose lives are detailed in local histories. Their economic power and, most often, their prestige and connections as old residents placed them in a dominant social position. They were well educated and active in politics and Freemasonry. They were the prime players in the towns' professional and religious associations and often thought of themselves as working for the general community welfare. Following a tradition of stewardship, they also held local elected offices. They were members of a wealthy elite, not of that middle class of craftsmen and smaller shopkeepers that emerged from the antebellum temperance and abolitionist movements and that defined itself in opposition to what it viewed as the extravagance and dissipation of both the poor and rich. If, as some historians have argued, the middling group craved for a homogeneous society,[18] the elite sought instead to maintain the stratified heterogeneous society that was the source of their local dominance.

Joseph Lybrand Stichter of Reading was in many ways a typical Pennsylvania merchant of the 1870s and 1880s and an embodiment of this local elite. Reading, located 55 miles west of Philadelphia in Berks County, was far enough from Philadelphia to have become by the mid-eighteenth century, like Lancaster or York, a thriving, independent county seat.[19] The German and Welsh settlers had located iron ore—both veins and surface deposits—and started iron foundries in the Schuylkill Valley.[20] The consequent prosperity of the Pennsylvania Dutch inhabitants was reflected in Reading's courthouse, built in 1799, a handsome building, with a portico borne by six columns of the local red sandstone.[21]

In the nineteenth century, the population grew at a rapid pace—jumping from about 16,000 in 1850 to 43,000 in 1880, to 59,000 in 1893—and the chief industry remained iron. In 1882, there were more than one hundred mines in operation in Berks county, whose foundries produced 95,000 tons of iron (bar, plate, nail plate, sheet) annually. The railroads were another source of economic prosperity. The shops of the Reading Railway employed about 3,000 men.[22] In 1858, Du Pont contracted with Joseph L. Stichter and Son, to distribute powder in the region, an arrangement that remained in force for thirty years.

The Stichters were an old family of German settlers.[23] The first Stichter, Conrad, was a weaver who bought a lot in Reading in 1751, just a few years after the city was founded. Conrad's son, Peter, was born in Reading, also in 1751. At the age of sixteen, he served in the Continental Army, wintering at Valley Forge with Washington in 1777. Joseph Lybrand Stichter, Peter's son, was born in Reading in 1813 and died in 1884. After receiving an education in the German and English schools of Reading, he was apprenticed to the iron and hardware trade at the age of fifteen, serving in the store of Keim and Drenkle. Nine years later, in 1837, he became a partner in the firm, which was then renamed Keim and Stichter. Four years later, James McKnight, another native of the town and son of the cashier of the Pennsylvania Branch Bank at Reading, absorbed Keim's interest and remained a partner until 1858, the year of the Du Pont contract and three years before reporting for military service at Harrisburg at the beginning of the Civil War. Stichter, after McKnight left, conducted the hardware business alone until 1871, when he established a partnership with his son, Thomas.

As the alliance of Stichter and McKnight indicates, by the second half of the nineteenth century, the merchants of German and English descent had abandoned many of their ethnic traditions and fused into a single local elite with common values. We can see this movement in Stichter himself. Although Stichter had been a member of the Trinity Lutheran Church, he joined the Episcopal Church in 1833, five years after he entered the hardware business. This sort of integration into American institutions could be found among other families of German ancestry in other county seats in rich, rural Pennsylvania.

This mercantile elite was well educated. McKnight followed the typical path in which a college education led to a clerkship, which itself served as springboard for a business career. McKnight studied at Princeton and, upon his return from college, entered the hardware store as a clerk. Joseph Stichter's son, Thomas, followed a parallel business career. After attending public school in Reading, he entered the University of Pennsylvania, graduating with honors. Then, like his father's former partner, he entered the hardware business as a clerk. An excellent liberal education, the privilege of a provincial elite, led to a clerkship, which was still in the late nineteenth century the most common form of apprenticeship for a business career.[24]

As a local hardware merchant, Stichter and his associates had directorships in local banks, railroads, and other industries they helped finance. When the Philadelphia, Reading and Pottsville Telegraph Company organized in 1847, Joseph Stichter was one of the commissioners from Reading. He was also elected a director of the East Pennsylvania Railroad Company in 1868, filling this office until his death. Thomas Stichter became director of the Second National Bank of Reading. Among Stichter's former associates, the Keims, Henry May Keim became president of the Valley Railroad in Ohio. Henry May Keim was also auditor of Reading in 1873 and 1874 and Democratic party county chairman in 1876.[25]

The Stichters' concern with commercial affairs spilled over into interest in the community. Their participation in community life, however, was not primarily in the form of holding office. Thomas, Republican in politics, served only one term in the Common Council from the Fourth Ward. Rather the Stichters preferred to play a prominent role in local associations and their related activities of social control. In 1849, Joseph Stichter was listed as an incorporating member of the Reading Library, an outgrowth of a reading society organized in 1837. He was treasurer of the Benevolent Society of the City of Reading from 1844 to 1870. He often served his new denomination as parish deputy to diocesan conventions, and, for years he acted as church treasurer and vestryman. And Joseph was longtime vice-president of the Berks County Agricultural Society and organized the Fourth of July celebration for 1869, training a chorus of seven hundred singers for the occasion.[26]

Thomas, in his turn, was a member of the Sons of the Revolution and sat on the board of directors of the Charles Evans Cemetery Company. He was a member of the vestry of Christ Episcopal Church and was an ardent worker in the Sunday School cause. Thomas was actively connected with the construction of the new Home for Widows and Single Women and, like his father, was a member of the Benevolent Society, Reading Library, Board of Trade, and Berks County Agricultural Society. Both father and son contributed generously to the local hospital. Thomas also took a deep interest in the University Extension movement, which he helped organize during the winter of 1892.

In the Gilded Age, masonry was still an upper-class activity, promoting self-improvement through industry, piety, honesty, temperance, and sobriety. Both Stichters participated in it and its search for a well-ordered, restrained personality in a well-ordered world.[27] Like many of their counterparts in other towns, the Stichters' role in masonry mirrored their elite status and their aspiration to community leadership. To be prominent in masonry was to exert moral authority. Joseph organized Huguenot Lodge, No. 377, Free and Accepted Masons, which was instituted November 29, 1866, as a lodge of the Ancient York Masons of Reading (with a membership of more than a hundred). Thomas joined Teutonia Lodge, No. 367, F. and A. M.

The Stichters of Reading are an exemplary case of the small town mercantile world on the eve of its demise, for they acquired their wealth and exercised their influence in the same place. Participation in regional financial circles, evident in the Stichters' case, is even more evident in the activities of the Smalls of York.[28]

The original family name was Schmahl, and they immigrated from Essenheim, Germany. The family elder, Lorentz, a farmer, died in 1749, the year that York County was formed out of Lancaster. By the Revolution, the Smalls had a general store in York, and during the nineteenth century, they expanded their commercial activities in the fertile valleys of York County, which were known for the production of fine wheat, rye, and corn. Philip Albright Small, born in 1797, was educated in York and trained for business in the mercantile firm of Schultz, Konig and Company in Baltimore. He returned to York and, with his brother Samuel, transformed the store into the leading firm in the region. He traded in grain and flour and established wholesale and retail hardware and grocery businesses. Capitalizing on urban growth and the cities' need for food supply, the Smalls expanded their business rapidly and diversified. In their heyday, the Smalls purchased one third of the wheat grown in York County, processed it in their mills, and shipped a large quantity of their flour to eastern port cities and to London. The Smalls' customers extended over a dozen counties of Pennsylvania and Maryland. They also built a number of furnaces in Maryland for the manufacture of pig iron. They did such a volume of business that the moving of goods and products to and from their various concerns equalled one-sixth of all the freight moved over the Northern Central Railroad between Baltimore and

York. Such activities led quite naturally to an involvement in regional transportation. Thus we find Philip Small director of different turnpike companies and, in 1835, one of the incorporators of the York and Wrightsville Railroad. His brother Samuel was a director of the York and Cumberland Railroad.

Both Smalls were prominent citizens of York, and their business and family connections extended throughout the region. Philip maintained a residence in Philadelphia, and Samuel extended the family business to Pittsburgh and then to Cincinnati, exploiting the growing trade of the Ohio Valley. Locally, the Smalls followed the Stichters' pattern of community involvement. Philip was director of the York County Bank and its president from 1858 until his death in 1875, trustee and president of the board of the York County Academy, and one of the promoters of the York County Agricultural Society. Brother and partner Samuel was director of the first building association in town. He established a home for the orphans of soldiers in 1865, became a liberal contributor to the York Benevolent Society, was among the founding members of the local hospital, a ruling elder in the First Presbyterian Church, a founder of the Collegiate Institute (with five faculty members and fifty students in 1873), secretary of the library, and a director of the York Bank. Samuel died in 1885 before the reordering of mercantile networks by large corporations. He was still part of a world where merchants like him were major investors in growth industries and prime players in the local institutions of social control.

The Stichters, the Smalls, and those like them thought of themselves as a class and were alert to social and economic developments outside their immediate sphere. Merchants like them consorted with the elites of other communities and cultivated relationships with the owners of major industrial firms throughout the country. This mercantile elite, controlling significant local resources, invested these funds in regional and national firms as a means of enlarging their local dominance.

When members of the southeastern Pennsylvania mercantile elite joined the growing professions, they used the new connections to reinforce existing ties among the local commercial, political, and legal milieus. Because of their prominence, members of these families often were selected as justice of the peace or prothonotary, offices that led to an apprenticeship in a legal practice in an age when law schools were only in their infancy.[29] It was not uncommon therefore for one brother to become a merchant and another a lawyer. This was the case of the third-generation Krauses from Lebanon. One brother was a hardware merchant who sold Du Pont powder among many other products and the other a lawyer who became a judge and the editor of the *Pennsylvania Intelligencer*.[30] In Harrisburg, the hardware store owner and Du Pont agent, Edwin D. Shellenberger, was the brother of a lawyer who had also been a merchant and an instructor at the Harrisburg Academy after graduating from the Pennsylvania College at Gettysburg.[31] In nearby Lancaster, George M. Steinman, who represented Du Pont, had in the 1860s sought a seat in the U.S. Congress but had been narrowly defeated by abolitionist Thaddeus Stevens. Steinman's brother, a lawyer, had been, with Thaddeus Stevens, among those who did free legal work for widows and orphans of the Civil War.[32]

When associated with other professional pursuits, southeastern Pennsylvania merchants also showed a significant degree of independence from corporations. Thus D. W. Cox, Du Pont agent in Harrisburg (Dauphin County), had first followed a railroad career, learning telegraphy as a young man on the Northern Central Railroad and ending his employment with it as paymaster of the road. In 1872, Cox went into business on his own, first in the retail coal business in Harrisburg, then in iron ore mining, and in 1887 as wholesale coal dealer. Cox, who served as city comptroller from 1876 to 1880, put both his railroad and accounting experience to good use in his new mercantile field by writing and publishing Cox's Calculated Tonnage Rate Book. Cox was no Charles Francis Adams or even Henry Varnum Poor, but he was typical of a growing number of men whose work lives were shared among civic and commercial ventures. They spent time codifying the various technological changes under way, participated in the emergence of a new corporate order, but remained largely autonomous.[33]

NORTHEASTERN PENNSYLVANIA

Merchants were significantly less independent from growing manufacturing concerns and corporations in the newer industrial areas. This was especially true in the northeastern section of the state that was being developed for the extraction of coal. Although Du Pont agents retained their autonomous status, they became, in effect, proto-executives, that is, agents who were primarily in the service of the powder interests. As corporate power increased in the region, some merchants tried to maintain their focus on the local community. In doing so, however, they found themselves increasingly dependent on the influence of the corporations. Still, the shift from an economic and social system controlled from within the community to one controlled from without was slow, and much ambiguity persisted, as the comparison of Mauch Chunk and Scranton, both towns at the heart of the coal trade, shows.

Mauch Chunk, at the south end of the anthracite region, was at the center of the immense coal trade carried on with surrounding states by means of a network of canals and railways. The town grew up around the Lehigh Coal and Navigation Company, which was dominated by the Leisenring family. The Leisenrings, of German origin, initially owned a general store and ran the local hotel. By the time they had anglicized their first names, they had greatly expanded their activities and achieved local prominence. John, Jr., became the Lehigh Coal and Navigation Company chief engineer and his son Edward, a third-generation inhabitant, became president. The Lehigh Coal and Navigation Company canal had the usual limitations of canals. It flooded in the summer and froze in the winter. Hence there was a need for a railroad, which was built by a new group of settlers, this time Yankees instead of Germans.[34]

By 1850, the activities of the wealthy Yankees, led by the Packer family, and Germans, led by the Leisenring family, together with funds pouring in from outside investors such as the Philadelphian Edward R. Biddle, had given Mauch Chunk the potential to become a regional center. Many coal operators, with ties to mercantile capital as well as to scientific and engineering societies in Philadelphia, joined the original two groups. Thus the Packers and Leisenrings extended their investments into regional iron, coal, and services. The Leisenrings dominated the First National Bank, the Packers the younger Linderman National Bank. But despite its location, the town never grew very large. There were 3,500 inhabitants in 1880, and only 4,000 inhabitants in 1893, clinging to the side of a steep valley with the coal bearing mountains above them and the Lehigh River, canal, and railroad below. By the last decade of the century, the Packers had left to reinvest their fortune in South Bethlehem Steel and the Leisenrings, in turn, had relocated in Philadelphia. Among the Leisenrings, only Alexander, president of the town's First National Bank, remained.[35]

Alexander Leisenring was a Du Pont agent, and his correspondence with Du Pont shows his ambiguous status. The growing corporation influenced his life considerably more than his counterparts in the better established communities. Leisenring had the connections to be an effective broker between the explosives manufacturer and the mine operators. Because he was selling large quantities of powder, he could occasionally negotiate with Du Pont for better terms for his customers.[36] He also managed local property owned by Du Pont. Leisenring's status depended on his connection with the Wilmington manufacturer as well as on his roots in the community and his family connection in Philadelphia. At times, his correspondence with Du Pont was on the First National Bank of Mauch Chunk stationery— reflecting Leisenring's position as an influential member of a local elite. Yet Leisenring prominently displayed his association with Du Pont on his hardware store letterhead.

The situation in Scranton shows Du Pont's more direct influence. Men with direct family connections with Du Pont were sent to Scranton, a coal center that soon came to displace Mauch Chunk and dominate the anthracite region. Such was the case of William Breck, who had married Victor du Pont's daughter (Admiral Samuel du Pont's niece) and moved in 1859 from Wilmington, Du Pont's headquarters, to Scranton where he represented Du Pont until his death in 1870. Henry Belin, Jr., succeeded Breck. Belin's grandfather, a planter of French origin from San Domingo, West Indies, had moved to Philadelphia following the uprising of the blacks in 1791 and formed a connection with Du Pont. His son Henry, a graduate of West Point, joined the newly formed corps of Topographical Engineers. He started to work for Du Pont in 1843. His sister Mary married Lammot du Pont and became Pierre's mother. As for Henry, Jr., he graduated from Yale in 1863, joined Du Pont, and moved to Scranton.[37]

The characteristics of these Du Pont agents were very different from those of agents in southeastern Pennsylvania. These men, who were also to become civic leaders in their adopted communities, owed their entire status, at least initially, to their connection with the powerful manufacturer. They were in Scranton primarily to exploit the anthracite market by selling Du Pont powder to coal and railroad companies. Ultimately, they became active in Scranton's economic life, but their local success was a consequence of their corporate connection. Belin provides a good example. As the head of Du Pont powder, Belin, like Breck before him, moved beyond his association with Du Pont and entered Scranton's financial and industrial circles. He became a director of the First National Bank of Scranton, director of the Lackawanna Trust and Safe Deposit Company, vice-president and director of a large lumber company, and vice-president and director of the Scranton Lace Company during a period when lace products were a major source of local revenue. A Democrat in politics and Presbyterian in religion, he was a trustee of the Second Presbyterian Church, and charter founder and treasurer of the Pennsylvania Oral School for the Deaf. He also served on the advisory board of the Hahnemann Hospital and as trustee and treasurer of Scranton Public Library. When the Scranton Club was organized in 1895, Henry Belin, Jr., became its first vice-president. Thus the Belins ultimately became local notables in their own right, but they reached this status because they represented the interests of a national firm.

WESTERN PENNSYLVANIA

The relations between Du Pont and its agents was different again in western Pennsylvania. Towns were generally newer, and the agents' association with Du Pont began well after the Civil War. Some towns were corporate creations, others rural markets, and others developing industrial areas. Some local merchants and Du Pont agents thrived as independents. Many independents, however, found that they had to redirect their efforts because the growing corporations bypassed them. Others never achieved much independence and, in effect, became protoexecutives.

In the many smaller towns of western Pennsylvania where the Du Pont Company maintained a correspondent, the merchants continued to balance local enterprises with partnerships with the outer world. Away from the main centers of activity, Du Pont agents were relatively independent. Often, benefiting from an inheritance, they carved out their own niche. Yet, it is precisely among this group—valued for their local status—that the Du Pont company would later recruit some of its first managers.

The Du Pont agent in Huntingdon, a small town of about 6,000 inhabitants in 1893, was Harry S. Wharton. Wharton came from a family of pioneers who had settled large tracts of farmland on the banks of the Juniata River.[38] In Bellefonte, agent William Keller Alexander was similarly independent. Alexander was educated at several academies before joining the mercantile and grain business with his father. He was elected to represent Centre County in the state legislature at Harrisburg.[39] In neighboring Phillipsburg, agent John Mills Hale, who bought out the hardware store of George Zeigler in 1878, also came from a family of old settlers. He attended the University of

Pennsylvania, then studied law with his father, then moved back to Phillipsburg, where he established himself as a merchant. He had considerable real estate holdings and invested in what were then growth industries: the waterworks, the telephone exchange, and the lighting company.[40] In a nearby lumber town, Lock Haven, agent George S. Good, son of a local businessman, was in the hardware business with his brother-in-law, Charles Datesman. As a local merchant and general contractor, Good constructed 500 miles of railroad. Good's social standing and his wide range of activities—he was a Presbyterian, member of the Grand Army of the Republic, the Lock Haven Business Club, the Hecla Park Club, and the Young Men's Republican Club—confirmed him among the small group of local businessmen who dominated the town.[41]

The same circumstances held true in Hollidaysburg, farther south. This was agricultural country, but after the Pennsylvania Railroad reached Altoona in 1852, ore was discovered right outside the small town, and furnaces erected. These furnaces, together with two rolling mills built some ten years later, made Hollidaysburg a modest iron center with 3,150 inhabitants in 1882. Among the wealthier local traders and merchant was A. L. Holliday, born in the hotel and general store that he was to inherit. He was the grandson of one of the two brothers who built the community, frontiersmen William and Adam Holliday, who had emigrated from the north of Ireland about 1750 and fought in the French and Indian War. When Du Pont started business in Hollidaysburg, A. L. Holliday was the company agent.[42]

Of all the truly independent Du Pont agents in small towns of western Pennsylvania, only one could claim to be a self-made man. In Ridgway, Elk County, Joseph S. Hyde did not inherit his local position from eighteenth-century settlers. Instead, local histories describe him as a Horatio Alger hero who was "clothed in overalls, and with all his possessions tied up in a handkerchief" when he reached western Pennsylvania in 1836. Born in New Hampshire in 1813, he had arrived in Ridgway after a brief stint in a sawmill in Maine. He opened a small store, bought a mill on credit, and soon thereafter became the leading lumberman in the county. In addition, Hyde exploited a paint ore mine that one of his partners had located on his land in the 1880s. As in *The Rise of Silas Lapham*, the chance discovery of mineral wealth contributed to the expansion of a local business based primarily on lumber.[43]

In other areas of western Pennsylvania, local entrepreneurs could not compete with a large corporate presence. S. I. Fries, of Altoona, is an example of one whose life was simultaneously molded by and removed from the new corporate order. Altoona, situated at the eastern base of the Allegheny Mountains, was during the second half of the nineteenth century perhaps the most representative railway town in America. Founded in 1849 by the Pennsylvania Railroad as a center for its workshops and workmen, it had grown by 1893 into a busy center of 30,337 inhabitants. The railroad works covered 120 acres, employed 6,000 men and produced 300 locomotives, 200 passenger cars, and 5,000 freight cars annually.[44]

In Altoona, the Pennsylvania Railroad was the salient force in community life. A hardware store merchant was obviously a small man compared to the representatives of the line. Yet S. I. Fries, a Du Pont agent since 1873, was still a leading citizen. Fries became the first vice-president of the newly formed board of trade in 1895. Not only was he known as a hardware merchant and coal operator, but also as someone who played a significant role in the social life of the community. Although on a smaller scale, Fries's activities are similar to his colleagues' throughout the state and are indicative of the status merchants managed to keep in the late nineteenth century even as their economic autonomy was declining rapidly in the face of large corporate growth.

Fries's relationship with Du Pont was diminished by the presence of the Pennsylvania Railroad, which purchased powder directly. Fries's trade in Du Pont products was consequently limited. This Pennsylvania merchant did not make more than $12/month on his Du Pont line.[45] In fact, most of his hardware revenue came from his investment in a series of stores outside Altoona in neighboring counties, including one his brother opened in the small coal town of Houtzdale. Yet he occasionally carried on a more complicated relationship with the du Ponts when searching for powder magazines that combined adequate protection against rain with easy access to freight lines. He and his partners also advised the du Ponts on competition with rival firms like Hazard.[46] Not integrated in the corporate hierarchy of Altoona and not counting the railroad among his customers, Fries had to pursue profits not available to him locally by expanding in the dense network of coal towns. Fries's strategies show the inevitable coexistence of the new corporations' own externally regulated system of commerce with the traditional, local system.

Yet it is from participants in the traditional system, independent men who were not entrenched in the well-established mercantile networks of older towns and therefore free from rigid commitments to the mercantile culture, that corporations found the representatives who became protoexecutives. Such was the case of Elliot S. Rice, who was to become the Du Pont agent in Chicago. Rice was, in his early career, a successful, independent businessman in western Pennsylvania. In 1878, he had established a wholesale grocery business with Charles Curtze, a budding entrepreneur in Erie, a town of 28,000 inhabitants. With a staff of thirteen, Curtze and Rice provided all manner of groceries and grocers' supplies in Erie and through western Pennsylvania. Rice and Curtze also sold hardware and Du Pont powder. Rice and Curtze followed, at least initially, the paths and preoccupations of the local elite. Charles Curtze was active in Erie's German voluntary associations. His brother Hermann was a lawyer who had been bookkeeper before returning to the old country to study law in Heidelberg and Leipzig. In enticing Curtze's partner, Rice, to work full time for them, the du Ponts drew upon local merchants to staff one of their newly created regional offices.[47]

EXIT PENNSYLVANIA

In 1882, Rice moved to Chicago to represent the Du Pont interests. From his Chicago office, he gave himself over completely to supervising sales in a large midwestern territory and acted as intermediary in many transactions such as contracting with the Burlington Railroad and supervising land contracts for Du Pont. During his tenure E. S. Rice sent about 350 items of mail a year from Chicago to the company headquarters. He was attentive to the changes in business conditions. Amidst his abundant correspondence, he noted with pleasure on January 17, 1888 that the typewriter had finally "found its way on-to the Brandywine in spite of the quill-pen."[48] These important agents, Rice in Chicago, Kneeland in New York, and Belin in Scranton, handled so much of Du Pont's business that they rapidly became company officials, protoexecutives paid partly in salary and partly in commissions as a percentage of sales. In this way, they are the direct precursors of the modern business managers, and the relationship that Du Pont established with them, especially after 1902, set the tone for the relationships that would become the norm between Du Pont and hitherto independent agents.

Rice remained a successful and prosperous general agent for more than a dozen years but his days as a protoexecutive—and indeed the days of the protoexecutive position itself—were numbered. Changes began almost immediately after the du Pont cousins consolidated the member firms of the Gunpowder Trade Association and the constituent companies of the Eastern Dynamite Company into the E. I. Du Pont de Nemours Powder Company.[49] These changes were formalized in 1904 with the creation of the sales department. Although large independent agents like Rice had already lost their autonomous status in principle and become Du Pont employees, they resented the change. Some large agents believed that the proposed organizational changes threatened their control of their districts. E. S. Rice bitterly fought Du Pont's plan for the new sales department and what he viewed as Wilmington's growing interference with his work.

Soon after the reorganization, Rice complained to Coleman du Pont that the Cincinnati agent, R. S. Waddell, had written Chicago railroad officials to discuss the recruiting of a "freight dept. manager" conversant with Chicago conditions and that he, Rice, had not been consulted. "I cannot believe that the foregoing was ever authorized by you," he wrote to the company president on May 22, 1902, "and I ask that the man who so far forgets himself as to write thus in your name, to the business associates of your Chicago representative, be required to apologise . . . and informed that any negotiation found necessary at Chicago in behalf of Messrs E. I. Du Pont de Nemours & Co. will for the present at least, be intrusted to the care of your Chicago agent." Coleman's answer was swift and unambiguous: "I beg to advise that your office in Chicago will be entrusted with just so much of our business as we think you can best handle, always reserving the right to ourselves to decide this question." Rice was flabbergasted. "After twenty-five years of honest effort and loyal services rendered to Messrs E. I. Du Pont de Nemours & Co., I have to acknowledge receipt of a first unkind letter." Then, he went on describing his achievement: "Today, as the result of my efforts and that of my assistants, you have an advantage in the way of carload rates not enjoyed by any other powder manufacturer in the United States." His protests were of no avail.[50]

That was only the beginning of Rice's troubles with the new lines of authority. Rice's office had come under close scrutiny as Du Pont's treasurer, Pierre, asserted that it cost Rice more to sell powder than the large agencies in Cincinnati, Wilmington, New York, and St. Louis. An auditor asked Rice to justify his expenditure of money under the vaguely labeled rubric "Street and Advertising Expense" that appeared in the Chicago report. Rice refused to comply. Coleman du Pont then requested the information himself. Rice explained that he had to contribute to the Chicago police and fire departments in order to keep his powder illegally stored near his place of business. To that end, he had to meet demands "for free powder upon the occasion of picnics, celebrations, firing of salutes, Fourth of July," to support the departments' benevolent associations and also to contribute to the campaign funds of "gentlemen of political influence." Although the new Du Pont president readily approved these expenses, Rice felt personally offended, for he thought the late Mr. du Pont's "verbal instruction" still carried weight in the new company.[51] At stake was his sense of freedom and business autonomy that he enjoyed as a protoexecutive.

One request led to another. Shortly after this incident, Rice was asked to justify the unitemized expenses of the Springfield agency, under the direction of his sister, E. E. Rice. Here again, he did not understand what the fuss was about and argued with headquarters that expenses at Springfield could not be lower. Rice pointed out that his sister hired help only for "the carting and storing of powder"; she had "no clerk, no book-keeper" and her pay was significantly lower than that of "a man for like service." Furthermore, Rice's sister was spending money from her salary to entertain coal operators who shopped in Springfield and to help wives of coal diggers. In the end, however, Rice had to comply with the auditor's request. The itemized statement for three months read as follows:

Contribution to fund for family of miner killed in mine	$20.00
Present to member Labor Union to get powder delivered to prevent strike	$14.50
Assisting miner in burial of child	$10.00
Bill Groceries for sick miner	$ 4.80
" " " widow miner	$ 3.00
" Clothing for family of sick miner	$11.50
" Groceries for sick miner	$ 9.20
Present to party for information regarding party who was said to use L. & R. powder	$10.00
	$83.00

Here again, Rice felt frustrated to have to report to some unknown auditor expenses that helped the business but could not be itemized in the standard accounting categories.[52]

The fight with Wilmington continued for three years on all fronts—definition of sales territory, authority in negotiating with railroads and other businesses, and the use of discretionary funds. The final blow came early in 1905 when vice-president for sales J. A. Haskell reached the conclusion that Rice's office was "inefficient," that Rice was overpaid, and that Rice carried too much overhead. The stubborn agent, however, put up a final fight, dismissing Haskell's authority. When Coleman du Pont declined to arbitrate between his vice-president and his agent, Rice vainly appealed to another du Pont, who was not connected with the new management. Finally, the old powder agent resigned.[53]

Rice felt vindicated when R. S. Waddell, the Cincinnati agent who had caused him so much trouble in 1902, not only resigned his new post as general sales agent in Wilmington (in 1903) but turned against his former employers by initiating an antitrust suit in 1907 (see chap. 3). But Rice's vindication had only symbolic value. Rice, who formed his independent outlook as a merchant in Erie and who had been chosen originally for his initiative, was now an impediment to the organizational overhaul the cousins sought to achieve. Given his background, he quite naturally viewed the creation of an integrated, centralized sales department as an affront to his personal and business integrity and failed to grasp its necessity.

By the end of the century, the changes around the Pennsylvania merchants were inescapable. Much of their dominance had been based on the relative isolation of their communities and on the merchants' ability to monopolize by virtue of their social status whatever connections existed with the outer world. The 1870s and 1880s, however, signaled the beginning of a changing role for the many local oligarchies as the diversity of interests encouraged by geographic isolation diminished. The heretofore independent merchants were absorbed in a new, hierarchical system of economic exchange. The silent corporate revolution that was taking place led the new generation of town elites to participate in the development of new knowledge, new professions, and new associations. Rice, who had already compromised when he gave up the grocery business to become a protoexecutive for Du Pont, was unwilling to go all the way.

THE PUBLIC ARENA

As the corporations became predominant, key aspects of the battle that was fought privately between E. S. Rice and the du Pont cousins erupted in the public arena. Progressive individuals dissatisfied with the changes around them yearned for a return to a past they now idealized. For most, the villain became bigness. The most widely debated episode in the progressives' fight against the incorporation of the American economy came in 1910 when Louis Brandeis, in a landmark rate case, fought the eastern railroads before the Interstate Commerce Commission on behalf of shippers. Swayed by the argument of the "people's lawyer," the Commission denied the railroads an increase in freight rates, even though it was needed.[54]

To be sure, neither inequality, nor the primacy of financial considerations over those of production, nor even class consciousness arose with the incorporation of America. Still the progressives, as Richard Hofstadter aptly remarked, reacted to "the changed pattern in the distribution of deference and power,"[55] such as we saw operating in the northeastern and western sections of Pennsylvania, as if it were a primal threat to the perfection of American life. In doing so, they sought to resist bigness, to impose a degree of social justice in society, and to improve efficiency. In effect, they sought a return to the decentralized society of the nineteenth century and resisted the more hierarchically integrated society big corporations helped create. The I.C.C. case clearly reveals those who felt themselves demoted by corporate change.

Brandeis well understood the mercantile milieu he was representing. The son of Jewish refugees who fled Europe after the defeat of the liberal revolution of 1848, he was born in Louisville, Kentucky. Brandeis's family was, in its own way, typical of the mercantile-professional elite we have seen operating in several regions of Pennsylvania. Louisville, on the Ohio River, was already the tenth-largest city in the United States and fast becoming the center of the grain industry. Adolf Brandeis, Louis's father, was a wholesale grain merchant along the Indiana border. The Brandeis family were professionals and leaders in the community. Adolph's brother was a physician, while Lewis Dembitz, Brandeis's uncle on his mother's side, was a lawyer who devised Louisville's tax-collection system and wrote such practical volumes as *Kentucky Jurisprudence*, *Land Titles in the United States*, and *Law Language for Shorthand Writers*. Dembitz was one of the nominators of Abraham Lincoln for president in 1860.[56] The Brandeises were an example of those merchants who had to contend with the rise of corporate power. As we have seen in Pennsylvania, many of them had invested their mercantile capital in the new corporate ventures only to find their economic dominance increasingly challenged.

In arguing the famous rate case, Brandeis showed that the corporations' claim to efficiency was unsubstantiated. He contended, and the headlines declared, that the railroads were so inefficient they could have saved $1,000,000 a day with proper managerial techniques, thus sparing their customers the price of a rate increase. To make his case, Brandeis struck an alliance with an unexpected set of allies, Frederick Winslow Taylor and several of his disciples. Although Taylor did not know enough about railroads to testify, he introduced Brandeis to James M. Dodge, Horace K. Hathaway, Frank Gilbreth, and other experts who did. Shortly after Brandeis met Taylor in Philadelphia, he met again with a small group of these engineers at the New York apartment of Henry L. Gantt, another Taylor disciple, to plan their strategy for the rate case; from that meeting emerged the phrase "scientific management," which had been used only informally by Taylor prior to the rate case. The lawyer forged an alliance with engineers to argue against financiers on behalf of merchants.[57]

Taylor had published numerous technical pieces with the American Society of Mechanical Engineers and worked as consultant for large firms for years. Among many others, Coleman du Pont, who was still with future reform mayor Tom Johnson's streetcar business in Cleveland, hired him in 1898 to apply his methods to the making of electric motors by installing a new cost-and-control system at several plants.[58] But after two decades of continuous consulting work, Taylor too felt cheated by corporations. Together, Brandeis and Taylor's disciples sent a message to those local governments and other organizations that looked to big business as a model of efficiency, that they were likely to be misled by financiers. Brandeis influenced Taylor's decision to publish his only popular work, _The Principles of Scientific Management_, which the ASME was reluctant to print, in Ray Stannard Baker's _American Magazine_. Taylor's view was that only disinterested engineers and professionals could create efficient business conditions and only they could look to the interests of all classes. The "rate case" gave new meaning to Taylor's work. After some hesitation, the engineer seized the opportunity to reassert the primacy of technical over financial control in industry. Some of Taylor's disciples would soon ally with Thorstein Veblen and influence the sociologist's dream of a "soviet of engineers."[59]

It did not take long for Henry Ford and others to disprove Brandeis's casual contention that the most efficient plants were medium sized. But that was beside the point. Beside the point also, at least for the time being, was the fact that the unions, who sought to protect the wage increases they had earned for their members, sided with the rail-roads. The specifics of Brandeis' argument on efficiency, his grasp of economics and social change, matter less than his intentions, for Brandeis's plea was essentially moral. The incorruptible lawyer FDR would later call Prophet Isaiah was staging his own battle for smallness and heterogeneity. As defender of the small against the mighty, Brandeis reacted against big business's tendency toward homogenization. Keeping parts separate meant resisting economic activities that unify and that flatten differences.

Brandeis's defense of economic independence, small units of work, and local autonomy was part of a large movement. That nobody should control the center to the point of absorbing peripheries became central to the pluralistic viewpoint that was emerging within progressivism. Indeed, by 1914, only four years after the rate case and two years before becoming Supreme Court Justice, Brandeis was openly to adopt a form of cultural pluralism that was revolutionary for someone of his standing. He became the leader of the Zionist movement within the American Jewish community. Having opposed a vision of America as a hierarchical society, dominated by wealthy corporations, Brandeis finally realized that his Jewishness need not take second place to his identity as an American, that it was possible to be Jewish as well as American. Thus, diversity, competition, and the right to be different became the very core of his vision of democracy.[60]

Such were the choices that Americans faced early in the century when the incorporation of the economy became deeply felt. Neither inequality nor the dominance of financial interests were new. What was new were the social and cultural manifestations brought about by the changing scale of the economy. The real problem was not the mere replacement of mercantile finances by corporate finances but rather the social and cultural consequences of such a shift. The fight against bigness was part of a larger goal of maintaining the heterogeneous character of society.

TWO

THE
FIRST
EXECUTIVES

The herd of men, which we call society, all act under the same circumstances exactly alike, unless very particular and powerful motives prevent them.

Jean-Jacques Rousseau, "Discourse on the
Sciences and Arts," 1750

Railway management in all its various departments may be said to involve the employment and the patronage of all the arts and sciences.

The Railway Review, March 19, 1892

With the spread of corporate bureaucracies, the influence of a very large, middle-level managerial stratum, neither rich nor poor, neither powerful nor powerless, became pervasive. But the appearance of the middle-level executive, whose activities so radically transformed American work culture and life-style, went largely unnoticed, at least initially. Bureaucracy building seemed too paltry an enterprise to enter the rhetoric of Republican representatives during Reconstruction. Nor was bureaucracy-bashing a feature of the speeches of Iowa populists who complained about rate discrimination by the railroads. Their targets were robber barons, not bureaucrats. The very power of the "iron monster . . . the galloping monster, the terror of steel and steam, with its single eye, cyclopean, red, shooting from horizon to horizon; . . . the leviathan, with tentacles of steel clutching into the soil, the soulless Force, the iron-hearted Power, the monster, the Colossus, the Octopus," to borrow just a few of Frank Norris's churning metaphors,[1] has traditionally been seen, by contemporaneous social analysts and historians alike, as being under the tight control of financial wizards. The key actors were seen to be the manipulators of capital, the Jay Goulds or the Daniel Drews—whether they used their own capital or that of others. These are the men Charles Francis Adams attacked in *A Chapter of Erie*, his masterpiece of muckraking. Adams observed that they looked more like a "gang of thieves . . . than like the wealthy representatives of a great corporation."[2]

When attention was ultimately turned to the managers who worked for corporations, they seemed to be, by contrast, mere foot-soldiers who implemented the robber barons' far-reaching financial schemes, hirelings in an economic system that increasingly favored bigness at the expense of equality. And yet the emergence of the bureaucratic personality has inspired some of the most significant chapters of twentieth-century social science. These works harken back to the founders of sociology, especially Max Weber and Emile Durkheim. In his posthumously published *Economy and Society*, Weber, describing "the types of legitimate domination," opposed "bureaucracy" to "charismatic authority."[3] Although Durkheim neglected to incorporate the emergence of bureaucracy in his concept of "organic solidarity," for him, the division of labor in modern life brought increasing differentiation and precipitated the decline of community.

Weber, who included the large modern capitalist enterprise among bureaucracies in his comparative framework and gave explicit references to the United States, reasoned mostly in terms of "the modern organization of the civil service."[4] Big business, however, not government, invented American bureaucracy. Government jobs were limited in number throughout most of the nineteenth century and were often sinecures unsuited for men of ambition, if Nathaniel Hawthorne's acid portrait of customs house officers in Salem bears any resemblance to reality.[5] Furthermore, it took decades after the passage of the Pendleton Act in 1883 for federal employees to feel the effect of the merit system.

Accordingly American corporate bureaucracies possessed many traits that do not fit into the Weberian model. Many decisions continued to be made in an informal way. General managers had broad, not always clearly delineated, functions and power. Consequently much depended on their personal priorities and their discretion. Improvisation in a rapidly changing business environment continued to be valued. Because profit was the final measure of success, salaries were, to a large extent, determined by market criteria, not simply by bureaucratic rank and seniority. While academic qualifications became more important, diplomas were not a prerequisite for a successful managerial career. Nonetheless, middle-level corporate managers did follow the Weberian bureaucratic model in that these men became specialized, adhered to formalized work rules, and advanced in a differentiated hierarchy. They attached increasing value to formal education and to committing themselves to a profession for life. In the United States, successful corporate management rested on reconciling the imperatives of the market and those of organization.[6]

The question raised by the division of the middle class into two distinct segments—one adapting to the corporate economy and the other resisting it—is therefore obvious. If the republican virtues of smallness and independence were so deeply ingrained in the middle class, how were corporations able to break into this class so easily and coopt large parts of it? Was it easy to take a successful professional away from private practice and entice him to work for a corporation? Did corporations offer other inducements besides a good salary? In other words, why did a part of the middle class participate in the corporate political economy and the other resist it?

The railroad executive in particular faced an unusually vast and diverse field of endeavor. The rise of railroad bureaucratic structures coincided with and was partly generated by the vast territorial expansion of the United States and the accompanying creation of new markets.[7] Executives needed to bring order to and wring a profit from operations in a variety of settings: the big city headquarters, the small-town hub, the rural farming region, and the frontier. Each place was subjected to the executives' autonomous energies and to newly established bureaucratic procedures of their devising.

The activity of these middle-level managers precipitated corporate change. Corporate change originated not only from the top but also at the middle, where it extended to either end of the corporate hierarchy. Middle-level executives were an intermediate corps between the top executives, whose options were often defined by those below them in the corporate hierarchy, and the clerical and blue-collar workers, whose working lives they ordered, and, as such, frequently innovated as well as arbitrated. These managers were, to a surprising extent, independent intermediaries, and their influence was felt not only on the job but also in the society at large. They adopted key organizational systems that would be felt in the larger society.

THE FIRST AMERICAN BUREAUCRACIES

The history of the Chicago, Burlington, and Quincy railroad makes it a representative case study of the making of a managerial workforce. Decision making in the C. B. & Q. occurred at three distinct locations. The C. B. & Q. originated in Chicago and maintained its headquarters in that great center. The Midwest shipped its wheat, corn, and hogs to market in Chicago, and it looked to Chicago for a steady return flow of equipment, clothing, and other necessities.[8] The general manager's office, by contrast, was located in Burlington, Iowa, in the rural heart of the C. B. & Q. network. The C. B. & Q. board, however, continued to meet in Boston, the city where the original investors lived. Railroads had been financed with eastern money, not local funds. Railroad securities were sold on the New York stock market, not on the Chicago exchange.[9] Among railroad magnates who operated in Chicago, only George Pullman, with his Pullman Palace Car Company, was a local entrepreneur.[10]

In 1870, the C. B. & Q. operated a little over 600 miles of track. By early 1881, it administered almost 2,800 miles, and by 1887, it had established a network of close to 5,000 miles. Under Charles Elliott Perkins's direction, the C. B. & Q. extended its tracks through Illinois between the Illinois and the Mississippi rivers, then through Iowa and Missouri to the Missouri River. In 1881, the C. B. & Q. crossed the Missouri River and penetrated into the states of Nebraska, Kansas, and Colorado and into the Wyoming territory. It opened a northern road through Wisconsin and Minnesota in 1886.[11] Although the offices of the railroads were of necessity spread over a variety of locations, such farflung outposts—made possible by improvements in communication—typified most new corporations. The new scale and complexity of the corporations required an organizational geography.[12]

In the late 1870s and the 1880s, C. B. & Q. general manager Charles Elliott Perkins promoted system building and, from his Burlington office, issued the tough decisions to make it work. The largest railroads relied on system building to establish direct links to the commercial and marketing hubs of the nation, free themselves from questionable and fragile rate agreements, and also rid themselves of speculators such as Jay Gould.[13]

System building required both capital and organizational skills. While investment bankers such as Jay Cooke and J. P. Morgan helped railroad magnates raise fresh capital,[14] it was the newly hired managers who administered the freshly laid rails. In the 1850s, large railroads were already employing from forty to sixty salaried managers.[15] As system building caught hold, this figure jumped. By 1880, the C. B. & Q. and its subsidiary lines employed 191 executives.[16] Whereas factory owners of a previous era dealt directly with foremen and even often with workers, top-level executives and board members of the railroads relied on this new middle stratum to run their businesses. System building, as we observe it, caused precisely the kind of differentiation that stimulated the social scientists like Weber and Durkheim.[17]

The organizational chart of the railroad was quite complex. As the C. B. & Q. reached maturity in 1880, its 191 executives were divided both geographically—distributed over seven states and twenty-five cities—and functionally. While the C. B. & Q. executives were clearly compartmentalized into over twenty departments (land, purchasing, auditing, freight, and so on), those of the smaller subsidiary lines—the Burlington and Missouri River Road; the Kansas City, St. Joseph, and Council Bluffs; the St. Louis, Keokuk, and Northwestern—were not yet clearly divided.[18]

Including affiliated roads, and according to distinctions and figures General Manager Perkins set, the entire C. B. & Q. system employed in 1880 a total of 23 top-level executives, all of whom made over $4,000 a year, and 168 middle-level executives at positions paying between $1,500 and $4,000. The largest line, the C. B. & Q. itself, employed a total of 10,204 people, of whom 148 were executives and several hundred were clerical workers.[19]

As the various listings Perkins's office prepared reveal, upper-level managers, paid above $4,000, were those whose tasks reached a sufficiently high level of abstraction that they went beyond the confines of a single department to involve the coordination of activities across and outside the company. By contrast, middle-level managers stayed within the confines of one department. Nonetheless, their positions were important. In 1880, Perkins urged the board of directors to review all appointments to posts paying more than $1,500. The money was not at issue, for as Perkins himself noted, $1,500 was "not in these days large pay."[20] Rather it was the responsibilities that went with these positions that required the board's supervision.

THE ORGANIZATIONAL GEOGRAPHY

The mix of middle management and top executives in the C. B. & Q.'s decision-making centers reflected the kinds of issues each group decided as well as their relationship to each other. Three top-level executives and seven middle-level executives worked in Boston for President John Murray Forbes and the board.[21] Forbes himself made his fortune in the China trade before investing in western railroads. As much a Bostonian in the eyes of the midwestern farmer as Charles Francis Adams, Forbes was the embodiment of the Yankee capitalist. He was assisted in his presidential duties by three of Perkins's own assistants (clerks paid between $1,800 and $2,000), seven of the eleven members of the treasurer's department (including comptroller George Tyson, $7,000), and the clerk of the board.

General Manager Perkins ($15,000) in his headquarters in Burlington, Iowa, employed nine other executives, among whom James Baldwin, the land commissioner for Iowa, was the only one with a top-executive salary. The others were Perkins's assistant and the middle-level executives of the Iowa division. Perkins's career with the C. B. & Q. had started with the Burlington and Missouri River Road in Iowa (B. & M., Iowa) in 1859.[22] The B. & M., Iowa was consolidated with the C. B. & Q. in 1872, and Perkins assumed the management of the Burlington and Missouri River Road in Nebraska (B. & M., Nebraska).[23] Later, in 1877, when he became general manager of C. B. & Q. while retaining responsibility for the C. B. & Q. Nebraska affiliate, he still remained in Burlington, the midpoint between Chicago and Lincoln.

Perkins's life in Iowa, although far from the board of directors in Boston, is a testimony not only to the old missionary spirit of New Englanders but also to the strength of extralocal allegiances, both personal and commercial, that counterbalanced the dispersion of corporate executives. Perkins's father, like John Murray Forbes, had worked in Boston's China trade, before relocating in the west and becoming a Unitarian minister in Cincinnati. These ties with the company president were reinforced when Perkins married his second cousin, who was also Forbes's niece. Although the Perkinses lived in Burlington, they remained Bostonians in many ways, as their daughter Alice explained much later to historian Frederick Jackson Turner: "The contrasts between our Burlington life and the summers in Milton with my grandfather and grandmother in my little girlhood were external. The dignity and the tradition existing in our Burlington house was very much the same, [the life was] much simpler . . . but I do not remember that I was very different from my New England Cousins in bringing up and in my ideals and standards."[24]

The C. B. & Q. headquarters in Chicago was not at all Bostonian. The Chicago office housed the largest departments, the ten top-level executives, and the forty-five middle-level executives who ran the departments. Although the railroad interests were interfused in every aspect of Chicago economic life and controlled the stockyards, only a handful of railroad executives intermingled with the local elite. In 1863, 216 Chicagoans already made at least $10,000 annually and by 1892, there were no fewer than 278 millionaires in the city.[25] Compared to the rich men of Chicago, railroad executives had limited means. Thomas Potter, general manager for the C. B. & Q. roads east of the Missouri, earned $10,000 in 1880, while General Solicitor James Walker made $10,800. Amos T. Hall, treasurer of the C. B. & Q., made only $6,000, and Paymaster Charles Bartlett, the next-in-line in Hall's headquarters, made only $3,300. Most railroad executives were part of a new bureaucratic middle class. Even the senior executives were far removed from the tycoons who had made great fortunes in Chicago. They were perhaps closer to the later generation of business leaders who joined existing bureaucratic corporations like the Harvester Company or Marshall Field.[26]

Most of the career railroad executives described in these pages earned less than $4,000 a year (the figure Perkins used to distinguish between senior executives and middle-level managers) and worked within large departments at headquarters. Purchasing had five middle-level executives and over one hundred clerks. The general auditor's department comprised six executives and about thirty clerks, while the freight auditor's department had two executives and sixty-six clerks. The executives of the purchasing and auditing department were among the best paid of the middle tier, making between $2,500 and $3,000 a year. The general freight and the general passenger offices, which processed all of the road's business, employed the largest number of executives, thirty-six (out of sixty employees) and fourteen (out of forty-two) respectively. These freight and passenger agents were paid between $2,000 and $2,300 a year.

In addition to functional departments, the railroad was also divided into large geographic divisions: Chicago, Galesburg, St. Louis, and Iowa. Perkins made every effort to reinforce the authority of division superintendents to balance the centralizing tendencies—reinforced by the need for standardization—of functional departments.[27] The division superintendent subordinates included office staff as well as freight agents and chief engineers. These divisions were mostly hiring and supervisory units, hence the small number of executives in each division. Only Iowa had as many as fifteen executives. Galesburg had five, Chicago only three, and St. Louis only two. Iowa division executives made an average of $1,875, and the division included such posts as chief operator and dispatcher, superintendent of bridges, superintendent of stockyards, track inspector, train master, and surgeon. Five engineers reported to the office of the chief engineer and had executive status.

Other executives were scattered among the railroad towns of Illinois, Iowa, Nebraska (General Manager Albert E. Touzalin, who controlled the roads west of the Missouri had his headquarters in Omaha), Kansas, and Missouri. The executives who lived in the small towns along the lines held a variety of middle-level jobs. They were superintendents of divisions, trainmasters, ticket agents, claims agents, freight agents, attorneys. Eleven of these men (the general foremen and master mechanics) reported to the superintendent of the locomotive and car department, a large organization that controlled 3,400 workers altogether. These master mechanics and general foremen, blue-collar workers promoted to supervisory positions, were generally paid below $2,000. There were also several freight agents in New York City.[28]

Then there were the personnel of stations. Only the Chicago station had seven people with middle-level status. They were three ticket agents, chief clerk, cashier, yard master, and assistant superintendent. Dining car personnel and telegraph repairers were classified under the executive supervision of Secretary and Superintendent of Telegraph Charles Levey.

Even the lowest paid managers were nonetheless part of a privileged group. While general managers regularly reminded their subordinates of the need to economize, most managers enjoyed regular salary increases. When salaries rose nationally between 1880 and 1885, as much as 75 percent of the railroad managers' salaries rose in nominal terms and 98 percent in real terms.[29] The favorable trend continued even after 1885, when salaries nationally declined and prices stabilized. Still, over half of the executives' salaries increased between 1885 and 1890.

There were also people on the payroll who did not fit neatly into hierarchical categories. Thus, General Solicitor Walker retained the service of members of the bar in various localities. Joseph Blythe at Burlington and O. F. Price at Galesburg had executive status without being fully integrated into the executive hierarchy. Other lawyers were hired full time such as Turner M. Marquett, the solicitor of the B. & M., Nebraska. The lawyers, who belonged to an already established profession, were increasingly brought into the corporate world where they performed critical tasks. They rationalized corporate practices through legal forms and served as brokers between management and such parties as investment bankers, underwriters, syndicates of foreign bondholders, and government officials.[30]

As the corporations grew in size and complexity, new levels of management were redefined often, on an ad hoc, experimental basis. Defining hierarchies was a constantly evolving process that required recruiting the best talent among the local middle class, a point General Manager Perkins made to the C. B. & Q. board in 1880 in explaining why the Iowa land commissioner was paid more than the land commissioner in Nebraska and why the two offices were not consolidated. The Iowa land commissioner ran his office independently and had to be lured out of private legal practice, while the Nebraska man worked under the supervision of the general superintendent of the B. & M. "There are many things to do on a big railroad which do not belong to any particular office or department. So long as a road is small, the general commanding officer can take such matters upon himself and manage them through his attorney and his clerks."[31] But with growth Perkins found it essential to hire competent people to help in miscellaneous affairs. "When Mr. Touzalin was made General Manager of the B. & M.," he explains,

> it was thought best by him and all of us, that the Iowa Land
> Department should be withdrawn from his jurisdiction, and
> in filling the place I selected Mr. Baldwin, not only because I
> thought he would make a good commissioner but because he

could also help me in many ways outside of the Land Department and I paid him $4,000 because I could not get him
for less (and we shall soon have to pay him more!) He has
earned his salary many times over in looking after our local
aid matters and extensions in Iowa and Missouri, helping us
in the legislature, etc., etc. He is an educated lawyer whom I
took out of the practice here in Burlington, is a democrat
and something of a politician, knows everybody, is a great
worker and withall a very upright and candid man.[32]

Although James Baldwin's title was identical to that of the land commissioner in Nebraska, he exercised a great deal more independence
and dealt with a greater variety of matters than his counterpart.

As Perkins attests, upper-level managers like Baldwin not only
went beyond the confines of a single department to involve the coordination of activities across the company, they also performed a great
many tasks outside the company itself, with other railroads, with state
legislatures, with farmers' organizations.[33] And these tasks often required diplomatic skills. Thus Perkins entrusted J. W. Blythe, an attorney at Burlington, with the task of lobbying for the company in Iowa
in order to protect the company from what he considered "unfair or
unwise legislation." General Manager of Roads East Thomas Potter
was also an important figure in behind-the-scenes Democratic politics
before his move to Chicago, although his only official activity in connection with the party was to serve as delegate-at-large from Iowa to
the National Convention of 1880. When Henry B. Stone became general manager, replacing Potter, who had gone to the Union Pacific,
Perkins supported Blythe's policy of giving passes to members of the
Iowa legislature over Stone's opposition. Too many issues were at
stake, ranging from the determination of rates to questions of incorporation to avoid such gestures.[34]

THE MAKING OF A MANAGER

Even though job definitions were subject to variations, a large managerial hierarchy was created in a few years and offered promotion
opportunities to those who joined it. Recruiting talented men was
only the first step in the larger task of organization building. Once
enlisted, executives busied themselves not only defining new career
profiles but also advancing their own. As other railroads built similar
complex organizations, an integrated world of railroading emerged

where managers experimented with the life-style they derived from a new corporate system of occupational mobility.

Like the Pennsylvania Railroad, the C. B. & Q. played a major role as a model for railroad management. Land Commissioner Baldwin made precisely that point when he directed attention to the fact that "the Burlington Service [served as] a sort of school from which have graduated many who have become prominent elsewhere in the railway world."[35] All those C. B. & Q. executives of the 1880s who ended their careers as vice-presidents or presidents of other roads held a succession of positions at C. B. & Q. To be sure, connections helped. Paul Morton, who ended his railroad career as vice-president of the Santa Fe system (before being appointed secretary of the navy in Theodore Roosevelt's administration and eventually president of the Equitable Insurance Company in New York [see chap. 3], started as a clerk in the land office in Burlington. His railroad career was significantly furthered by his father, J. Sterling Morton, who was an influential political figure in Nebraska. As a member of the state legislature and president of the state board of agriculture, the elder Morton helped the railroad behind the scenes. During his years in the Nebraska legislature (and before serving as secretary of agriculture in Cleveland's second administration [1893–97]), he was actually, although unofficially so, on the C. B. & Q. payroll.[36]

But most top executives who were promoted through the ranks made it on their own.[37] After graduating from high school at seventeen, E. P. Ripley started his working life as a clerk in a Boston dry goods store. In 1866, at twenty-four, he entered the employ of the Union Railroad as a contracting agent in the Boston office. Two years later, he was hired by the C. B. & Q., where he was promoted to general freight agent with headquarters in Chicago in 1878. He became traffic manager in 1887. The following year, Ripley replaced Henry Stone as general manager and succeeded in ending the great strike of 1888. In 1890, Ripley was elected third vice-president of the Chicago, Milwaukee and St. Paul Railroad Company with his office in Chicago and in 1896 moved on to the presidency of the Santa Fe.[38] Others who rose through the executive ranks at C. B. & Q. experienced similar career patterns, crowned by the presidency or vice-presidency of a road. Henry B. Ledyard, president of the Michigan Central, had begun as a clerk in the office of a division superintendent; W. C. Brown, vice-president of the Lake Shore, had started as a train despatcher in Burlington; William F. Merrill, vice-president and general manager of the New York, New Haven & Hartford, had entered the Burlington in the engineer corps. Thomas Potter, who died while vice-president of the Union Pacific, had begun as a station agent at Albia, Iowa.[39]

Movements among firms were essential to the evolution of an integrated business hierarchy of managers. This process worked both ways. Other executives brought to the Burlington railroad experience they had acquired with other roads in the United States or abroad. L. A. Howland, trainmaster of the Chicago division, started as a teen-aged brakeman in New England. John Lathrop worked with a New England railway in the 1850s before moving west, becoming secretary and treasurer of the Hannibal & St. Joseph Railway, auditor of C. B. & Q. in 1878, then general auditor. William McCredie, a freight auditor, started as an office boy of the Edinburgh & Glasgow Railway in his native Scotland.[40] The new world of railroading involved the creation of a pool of capable managers, recruited in part for their recognizable professional skill and demonstrated experience.

Some executives were well educated. Forbes personally selected a number of executives and sent them west, thus duplicating many times over the process by which managers who maintained extra-local ties penetrated local elites. Forbes picked young men from Harvard University who ended up in high level jobs. George W. Holdredge, who had left Harvard before graduation in 1869 because of family misfortune, became general superintendent of the B. & M. in Nebraska and, then, general manager of lines west. Henry B. Stone, five years younger, ran the locomotive and car department before assuming the post of C. B. & Q. general manager. Thomas S. Howland, who graduated from Harvard in 1868, where he had taken science courses, began his C. B. & Q. career as a civil engineer for the B. & M. in Iowa in 1868, became secretary to Perkins in 1876, and in 1884, secretary of the company with headquarters in Boston. In addition to these three Harvard-trained men engaged by this Bostonian institution, a western railroad, T. E. Calvert, chief engineer of the B. & M., had graduated from the Scientific School at Yale. He would later succeed Holdredge as superintendent.[41] If Forbes and Perkins favored Harvard, midwestern associates like Detroit lawyer James F. Joy, the aggressive promoter of the Michigan Central, had ties to a growing midwestern center of higher education, the University of Michigan. From there, Joy recruited James Walker to work for the Michigan Central. Walker, who later became C. B. & Q. general solicitor and then president, selected another Michigan Law School graduate, L. O. Goddard, as his secretary. The trend in the 1880s was to hire a growing number of employees who had received academic training.[42]

While the majority of middle-level managers of the C. B. & Q. in 1880 had risen through the ranks without having had the benefit of higher education, the scattered evidence suggests that most were already among the 8 percent of the American population who had graduated from high school, and some had gone beyond high school. F. C. Smith, cashier, had gone to the St. Lawrence Academy in Postdam, New York, then acquired mercantile experience in a Boston firm before working for Treasurer Amos T. Hall. N. B. Hinckley, assistant to General Auditor Lathrop, graduated from the select Milton Academy. Son of an artist from Milton, where the Forbeses had their home, he started his career in the China trade, where John Murray Forbes had made his fortune. William Irving, purchasing supply agent, prided himself on having received a good education in Boston. C. M. Higginson, also assistant auditor, went to the Lawrence Scientific School before starting office work for the B. & M. While working for the railroad in Scotland, William McCredie attended night school for five years and attained a position of senior clerk in the office of the Caledonian Railway before migrating to the United States.[43]

BUILDING THE BUREAUCRACY

The majority of executives at C. B. & Q. were career men who spent most of their lives in the middling ranks of the hierarchy. What, then, was the attraction of such seemingly uneventful careers for these middle-level managers? A close look at the C. B. & Q. reveals that, although only a few would rise to the top of the hierarchy, even those who did not had responsibilities unmatched in the world of small business. They exercised a great deal of autonomous judgment largely because the job of building the new bureaucratic structures fell to them. In the process, they had significant power over large numbers of personnel, and they controlled large financial resources. They relinquished individualism, to be sure, but in exchange gained the opportunity to set in motion the capital of the new giant corporations. In helping allocate and expand that capital, they participated in some of the most significant and challenging tasks of their generation.

The most direct way in which middle-level managers developed the bureaucracy was through the hiring of both clerks and workers. They were given full authority; the only advice they received was to encourage internal promotions whenever possible by hiring employees at the lowest possible level, as brakemen in the train service, as firemen in the engine service, as clerks or assistants in the station service.[44] In assuming control of hiring, these men removed it from the hands of both the senior executives and the foremen and laid the basis for managerial power.[45]

Control only began with hiring. Middle-level managers spent much of their talent in developing well-oiled bureaucratic mechanisms within a single department. Such men, we often forget, imposed work rules on white-collar workers long before Taylorism imposed scientific management on millions of factory workers. The career of A. E. Touzalin demonstrates the zeal with which middle-level managers approached the task. Touzalin was ultimately rewarded for his efforts as a middle manager by being appointed the head of the B. & M. and, then, general manager of lines west. His earlier career, however, is a good illustration of the trend toward middle-level managerial independence and power over organizational matters.

Touzalin was an Englishman by birth and spent his entire career in railroading. Before his promotion and the separation of the land department into Nebraska and Iowa divisions, Touzalin was head of the B. & M. land department in Lincoln, Nebraska, reporting to the central land office in Burlington, Iowa. In that function, he oversaw a large part of the railroad efforts to populate areas touched by the B. & M. network by advertising and selling the company land. Touzalin began by reorganizing the department, defining tasks, and writing job descriptions.[46] What should a cashier do? How do his responsibilities differ from those of an accountant? He also delegated specific tasks to his subordinates. One man wrote the contracts, another one responded to inquiries made by parties in person, while another tracked down delinquent accounts. Taxes also had to be attended to. So did land assessments and lawsuits. Each task was the responsibility of a specific person in his department.

Touzalin also set out to define procedures for particular situations: the issuance of contracts whenever land was purchased from the company and payments not completed in full, the evaluation of credit risks, the mode of dealing with delinquents. He also concerned himself with the problem of advertising land for sale. He instructed his agents in a circular of January 1875 to give five-year credit instead of ten-year credit on Iowa sales and discounts for cash receipts. Elsewhere, he reminded land department employees that they had no obligation to show land to land hunters. Just as the general freight agent asked his executives, who were setting freight rates, to abstain from investing their own money in elevator companies, Touzalin charged his land department subordinates with fiscal discipline: no rebates to employees on land they purchased for themselves![47]

In addition, Touzalin reorganized the payroll, asking his employees to place the payroll of Iowa Department on a sheet by itself and to prepare a separate sheet for employees working both in Iowa and Nebraska. Seemingly no detail was too small. He instructed them that the Iowa and Nebraska sheet should be titled, "Pay Roll of Employees engaged in the joint work for Iowa & Nebraska." And he noted that "Mr. Lawrence's services [writing contracts] can be placed on a voucher & recorded as services." Then, the "employees in the folding Department & advertising will have to be paid weekly & the memo held as cash items until close of month, which J. C. Bonnell who has these girls to look after can arrange as he used to do."

Touzalin went to a great deal of effort even though his staff was small. The payroll for 1875 included nine employees: a secretary, a salesman, an accountant, a cashier, a man employed for the preparation of vouchers paid monthly, and three other men, including a porter, paid by Iowa and Nebraska jointly. He also supervised a small number of white-collar assistants, including young women in the folding department who were paid by the letter. Touzalin insisted on the importance of office hours (heretofore not respected) and the importance of someone minding the office during the lunch hour.

Touzalin's activities at a time when his work was confined to a single department are typical of those pursued by other middle-tier executives. Executives of different departments in the main C. B. & Q. line had free rein over internal department policy. The system required upper-level management signature or authorization, but it was only in exceptional cases that general managers were really consulted.

Middle-level managers addressed questions of white-collar crime, theft, and disobedience. They decided cases of clerical errors involving financial loss to the company, although, strictly speaking, the procedures were a matter of company policy. George B. Harris, who by 1890 was Perkins's right-hand man on the C. B. & Q. (and who would succeed him in the presidency of the road) recognized the importance of relying on the middle-managers' discretion. He advised the treasurer, J. C. Peasley, that the policy of charging a clerk or any employee of the company for pecuniary errors was too vague to be applied indiscriminately. Reflecting on his experience as assistant general freight agent for the B. & M., he added: "About clerks at freight or passenger stations, I do not think any general rule can be made.

The character of the man, his work, and all the surrounding circumstances must be considered in each case." This was a task best left to his immediate supervisors.[48]

Only controversial cases or cases that exceeded the boundaries of a single department were referred up the managerial ladder. Thus Treasurer Peasley intervened in 1890 after having been informed by a station cashier that an agent fired at the Stone Avenue station in La Grange (Ill.) for accepting worthless checks had been rehired there a short time later.[49] Routine cases were dealt with at the local level with only occasional reporting upstairs. Once "bad behavior" or breach of loyalty to the company was uncovered, it was the middle-level executives' responsibility to mete out punishment. For example, the superintendent for the general freight and passenger agent disciplined an assistant treasurer in Lewistown, Illinois, for drinking, speculating on the Board of Trade, indulging in extravagance, and running up substantial debts. The superintendent, using his discretion, did not fire the man but transferred him to the Chicago office with a loss of pay![50]

Middle-level executives had the power not only to discipline their subordinates but also to determine their take-home pay and to further their careers. Even under exceptional conditions, when their ability to control wages and promotions was suspended, middle-level managers could exercise considerable influence. For example, clerks were promoted in the East St. Louis Freight House in 1893 but without an increase in salary "in view of the necessity of economy at this time." Because they had to pay a larger bond premium, the promotion actually decreased their take-home pay. In this unusual case, Fletcher C. Rice, superintendent of the Illinois lines in Galesburg, negotiated with his superior, General Superintendent Besler, for the company to assume the premiums on their bonds.[51]

Middle-level executives made policy recommendations regarding payment to other firms on behalf of the workforce. While payment of insurance premiums was common practice, no payroll deduction was admissible on behalf of other companies such as the International Correspondence School of Scranton.[52] Occasionally, however, middle-level managers made exceptions for garnishment. R. W. Colville, master mechanic in the Galesburg division (1889), explained to G. W. Rhodes, superintendent of motive power at Aurora, that he had told Fireman J. H. Whalon, a faithful employee who stayed with the company during the strike of 1888, that in his case garnishment of parts of his wages to settle old debts would be acceptable for a short while but that this was an exception to company policy.[53] Only occasionally would general managers step in to discourage leniency and standard-ize ad hoc policies developed in local offices. Thus the paymaster wrote to the vice-president in 1893 pointing out that while 57 percent of all the garnishment cases for May 1893 originated from Galesburg, the number of men at Galesburg represented about 13 percent of the workforce. He went on to complain that the discipline at Galesburg was not nearly as tight as it should have been, pointing to drinking, gambling, and "general extravagance" as well as "undue leniency generally and favoritism in certain cases."[54]

Department executives also administered a variety of corporate programs which affected their clerks' prospects, such as the availability of company credit for clerks to buy their own typewriters.[55] They also exerted control over their clerks' release time. Only occasionally did the company set policy in this area. For instance, on the eve of the World's Columbian Exposition, George B. Harris made a special point of instructing department heads (through Peasley again) not to grant special holidays to employees to visit the fair.[56]

The middle-level executives' role in hiring and promotion reflects their significant financial responsibility. They had other duties that influenced railroad finances as well. Admittedly middle-level managers constituted only one voice among many in the most controversial chapter of railroad economic policy, rate setting. Rate setting was the economic issue of the day that captured the attention not only of railroad men and their customers but also of politicians of all stripes, state legislatures, and courts. In the continuing negotiations among competing roads, between individual roads and state assemblies, regulatory commissions, and federal courts, senior executives and lawyers rested their case on the data and evidence provided by those who knew the market best, the middle-level executives who routinely collected the data necessary for forecasting. Forecasting became increasingly significant as the margin of flexibility the railroads enjoyed was narrowed when Congress passed the Interstate Commerce Act of 1887, forbidding pooling arrangements—thus reinforcing the trend toward system building—and making illegal the various preferential rate schemes.[57]

Other areas where forecasting was important were directly in the middle-level managers' purview. Once the bureaucracy was established, it became necessary for bureaucrats to predict business flow and estimate the need for appropriate growth in the bureaucracy. Traveling auditors were responsible for considering business conditions and recommending staffing levels in local offices.[58] Economic forecasting was also needed for the smooth functioning of the road. Each spring the railroad needed estimates of the wheat crop based on number of acres under cultivation and yield per acre. It secured its own figures and compared them to those of the government.[59] Much of this work required extensive travel, often under difficult conditions.

The results of these various surveys were also used for public relations, in the railroads' efforts to secure settlers along the lines. When George S. Harris[60] was land commissioner of the B. & M. prior to Touzalin, he hired a man of letters and well-known lecturer, J. D. Butler, who not only conducted a variety of surveys on farming conditions in the west but broadcast the results of these surveys across the country and in lecture tours and in numerous editorials. So involved had Butler and Harris become in this colonization work that Perkins concluded that Harris senior had lost sight of his business responsibilities.[61]

Some middle-level managers controlled large sums of money directly, and they were legally liable for their mistakes. As paymaster, Charles S. Bartlett disbursed from $500,000 to $550,000 every month among the company's 15,000 employees, of which from $150,000 to $175,000 was in currency and the remainder in paymaster's checks. He handed out an average monthly pay of $33 (or about $400 a year) from his safe in the pay car on the C. B. & Q. line. The bond that he had given to Amos T. Hall, then treasurer, consisted of railroad bonds and bank stock. The assistant paymaster, who accompanied Bartlett on his monthly trip in the paycar, was also bonded.[62] Bartlett had a long career with the road. By 1886, he had worked for the railroad for eighteen years, first as general accountant for about three years, then as cashier for five years, then as paymaster for ten years. He was paid a mere $3,300 a year.

COMMUNITY PLANNING

Community planning is another area in which railroad executives exercised their considerable talents. For many executives, town building was an imperial adventure. When the Burlington line was laid through Nebraska, the townsites were selected by a group of railroad officials and their friends who organized themselves as the Eastern Land Association. Thomas Doane, a founder of the association and the chief engineer of the Burlington and Missouri River Railroad Company in Nebraska since 1869, traveled from Fort Kearney in 1870 to the Republican River with a military escort of six men. The area was deserted. He reports, "We saw tens of thousands of buffalo. No

Indians were in sight."[63] Because he feared that later settlers might disregard the railroad's claims to land grant sections, he erected four two-story frame houses near each of ten of the stations on the line between Lincoln and Kearney. He drew names for his still imaginary towns from a variety of sources and arranged them neatly in alphabetical sequence: Crete, Dorchester, Exeter, Fairmont, Grafton, Harvard, Inland, Juniata, Kenesaw, and Lowell. He imposed a gridiron street pattern on each of the towns with the Burlington running right through its center.[64] On a map of Harvard drawn shortly after the town's founding, one could already see a metropolitan house, a hotel, a bank, a post office, two lumber yards, a livery stable, a carpenter and wagon shop, a Congregational and a Methodist church, the B. & M. railroad station, and a high school.[65] Because the eastern part of the state by 1870 had been settled by homesteaders, it was necessary in some cases for the group to purchase land. Thus, they bought 120 acres adjoining Beatrice in 1872, laying off the tract at South Beatrice. In one of these new towns, Doane later created and raised money for a small educational institution bearing his name, Doane's College.[66] The railroad executive had become institution builder.

In addition to laying out station towns, the railroads built complexes at division points. Here were the shops, roundhouses, yards and sidings, warehouses and other buildings needed at these regional centers of railroad activity. Their plans, although somewhat larger, scarcely differed from those used for the smaller station towns. North Platte was the farthest west of the Union Pacific division towns in Nebraska. Grenville M. Dodge, the chief engineer responsible for the completion of the first transcontinental railroad, laid out the town of North Platte in November 1866 to serve as an end-of-track construction base. The population immediately soared to 5,000 and remained at that level over the winter until the terminal moved to Julesburg. Although the population plummetted to 300, completion of the railroad shops and roundhouse provided a stable and growing economic base. The railroad workforce increased from 100 in 1867 to nearly 500 by the early 1880s. North Platte soon became the county seat of Lincoln County. Following Dodge's plan, two blocks were set aside near the center for a courthouse and school. These two blocks were divided by the principal business street, which led to the station.[67]

ENGINEERING THE ROAD

Not all executives were administrators or planners. Also among the middle-level executives at C. B. & Q. were the master mechanics, roadmasters, superintendents of bridges and buildings, general fore-men, and so on. These men often had different backgrounds from other executives. There were, as yet, few degree programs in engineering; consequently, these men developed their expertise on the job. While mechanical engineers received training at the Naval Academy early in the nineteenth century, and while Yale and Rensselaer recognized the "possibilities of curriculum specialization" in the late 1850s, it took several more decades for colleges to have an impact on the field. As a result, many technical executives rose from the 'working ranks to positions of considerable responsibility. Their experience was distinct from other executives in that they emerged from the "shop culture complex."[68] Together with the machine-tool shops and engine-building shops, railroad shops became an important training ground for mechanical engineers. Later, in fact, many railroad superintendents would figure among the founding members of the American Society of Mechanical Engineers in 1880.[69]

These mechanical engineers were conscious of the role they played in changing the society in which they lived. W. S. Perry, who ended his career as superintendent of bridges for the B. & M., is a typical example.[70] Born in a small town on the Ohio River in 1851, Perry headed west at sixteen. He tried his luck in Omaha but did not succeed. He moved on to Lincoln. To go from Omaha to Lincoln, he took the Omaha and Southwestern Railroad to the north side of the Platte River to a point opposite Cullom, crossed the Platte River on a ferry boat, then went to the B. & M. platform at Cullom in a wagon and took the B. & M. to the Lincoln depot. In Lincoln, he landed a job as a carpenter. The builder who hired him was organizing a colony of homesteaders to settle in Clay County, Nebraska, ahead of the C. B. & Q. line from Lincoln to Kearney. The young man entered on a 160-acre preemption four miles from the town site that is now Harvard. Track laying reached Harvard at the end of 1871, when Perry was twenty-one. Perry then secured a job as a track layer but continued to struggle on the farm. The prairie was uncultivated and burned over; there were no cornfields, no stubble, not even any trees, and much of Perry's stock died in a snowstorm. Finally, after renting out his homestead, Perry took full employment with the railroad in 1875.

He was employed in Plattsmouth with the bridge and pile driver gang; his first job was replacing a pony truss with a pile trestle. These trusses, built of white pine timber with uncovered oak packing blocks, rotted away in a few years. They were replaced by timber bridges with cast iron clamps and packing blocks. In the spring of 1878, Perry became foreman of a pile driver crew. He found himself constantly out in the weather under dangerous circumstances. The "thrill of my life," Perry noted ironically, was when the ice movement shifted the entire bridge at Plattsmouth out of line with the tracks. This was in 1879, the year that he returned to visit his home town in Ohio and met the woman he was to marry. In 1880, he was appointed bridge foreman of the eastern division with headquarters at Red Cloud, the railroad crossing where Willa Cather grew up and which became the typical small Nebraska town of many of her novels (see chap. 6). The line was soon extended to Campbell Siding, later appropriately renamed Perry, where large cattle-shipping pens were built to accommodate shippers from western Nebraska and eastern Colorado.[71] In the fall of 1882, Perry and his two immediate superiors, Superintendent Campbell and Roadmaster J. R. Phelan moved their headquarters from Red Cloud to McCook, Nebraska, where they built homes with lumber bought at Burlington, Iowa. That year, track was completed from Campbell Siding to Denver. In 1892, Superintendent Calvert decided to replace the wooden bridges between Oxford and Denver with stone masonry and steel. Perry suggested "building roofs of concrete between the eye beams." In the spring of 1906, Perry was appointed supervisor of bridges, lines west, with headquarters at Lincoln. He had become one of the top executives of the engineering department.

Other railroads such as the Central of New Jersey, which imported at the turn of the century a two-way bar system of reinforcing bridges, provided a more advanced technological environment for their employees than the C. B. & Q. and depended more on engineers with formal training.[72] But Perry, on his own, using the opportunities afforded him as a middle-level executive and the engineering information that circulated among railway managers, was responsible for building, maintaining, and improving the road itself and, it can be said, played an important role in the settling of the frontier and in pioneering new technology. These challenges were available to him only as a member of the expanding railroad bureaucracy.

Other executives who were responsible for technical matters contributed to and benefited from the same advances in engineering, and their careers are remarkably similar to Perry's. They combined a talent for innovation and attention to detail. Joel West, master mechanic of the Iowa division with headquarters at Burlington, was noted for his remarkable memory and his obsession with detailed instructions, which he insisted must be carried out to the letter.[73] At the time of his death in 1897, West had finished nearly forty years of continuous service. He had started as a journeyman in Quincy, Illinois, a border town where fugitive slaves settled in the hills. At the end of the Civil War, West was fireman on the C. B. & Q. Before he was promoted to master mechanic of the Iowa Division, he was master mechanic of the Quincy shop. In the C. B. & Q., West found a wide field for his talents. He was interested in improving the quality of tools and in developing safety devices to reduce the alarming number of wrecks. Improving safety (a problem also at the heart of Charles Francis Adams's writings) was an issue which concerned the entire C. B. & Q. hierarchy, although the realities of railroading often led engineers to improvise rather than follow prescribed guidelines. West also did bridge work.

After West died, one of his co-workers wrote his eulogy in a tone revealing of the great enterprise these men had undertaken. As he put it, "when Joel West commenced to work for the Burlington road the Mississipi River was almost the western border of civilization. At that time the great railroads which now span the states of Missouri, Iowa and Minnesota, stretching thence to the Pacific ocean, giving employment to tens of thousands of men, were practically unthought of, and the roads in existence when he entered railroad service did not employ a tithe the number of men they now employ." The sense of mission and accomplishment inherent in these remarks is typical. This then is what Joel West's career meant to his fellows. He took part in the creation of a vast and sophisticated organization and in essence grew with it. He conquered new territory, supervised larger gangs of men, and was at the forefront of technological innovation.

C. W. Eckerson, general foreman at Creston, Iowa, locomotive and car department, is another example of a life dedicated to the technical side of railroad work. He was not at ease in writing. He asked those who sought advice from him to visit him, for, in the words of one of them "we could talk better than we could write." But he had a talent for finding technical answers. Another railroad man recollected:

> I worked with Mr. Eckerson at Creston in 1884 in the equip-
> ment of the new machine shop there. When there was any
> difficult detail about the machinery, I had but to state the
> problem and Mr. Eckerson would find some successful way
> of working it out.
>
> The locomotive grate and ash pan which bear his name
> are good illustrations of his capacity as a mechanic. The coal
> used in Iowa was so poor that it required nearly one hour to
> clinker our consolidation engines, and when business was

brisk it caused a serious delay to engines entering the round-house in winter, and the manager said we must reduce the time by some change in the grate and ash pan. I explained to Mr. Eckerson what we wanted to accomplish, and he soon devised his improved grate and ash pan, which reduced the time of clinkering to less than twenty minutes. . . . I have come to look upon the big machine shops (of West Burlington and Creston) as monuments of the men who helped so much in building them.

Eckerson and West are examples of those mechanics who rose to the executive rank by finding efficient uses for equipment. They are representatives of a much larger shop culture that grew from the concentration of resources in a few large corporations that needed talent and inventiveness. The gifted mechanical executives tapped these enlarged resources to make a genuine impact on their time. Mechanical engineering was only one of the technical fields where such talents found an outlet. Others ranged from the design of passenger cars to the design of train stations, which have become symbols of the nineteenth century.[74]

PROFIT

Looking at middle-level management as we have so far, one might form the impression that managers used their entire energy setting up administrative mechanisms, laying tracks, and providing markets and support networks. What about profit making? Railroads were businesses, and the purpose of those who made the rules and regulations was to win markets and overcome competitors. When looking at middle-level managers in this context, another view of their world emerges. Their work lives combined, in a complex way, the search for order and method with the often irregular and improvisational strategies necessitated by the search for profit.

Land speculation was essential to the railroad business, and railroads resorted to what can mildly be called imaginative methods of land acquisition. Thus, in a practice that was not atypical, four agents of the Eastern Land Association built a single house in Lowell at the junction of four quarter-sections. Each lived in one of the four corners of the house, plowed a few acres of land on his side, and entered a claim as a bona fide settler. Once ownership was granted, the agents transferred their titles to the association, which promptly cut the section up in 22 by 140 foot lots.[75]

The story of Edgar Mott Westervelt provides another example of the tactics managers resorted to. Born in Illinois in 1861, Westervelt worked on the C. B. & Q. telegraph service as a young man, a good school for accuracy and rule. From 1885 to 1893, he was assistant right-of-way agent, then became right-of-way agent and real estate agent. He lived in Lincoln and worked for the B. & M. land department. "Those were the days when things happened," he begins his memoirs somewhat sentimentally.[76] The things that happened often reflected the combination of deception and profit making many middle-level railroad executives, Westervelt included, resorted to. "During the fall of 1886," Westervelt reports,

> it was decided to buy some additional property at Beatrice to fill out our station grounds in preparation for the construction of a new passenger station. A part of the property that we needed was (two lots) owned by Mr. John H. Von Steen. Our people and the Union Pacific had both been negotiating, or trying to negotiate, for the purchase of these two lots. Mr. Von Steen had taken the position that inasmuch as he was friendly to both companies, he would not sell to either one of them; therefore, as I was new in the railroad world and not known at Beatrice, I was sent there to get title to these lots. I called at the First National Bank, and introducing myself to Mr. John Smith, then cashier of that bank, told him I was from New York and looking for a location in Beatrice on trackage. . . .

To make a long story short, Westervelt bought the land under false pretenses and transferred it to the railroad, which infuriated the owner, who for a short time took his business away from the Burlington. "But after a time," Westervelt notes, "it all righted itself, and then I went to Mr. John Smith to apologize for the misrepresentation that I had made to get his assistance."

These memoirs make an interesting contrast to the sort of bureaucratic order reflected in Touzalin's activities when he headed the same land department. But the contrast is only superficial. The pursuit of profit required both the habit of order and a penchant for flexibility, even deception. The capitalist bureaucracy in America began as a peculiar form of bureaucracy, hierarchical and rigid, geared toward planning and long-term profit, but also highly sensitive to market circumstances.[77]

As the first American bureaucracies were fashioned to meet corporate goals, they were subjected to profit imperatives. Managers
who were responsible for implementing bureaucratic structures in
the United States were also profit-conscious businessmen whose concerns reflected the dual imperatives of order and gain. Both order
and flexibility coexisted within their lives. Achieving this mixture, and
achieving it within a large organization, became the middle executive's
contribution to American work culture.

DEFINING THEMSELVES IN OPPOSITION

The middle-level managers' achievements, however, were overshadowed by the prominent role they played in defending the most un-
popular causes of the railroad. They came to be represented as
indifferent, if not overtly hostile, to community interests. Frank Norris, for instance, portrayed a harsh Pacific & Northern agent who
fought the ranchers viciously.[78] Such feelings were solidified after
1877. Labor problems had been mostly the province of lower-level
management before the violent railroad strikes of 1877, which were
ended only through the intervention of federal troops. At C. B. & Q.,
Perkins had mobilized his managers to take a hard line and averted
the strike in Iowa, while the more liberal Robert Harris in Chicago
had failed to head off the union. The success of Perkins's methods led
to a shakeup in upper-level management and to Harris's departure
from C. B. & Q. Although the episode did not close the controversy
among railroad managers, Perkins's position reinforced the view that
management must stand ready to oppose labor.[79] Too often by their
unrelenting commitment to maintain the rail operation they built and
by their willingness to fight against labor, managers defined themselves in the public realm. Drawing the line between management and
labor became another way to identify the new managerial class.

Labor conflicts were violent, and all who participated knew it. For
middle managers, such conflicts involved much more than finding
scabs to replace striking engineers and enforcing the blacklists. They
demanded a constant effort to sway public opinion. In the public's
mind, the managerial hierarchy, from the president of the railroad to
the foremen were judged together as part of the same world. The
railroads appealed to the middle-class sense of law and order to justify
violent reactions to violent struggles, no matter what issues of social
justice were involved. And the executives relied on the prevailing social Darwinism of the same middle class and the individualism that

usually goes with it to justify both their companies' lack of welfare programs and fight against labor organizations.[80]

Yet the railroads could not dismiss the questioning of those views by an increasingly large segment of the population. William Dean Howells captured these doubts in his reflections on the great Burlington strike in 1888. "When the strike began," Howells wrote in *Harper's Weekly*,

> I suppose that nearly every humane person said to himself, "Well, between men who want to make a better living and a corporation that wants to make more money I can have no choice." I said something like this to myself, not remembering my C., B., & Q. stock in my magnanimity. But of course when the strike came, as strikes must, to involve violence, the general sentiment changed, and many lectures have been read to the engineers on their misbehavior, but to the road none. . . . Shall the railroads fulfil their public obligations by agreement with their employés, or shall the government take possession of them and operate them? It is folly to talk of the withdrawal of capital, and the consequent ruin of the country. The country belongs to the people and they are not going to let it be ruined. . . . Let us understand that it is not engineers or switchmen or brakemen who can bring it to the worst; it is only directors and managers and presidents who refuse to arbitrate, and who forget their public duties so far as to talk of a railroad's affairs as private affairs.[81]

The fight against the great Burlington strike became an enduring test of corporate solidarity. Jay Gould's "surrender" to the assaults of the Knights of Labor only reinforced Perkins's determination. Shortly before Vice-President Potter resigned in 1887 to take a position with the Union Pacific, Perkins wrote him a letter reflecting on the Gould strikes. He told Potter, who had a good record of negotiating with the brotherhood, "When you have the enemy on the run is a pretty good time to go for him vigorously, and the question occurs whether this may not be a good time to go for the Knights of Labor."[82] Potter's replacement, Henry B. Stone, general manager of the C. B. & Q., formerly superintendent of locomotive and car department, was a hardliner. The army of Pinkerton detectives hired by the railroads sent Stone daily reports of their detailed investigations. More than anybody else, workers held him responsible for the inflexible stance of management.[83]

Top management's efforts to crush the strike were vigorously sec-
onded. Middle-level managers were also very much involved and at
dangerous places. Reading through the notes of Trainmaster Oscar
Eugene Stewart written during the Burlington strike of 1888, one
finds testimony to the same attitude toward labor from the lower end
of the managerial stratum: "This is the third day of the strike," wrote
the trainmaster. "Everybody is hard at work hunting up new engineers and taking care of those we have. We have an abundant supply
of applications for firemen, many of them country men who were
never on an engine. . . . Chicago papers are coming out on the side of
the Company and are eagerly read."[84] To keep the trains operating,
Trainmaster Stewart even slept in the cars. Edgar Mott Westervelt, the
land agent involved in dubious schemes, remembers that year as
"never to be forgotten." Westervelt helped replace engineers and firemen and "made running time and came into Lincoln on time."[85]

Such managerial solidarity cannot be explained simply as the result of the pressures upper-level managers applied on their subordinates; indeed few middle-level managers needed to be coerced into
fighting the labor movement. Although most were forward-looking
men in organizational and economic matters, they were backward-
looking when it came to social issues. To them, the new organizational
structure they had helped create gave them opportunities for superior
individual achievement. And they were not about to subject these opportunities to collective bargaining.

Managers, who often outplayed their bosses in the fight against
the labor movement, could not escape unfavorable characterizations,
no matter what their accomplishments. The managers' need to defend their handiwork caused them to take refuge in social Darwinism
and to hold the line against the labor movement. They assumed that
the public shared their Darwinian view, but wrongly so, for their
ability to coopt the state was increasingly challenged by the state itself. And the managerial insistence on fighting labor aroused the
fear of many Americans that bigness would crush democratic ideals.
Thus parts of the middle class stood aloof from the managers' aspirations and repudiated their fears. William Dean Howells's reflection
on the Burlington strike expressed a spreading sense of unease with
corporate growth and the conflict many people—not just workers—
felt between economic innovation and social aspirations. Howells
voiced the increasing concern of those reformers influenced by the
Knights of Labor's call for the eight-hour day and shocked by the violent repression at Haymarket only two years before. This sense of

grievance is why the labor movement enjoyed a new degree of solidarity beyond the ranks of the working class in the 1880s. Working-class subculture gathered unusual strength when members of the society at large became convinced that "unbridled acquisitive individualism had to be restrained."[86] The motives of these other groups were not entirely altruistic. Many an independent entrepreneur who felt the pinch of corporate growth and power joined in the protest. In local associations, independent businessmen, motivated both by idealistic and financial considerations, fought against the alliance of corporate influence and political corruption they saw infiltrating and sometimes overtaking municipal administrations.[87] Such middle-class local entrepreneurs even lent occasional support to workers striking the railroad lines, for their vision of a nation founded on independence, social justice, and fairness was at issue in these disputes.

In some communities the sympathy of the majority of the citizens was so clearly with the strikers that elected officials hesitated to apply the protective measures demanded by the company. "A Pinkerton man at Aurora reported that the marshal was willing to help the company but "the mayor was afraid of the strikers and was trying 'to keep the marshall down.'" Another Pinkerton reported from St. Joseph that the mayor and the local police had sided with the strikers and that the sheriff was "doubtful."[88] If working-class organizers succeeded in reaching new audiences in the 1880s, it was in part because they forged a motley alliance against the rising class of managers with a middle class alert to the disruptions caused by corporate power.[89] Because workers were not alone in distrusting the coming of the corporate order, managers became embattled, regardless of their lack of personal wealth and middling position in the hierarchy, with the larger community. Opposition to their views reinforced their sense that they belonged to a new class, distinct both from those who did manual labor and from those who were individual entrepreneurs.

THE MANAGERS' INFLUENCE

What does this incursion into the C. B. & Q. managerial stratum tell us? First, managers invented a new work culture within the large corporations, a culture that balanced order and rule with competition and a search for profits and that sought to resolve large problems with increasingly specialized knowledge. In the emerging corporation, managers shared a technical culture, business aspirations, and supervisory responsibilities. Taking advantage of a new corporate synthesis, they channelled their energies through a wide geographic area while deriving their expertise from a combination of formal knowledge and experience. These men were motivated to join corporations, for they saw in them a means to live an interesting life and participate in innovation beyond the reach of any single entrepreneur without exposing themselves to as much personal risk. There was also a utopian impulse behind their work. Pooling their talents and resources to achieve a unique combination of innovation, order, and profit, middle-level managers enabled business organizations to succeed in a task as ample as that of the railroads.

Developing a managerial system was only part of the story, for the managers' influence was felt far beyond the office, not only in the towns they helped build along the railroad lines but also in the country at large. It is often said that the famous Wabash receivership case of 1884, in which the Federal Court of the Eastern District of Missouri consented not only to place the road into receivership prior to actual default but also to appoint receivers close to Jay Gould, was yet another stroke of genius from the ever resourceful railroad tycoon. By declaring bankruptcy, the Wabash freed itself from immediately payable promissory notes, kept running, and retained control of its affairs.[90] The endless commentary and legal controversy over property rights the Missouri court decision generated missed a simple fact of critical significance. For the first time, a court acknowledged that a system of transportation had become more important than its individually owned parts. At stake beyond the interest of the bondholders was a new notion of public interest that resulted directly from the work of managers. Keeping the road operating meant keeping the managers in charge, for too many people and towns depended on the functional system these men had built to dismantle it.[91]

By the 1890s, college professors recognized the importance of business managers. They argued that "the success of the great corporation today depends primarily upon the possibility of securing not capital but brains."[92] Initially because corporations had no model for the development of the bureaucracy, practical experience was placed at a premium. But gradually, as the work of the first executives was completed and bureaucratic procedures were codified, management training gained in importance. Specialized education was becoming a prerequisite for a middle-level manager. And articles in the *North American Review*, *Harper's Weekly*, *Popular Science Monthly*, *World's Work*, and *Munsey's Magazine* echoed the new prophecy.[93] In the words of *The Outlook*'s editor, "the man who is not specially trained in his own field of enterprise is a man doomed to failure."[94] The first executives established the curriculum for this training. Specialization alone perhaps was a limitation but in the corporate structure, the coupling of individual talent and expertise would more than offset the limitations of any single individual.

The establishment of a working corporate bureaucracy is one reason that during this period American corporations became the model for government. Max Weber had accurately remarked that "the idea that the bureau activities of the state are intrinsically different in character from the management in private offices is a continental European notion and, by way of contrast, is totally foreign to the American way."[95] This is because in the United States, the reformers who sought to fight corruption in public life, do away with spoils, integrate efficiency in government, and deliver technologically advanced services in the end turned to modern business methods for guidance.[96]

As the capitalist bureaucracy spread and became more influential, middle-class opposition to corporations also became more pragmatic. With the corporations becoming permanent institutions, the abstract visions and principles of the socialist utopians that had marked the 1880s[97] and that had penetrated local associations were replaced by a more matter-of-fact agenda based on an analysis of the new capitalist bureaucracies' impact on the American class structure. As we will see, members of this large managerial stratum—both hierarchical and fluid—took an increasingly active role in the larger society and contributed much to the spread of the principles of big business, which they were helping to shape. Their decisions reached an ever greater proportion of the society or influenced it indirectly. Such a stratum—so large and so well entrenched today—had only just been invented in the 1870s. Its coming to the scene signaled the creation of a managerial middle class forsaking the ideal of small independent entrepreneurship. What happened on the C. B. & Q. line between Chicago, Burlington, and Denver in the 1870s and 1880s, duplicated many times throughout the country at the same time, marks the start of the twentieth century.

THREE

THEORIZING, TINKERING, AND REFORMING

Speak your latent conviction, and it shall be the universal sense.

Ralph Waldo Emerson, "Self-Reliance," 1841

Popular sentiment in this country will not tolerate the assumption of responsibility by the technicians, who are in the popular apprehension conceived to be a somewhat fantastic brotherhood of over-specialized cranks, not to be trusted out of sight except under the restraining hand of safe and sane businessmen.

Thorstein Veblen, *The Engineers and the Price System*, 1921

CHAPTER THREE

T he middle class was ambivalent toward the redistribution of economic power that characterized the late nineteenth century and the early twentieth. But despite what was referred to in the legal language of the day as efforts to combat unreasonable restraints of trade by monopolies, the corporate form of organization became widely adopted.[1] The new communications technology—the telegraph and the telephone—and the managerial techniques first perfected by the railroads were strategically suited to the peculiar economic circumstances of the late nineteenth century. Expanding output and falling prices, a combination that placed small firms with obsolete equipment at a serious disadvantage, forced even large industrialists to look at new modes of financial, structural, and operational organization that would reduce production costs and eliminate ruinous competition.[2] In the late nineties, the postdepression merger movement virtually completed the domination of most capital-intensive industries by publicly held corporations, a move facilitated by the liberalization in the "traitor state," New Jersey, of general incorporation laws.

The belief that larger enterprises were more efficient than smaller ones was firmly reinforced by Andrew Carnegie's success in drastically reducing the cost of making steel rails and Standard Oil's efforts to lower the price of kerosene. Few of the new corporations were trusts in the sense that they cornered a whole industry, leaving no room for smaller firms specializing in high quality or specialized goods. But mass-produced consumer durables such as agricultural machinery, sewing machines, typewriters, cash registers, bicycles, and, by the 1910s, automobiles came to conquer the manufacturing sector. This transformation required no less than a complete overhaul of the ways in which a society produced and exchanged goods. This is a well-known chapter in economic history.[3] Corporations, however, became not only the dominant economic force of the twentieth century but also a crucial element in social change, for organizations, especially pervasive and successful ones, have powerful sociological and ideological consequences.

The two primary schools of thought that sought to explain the incorporation of American society are also well documented. The first, initially found in expressions of muckraking, underscores the manipulative abilities of "robber barons" and, by extension in our era, of "the power elite." The second explanation, proposed by the advocates of organizational synthesis, is simply functional: the technology of production and distribution imposed work reorganization.[4] This chapter does not invalidate either of these explanations but rather posits a third premise: that corporate influence on American life became pervasive because the corporations' reasons for being—whether it was to create products of synthesized chemicals, to manufacture an automobile, or to offer a service—were not one but many. Thus their influence entered American life through a variety of channels.

Different types of corporations required different mixes of skills and turned to different strata of the population and different intellectual traditions and technical cultures. When they emerged, there existed no set vision of how corporations should be structured, and each segment of society pursued its own methods of organization. Although corporations may appear monolithic today, the history of corporate America is an instance where the privilege of hindsight turns out to be no advantage at all.

THEORIZING

Over the years, the idea of the corporation has come to refer to corporate bureaucracies, the lives of its managerial groups, as well as to the type of organization responsible for the development of mass-production and mass-market techniques. The Du Pont Company, a prototype of the modern corporation that best embodies the principles of big business as we commonly understand them, is an exemplary case of the amalgamation under one structure of corporate functions such as manufacturing, sales, investment, and research—all of which had occupied related but distinct spheres in the Gilded Age. But Du Pont and the paradigm that has been derived from it should be understood as one of several competing models that, for historical reasons, has become most common. Many corporations initially followed alternative models, two of which I will explore by looking at the formative years of the Ford Motor Company and the Metropolitan Life Insurance Company.

Alfred Chandler and Stephen Salsbury, Pierre du Pont's biographers, point to the du Ponts' central role in creating the modern corporation: "Pierre, his cousin Coleman, and their associates brought the ways of both Carnegie and Taylor to the Du Pont Company, modifying them to meet the special needs of the explosives industry. Then, as the Du Pont Company moved into chemicals, these big business techniques were carried into that industry."[5] After having helped transform Du Pont into a firm at the frontier of managerial tech-

niques, Pierre du Pont and his younger colleagues rescued General
Motors from the disorder created by William C. Durant's erratic management. Having amassed a fortune during the First World War,
which it partly reinvested in the automobile industry, Du Pont "played
a pivotal role in spreading the techniques of modern corporate enterprise within the American economy."[6]

Pierre du Pont came from a family of industrialists who, as we
have seen in chapter 1, successfully dominated the production of gunpowder in the United States. Whereas the du Ponts of the Gilded Age
had sought to control a national market through horizontal combination (in this case the Gunpowder Trade Association) rather than
through vertical integration, the three du Pont cousins who bought
the firm from the older generation in 1902, pursued an aggressive
policy of absorbing all the constituent companies of the old trade association and moving into distribution and sales. By the time of the
1902 purchase, the Du Pont Company had a payroll of about 1,500
employees. Only three years later, the firm employed over 16,000 employees. The number jumped to 60,000 in 1915, once hostilities had
broken out in Europe.[7] Such intense growth was partly the result of
an aggressive expansionist policy, partly the result of circumstances.
The key decisions that were taken because of such pressures add up
to an impressive story of the diversification of a powder manufacturer
into an integrated, full scale, chemical empire.[8]

By this time Du Pont was not only vertically integrated, it was
diversified. Diversification came at Du Pont initially as a response to
the antitrust suit brought against the company in 1907 for its monopoly in the manufacture of military powder. When the navy—as a
consequence of Du Pont's alleged violation of the Sherman Act—
expanded its capacity to produce its own powder in 1909, the du Ponts
were faced with the possibility of severe losses. Furthermore, the final
court decree of 1912 ordered Du Pont to spin off two new explosive
companies, Hercules and Atlas, which would then compete.[9] Although these losses did not materialize, their prospect induced diversification into the production of celluloids and artificial leathers. The
principle of diversification was well established at Du Pont by 1913,
although nonexplosives accounted for only 3 percent of the company
business. It was bound to increase, however, in the face of low military
appropriations for munitions in 1912 and 1913. In January 1914,
Colonel Edmund Buckner, the Du Pont vice president in charge of
military sales, the man who directed a successful lobbying effort in
Washington to minimize the adverse effects of the antitrust suit,

wrote to Coleman du Pont, company president, that "government business was almost a thing of the past."[10] History, obviously, decided otherwise.

The demand for powder created by the European war generated not only a great expansion of the company's production but also excess capital, which stimulated a new round of diversification. The war left the United States textile industry without dyestuffs, heretofore a German monopoly. As the intermediate components needed in both dyes and powder were similar, the company saw an opportunity to create an American dye industry. This venture took Du Pont into organic chemicals, its area of greatest expansion in the postwar era.[11]

By 1917, the Du Pont Company was selling, in addition to eight types of military powders, two types of powder for railroad work, and eight kinds of sporting powder, fourteen different types of dynamite to be used for activities ranging from ditch blasting and underwater blasting to quarrying and tunnelling, as well as a score of different blasting machines and other tools. Nitrated cotton and the same group of acids used for explosives were also used in making artificial leather, cellulose, and plastics. Leather substitutes (marketed as "fabrikoid") were developed for automobile upholstery, furniture, bags, book binding, and waterproof materials. Plastic and cellulose (marketed as "pyralin") were used to produce lacquers, enamels, ivory toiletware, plastic sheeting, and cleanable collars. The company further diversified into paints and varnishes and commercial chemicals (acid, ethers, leather solutions, lacquers of all kind), colors and pigments and general purpose dye stuffs. Soon, the 1920s would see the growth of such popular products as rayon, cellophane, and the cellulose films used by the booming motion picture industry.[12]

The Du Pont diversification was a response to major pressures brought about by law, international events, and economic opportunities. It took years before the dyestuff venture paid off, for much of the German leadership in this field had been due to tricks of the trade American chemists had to reproduce from scratch.[13] A similar story can be told about the investment in paint, which brought minimal return until the Cellulose Products Department inadvertently invented Duco lacquer in 1920.[14] Other investments had dramatic returns. By investing massively in the automobile industry, Du Pont ensured a growing market for many of its new products (like artificial leather), and the profit from these ventures sustained the expenses of product development.

Such massive expansion and diversification required a new organization. In creating this new structure, Coleman, Pierre du Pont, and their older partner Hamilton Barksdale—a civil engineer who had graduated from the University of Virginia, worked at Repauno dynamite works (see chap. 1), and married a du Pont—brought in a new generation of business executives to maintain a high level of management activity. After one reorganization in 1911 and two in 1914, Coleman and Pierre gave Irénée du Pont, Pierre's younger brother and future president of the corporation, a major role.[15] They instituted a three-tier structure of authority. They appointed to the executive committee the younger people they had hired, and charged them to diversify the company, to carry out its commitment to research and development, and to implement long-range planning and coordination. The second, actually a transitional tier, was composed of the former members of the executive committee who were promoted to vice-presidencies. They were removed from the responsibilities of daily operations and were dedicated to developing long-range policy in major organizational areas. Managerial responsibility, the third tier, was placed with the heads of each department and the managers who reported to them. The executive committee rotated again in 1919. By then, many of the young graduates with engineering degrees from the University of Virginia, M.I.T., Princeton, or Virginia Polytechnic Institute hired by the cousins were running the organization.[16]

There was naturally some resistance to change. Hamilton Barksdale, whose promotion to one of the new eight vice presidencies was, in his case, a way to separate him from managerial responsibilities, immediately offered his resignation. He withdrew it only after President Coleman du Pont assured him that the ultimate goal of the plan was to give men of his talent and importance the time to think about the larger issues. "Dear Barkie," Coleman wrote, "I really think you are so absorbed in your work that you do not realize how little you see of the outside world and how little you meet the leading men of the day and the men who are doing things. . . . The new position is one which will tend to broaden your views, enable you to get good ideas elsewhere, bring them to the Company, go into other enterprises if you want to where, if you don't sharpen your wits to the razor edge, some fellow will get the best of you." The duties of the president and new vice-presidents included working on special committees on "various subjects either in our company or in other companies"; for instance, one would look "into the way the Development Department of the United States Steel Corporation is handled; another . . . into the methods of purchasing by other companies"; another into bonus and pension plans.[17] This frequent consultation with other firms was part of the du Ponts methodical effort to formulate a system of management.

Although the head of the department was responsible for developing his own managerial organization, the executive committee always reserved the right to intervene. And the executive committee (and at least theoretically the board of directors and the finance committee) kept direct control of companywide programs and procedures affecting employees' benefit plans, salary approvals, appropriations, the division of departments, and the power of affixing official signatures. The executive committee formed specialized committees composed of executive committee members and heads of departments (manufacturing and sales, purchasing, appropriations, development, legal, employees) including a board on pensions and one on benefits and awards.[18]

As Chandler and Salsbury recount clearly, Pierre was the primary force behind the initial transformation of a manufacturing concern into a large integrated chemical empire. He championed vertical integration early on, from assuming sources of supply (by purchasing nitrate plants in Chile—an investment that turned out to be less advantageous than hoped for) to distribution (by creating a complex sales organization).[19] He implemented a significant degree of separation between ownership and management, although always being careful to keep family members (such as his brother Irénée and his brother-in-law R. R. M. ["Ruly"] Carpenter) in key positions. He foresaw the need for diversification, although the real push for diversification came under the leadership of the younger people he put in place in 1914.

Pierre himself was an organizational wizard, but his work should be seen in the context of the overall experimentation with organization that characterized the age. Organizational structures were adopted in a variety of settings, and Pierre expressed curiosity about them. Amid Pierre's abundant notes and schemes for the 1914 reorganization of the company into a complex hierarchy of departments and committees is an interesting page torn from a magazine: a printed sketch showing in schematic form the various departments comprising the organization of the Hotel McAlpin in New York.[20] In satisfying the typical guest, the hotel manager relied on no fewer than seventeen different departments, some controlling as many as fifteen functions vital for the hotel. Plumbers and the silver-plating plant, together with eleven other groups, reported to the chief engineer; cashiers, auditors, the stationer, and others reported to the hotel's chief accountant; while the headwaiters and the restaurant and banquet departments, captains, waiters, busboys, and room service pantries reported to the maître d'hôtel.

The reorganization of 1914 created a centralized organization not without analogy to that of the hotel. But as the company continued to diversify, the ineffectiveness of centralized departments (such as purchasing or sales) in responding to the requirements of Du Pont's varied product lines made itself felt in the balance sheet, especially in the postwar recession years 1920 and 1921. To compensate for these problems the younger executives Pierre du Pont had put in place, after several trials, created a hybrid: the "decentralized, multidivisional structure," with autonomous departments, each with its own managerial structure, and "a central office to coordinate, appraise, and set the goals and policies of the functional departments in the interest of the enterprise as a whole."[21] This new structure, which became the model for the modern corporation, Pierre took to General Motors, where he instituted a central office to coordinate the existing autonomous divisions.

Three other aspects of Du Pont—in addition to diversification and decentralization—make it an exemplary case of corporate capitalism: expertise in corporate finance, massive investment in science, and managerial policies aimed at wedding managers to the company, thus reducing what economists call agency risk, that is, the risk that managers will value their perceived interest over that of the organization.

In the domain of finance, Pierre du Pont maintained a lifelong association with John J. Raskob, who succeeded him as treasurer of the company. Raskob was the only executive at Du Pont who came from a lower-class home. If Pierre was an organizational wizard, Raskob was a financial wizard, primarily responsible for many of the stock schemes that led to Du Pont's success in the initial years of reorganization—in effect freeing Du Pont from hiring the services of New York investment bankers. Although Raskob was effectively out of the picture at Du Pont after the war, he was the primary force behind the decision to pour huge war profits into William C. Durant's ailing company and, in this instance, to negotiate a partnership with New York investment banker J. Pierpont Morgan, Jr.[22] While investment bankers had raised capital for the government and for railroads in the nineteenth century, it was only at the beginning of the twentieth century that their influence was deeply felt in industry, as they moved to reorganize the larger corporations. The senior Morgan and his partners had successfully reorganized and played a major role in the subsequent management of U.S. Steel in 1901, International Harvester in 1902, and A. T. & T. in 1906.[23] But the House of Morgan had heretofore stood clear of the volatile world of the early automobile industry. Durant, who was scrambling for money in 1908, had told George W. Perkins, the Morgan partner most influential at U.S. Steel and Harvester, "The time will come when a half a million automobiles a year will be made and sold in this country." The unimpressed Perkins reportedly commented "If that fellow has any sense, he'll keep those observations to himself when he tries to borrow money."[24] A decade later, not only had the outlook drastically changed, the Du Pont investment gave the House of Morgan the guarantee of sound management it needed.

With the creation of a chemical empire, Du Pont also created one of the first large, research establishments in American industry. The Du Pont brain trust quite early understood that the era of the lone scientist who tested steel for Carnegie was over. All scientists hired at Du Pont combined middle-class background with a solid scientific education. But they lacked a model for the laboratory they set up in 1902. The only existing models of collective, organized, research were laboratories established by Edison and General Electric.[25] Thus creating, managing, and devising policies for research became a major challenge for the development department that was set up in the 1911 reorganization. What role should the laboratories play in diversification? How should research efforts complement the acquisition of existing companies for their trade secrets? How much should be invested in basic research? How should scientific invention be rewarded? How should scientists be recruited and what relationships should Du Pont maintain with research universities? All of these questions remained relevant.[26] The old company had had ties with scientific research in several institutions, notably the University of Pennsylvania, MIT, the University of Virginia, Virginia Polytechnic Institute.[27] But the new company contained a much more dramatic symbiosis of managerial and scientific expertise.

The salient fact is that by 1920, most of the scientists who worked in R&D at Du Pont had Ph.D.s.[28] Several had received training in the German academic institutions that became models for American research universities. Many were initially recruited at Johns Hopkins, where the first research director, Charles L. Reese, hired in 1902 to run Du Pont's first experimental laboratory, had received his training (he also studied at the University of Heidelberg). But the network widened rapidly. During the First World War, the National Research Council induced corporations to fund basic research at universities across the country and was instrumental in bringing about an enduring cooperation among corporations, foundations, and universities.[29] By the 1920s, Du Pont supplemented the in-house expertise through a wide program of academic consulting, through fellowships to support academic research, and, especially, by recruiting many young Ph.D.s from the University of Illinois chemistry department. The Du Pont R&D structure also maintained ties with other corporate labs such as Kettering's at G.M.[30] The high level of training required from R&D personnel had consequences in many other areas of the company, for it was common for researchers to move out of the lab and assume executive positions in manufacturing or marketing.

Du Pont also took a cautious but forward-looking approach to the problem of reconciling their employees' quest for security in their careers and the company's quest for greater efficiency and profit. The company moved early in giving stock options to management and thus interested them in the future of the company. There were 809 stockholders in 1907, of whom 218, or 27 percent, were employees of the company. By 1912, the percentage of employee-stockholders had doubled either through awards granted by the company since 1909 (as profit-sharing or as rewards for inventions, unusual sales performances, etc.) or through direct purchase. Of 2,697 stockholders in 1912, 1,440, or 53 percent, were employees.[31]

At the same time, the company systematized its effort to regulate salaries and to create salary scales, limiting salary increases but distributing profits above a certain percentage. Coleman had written to Morgan partner George Perkins to ask advice on regulating salaries and governing the promotion of employees. Did Perkins know of any firm with a good system? The company president sent similar inquiries to the Pennsylvania Railroad, G.E., and U.S. Steel.[32] Perkins's response served as encouragement to the implementation of the pension plan under study by Raskob and other executives. "If you people have not any such plan in operation, I strongly urge you to get busy and adopt one." The New York investment banker went on to argue that "the right sort of pension plan comes pretty near being a panacea for most of the ills that exist between employer and employee!"[33]

All these characteristics show that the structure of Du Pont and the corporations that followed its lead emerged from a concerted effort on the part of men in charge to think about managerial struc-

tures, investment strategies, expert knowledge, and employee relations. These men, many of whom came from privileged families and
graduated from institutions of higher education, were inclined to
theorize about their tasks.

A salient point about Du Pont's theoretical approach to capitalism,
however, is that the evolution of Du Pont theory did not reflect a cor-
responding evolution in Du Pont's view of society. The Du Pont commitment to rethink managerial strategies constantly and create a new
science of management did not supplant an older worldview and older
philosophical principles. Like the railroad managers who preceded
them, Du Pont leadership was at once forward-looking and backward-
looking. While the management system and the organizational philosophy that animated men like Pierre du Pont, John Raskob, and
other members of the corporation's executive committee quickly entered the mainstream of American life, their ideology retained the
Gilded Age beliefs in laissez-faire and the social Darwinism of their
forebears. They rejected regulation and "progressive" state intervention. In fact, all his life Pierre du Pont forcefully attacked the notion
that his corporation ever was a trust. In his mind, there had never
been a restraint of trade during the first decade of the twentieth century or an attempt at monopoly, just a search for efficiency. In 1922,
recalling the court decree ten years earlier forcing Du Pont to spin
off two explosive companies, he wrote to his nephew Samuel Hallock
du Pont:

In the year 1907 the U.S. government brought suit against
E. I. duPont deNemours Powder Company on the claim the
company was a trust. The suit was "set up" by one R. S. Waddell, a former employee of the company who became dis-
gruntled, started in the powder business and failed. This
suit, brought at a time when "trust baiting" was at its height,
was filled with a great amount of irrelevant evidence. Finally,
after five years, settlement was reached by accepting a decree
written by the Government agents, the court taking practically no part. The whole performance was an outrage on
proper conduct of law, much of it in the nature of comic opera farce. I have always severely condemned the judges for
the part they played. The result of the suit was a "dissolution" of E. I. duPont deNemours Powder Company by splitting off from it the Hercules Powder Company and the Atlas
Powder Company. . . . The dissolution was appropriate to

the completion of the farce. Nothing was accomplished by it, for the reason that there was nothing to be accomplished.[34]

On the issue of war profits, both Pierre and Irénée, his younger brother who succeeded him in the presidency, argued publicly that these massive profits that benefited the company were just rewards for heroic work done under difficult conditions. While the United States Congress worried about unethical profiteering (and intellectuals questioned the notion of human progress in the aftermath of the Great War) war profits at Du Pont were viewed as a stimulus to better the lot of mankind.[35]

Ultimately Pierre du Pont believed that each individual was responsible for his own welfare. He even had reservations about the social and moral value of the corporate pension programs he had helped promote. In 1950, years after his retirement from active management, Pierre's response in a letter to a former employee revealed his second thoughts: "I have always been a believer in trying to make people conscious of their obligations to themselves and to society. Pension plans discourage such an idea. . . . This does not mean there are not some unfortunates, who, from lack of brain powder [sic], fail to make a provision but, fortunately, that class must be comparatively small, else all would have gone to pot long ago."[36]

The du Ponts found it essential to maintain a political climate not antagonistic to such views. The intensive lobbying by Coleman du Pont and Colonel Buckner in Washington during the antitrust case was characteristic of the ways many large firms fought regulation.[37] Concern with regulation led to concern with a whole panoply of larger issues. As a result, more businessmen took an open role in national politics. Coleman du Pont had himself been a member of the Republican National Committee and had a vast political acquaintance. Although Pierre du Pont's role in public education in Delaware was a personal commitment fulfilled only after he had retired from the company, his old associate John J. Raskob had his day in the limelight as chairman of the Democratic Party during Al Smith's unsuccessful campaign in 1928. Later on, he became secretary of the conservative, anti-Roosevelt, American Liberty League. Well endowed with du Pont money, the league rejected "the demagogical theory that legislation provides cure for all ills" and dissented "from the doctrine that rigid regulation, even when given the sugar-coated title of 'economic planning,' has merits superior to the American system of private enterprise."[38]

Du Pont and the reorganized General Motors are textbook examples of "center" firms, that is, firms that were large, capital intensive, and vertically integrated.[39] These firms pursued technological and organizational innovation emphasizing mass production and economies of scale. They developed complex managerial hierarchies and committed themselves to long-range planning.[40] These well-managed corporations were run by men with strong conservative beliefs, brilliant capacity for organization, and links to the financial and scientific establishments.[41] The big corporations that did not fit into this pattern were usually framed either as failures or as exceptions, odd cases. Most of the exceptions, if they were to succeed, eventually conformed to the "center" paradigm.

TINKERING

A case can be made that the Ford Motor Company, after an extraordinary start in the 1910s, fell onto hard times in the 1920s because the peculiar conditions that had made it successful were no longer operative and because the idiosyncracies of the older Henry Ford defied managerial common sense. So infatuated had Ford become with his invention and so enraptured was he in his autocratic ways that he missed ample cues from car buyers for model diversification. General Motors, reacting to this need, was able to use its organizational flexibility to make inroads into Ford's market. Ford's success was short-lived in a world where the rules had been reshaped by other companies.

The case needs further examination, however, for Ford's initial success constitutes a major chapter of the American industrial experience. The Ford assembly line and the distribution system to market the Model T were the prototypes of the systems that would be installed by all major manufacturing concerns. Thus, although the Ford Motor Company was forced to adapt the more orthodox practices that enabled its competitors to measure and react quickly to market conditions, in its original form, it was an extraordinarily influential organization that contributed significantly to our modern notion of the corporation. Sigfried Giedion somewhat underestimated Henry Ford's genius when he suggested that Ford's assembly line simply marked the "end of the mechanistic phase," of American industry.[42] Giedion saw the assembly line as the culmination of decades of progress in designing machine tools capable of providing identical, interchangeable, parts, thus setting the basis for what became known as the "American system of manufactures." This system, first perfected in clockmaking and firearms, greatly expanded with the bicycle craze of the 1890s. But it was mass production on an unprecedented scale— such as Ford achieved—that required absolute standardization. Ford and his associates not only found new ways to apply standardization, they also installed a system of conveyors and moving assembly far more complex than any found in slaughterhouses and can making.[43] Historians of technology argue over the exact chronology of innovation at Ford that led to the creation of moving assemblies for the flywheel magneto, the transmission, the engine, and finally the chassis, but all was accomplished rapidly once the initial goal was identified.

The sheer technical virtuosity of the Ford assembly line made it the forerunner of modern automated factory systems in use today. But Ford was obsessed with mechanizing the lives of his workers as well as the production process. No other corporate production technique better illustrates the dilemma that Charlie Chaplin captured in *Modern Times*. Even though workers could probably maintain a small degree of autonomy on the shop floor,[44] the endless repetition of the job, as Chaplin pointed out, could drive the worker to the point of distraction. And when Ford instituted the $5.00 day to help stabilize a restless workforce, the ultimate message to the foremen was to learn "hurry up" in every language possible.[45]

"Fordized industry," in the eyes of the Italian communist Antonio Gramsci writing in his prison cell between 1929 and 1935, took the play out of life. What Ford had to offer to the worker was a drab, sterile, eventless, machinelike routine. Insanity was not what Gramsci feared but too much sanity. In his *Prison Notebooks*, Gramsci presumed that Ford's concern with the family life of his employees was yet another way to enforce factory discipline, another way to make sure that Ford workers would return home in the evenings to the peaceful "'venerem facilem parabilemque' [easy and accessible love] of Horace." The Ford worker should love "his own woman, sure and unfailing, who is free from affectation and does not play little games about being seduced or raped in order to be possessed."[46]

To be sure, the introduction of the assembly line was not merely a technical coup. It was in effect, as Gramsci correctly sensed, a sociological one, and one that depended, at least in the formative era of the company when the assembly line was designed, on the peculiar corporate structure Ford devised. Actually, Ford built an organization that appealed to exactly the type of managers he needed to create an automobile.

Ford was not interested in the managerial issues that dominated Du Pont executive committee meetings. He did not believe in job titles, and there was little compartmentalization of the workforce. In 1910, ninety-one of the 446 employees on the salaried payroll were listed without a department. It is only in 1913 that A roll distinguished senior men from the lesser executives and white collar workers listed in B roll. Although B roll was roughly organized by department, the sixty-eight top men in A roll were simply listed in decreasing order of pay.[47] Insiders knew who was doing what. Even though James Couzens, Ford's general manager who would later become mayor of Detroit, had started his career in the more systematized organizational structure of the railroads, Ford management practice did not extend much beyond issues not directly related to production.[48]

Ford's approach to the production process itself was both traditional and highly original. Ford was a tinkerer who preferred trial and error, ingenuity and intuition. In this, he stood apart from the mainstream of corporate development. David Noble, looking at the formation of the scientific-corporate complex in *America by Design*, notes that he omitted Ford deliberately: "Ford—like Taylor but unlike most of the [others]—was neither a college-trained professional engineer nor one tutored in science. Unlike Taylor, Ford laid the technological bases for mass production more in the manner of a mechanical-minded inventor than as a proponent of scientific management."[49] While Taylor's work—focusing on time and motion techniques—directly addressed the theory of management, Ford, adopting motion studies, was more interested in devising ways to replace men with machines.

Ford's individualism also comes through in his attitude toward finances. Ford resisted any resort to the financial markets. He hated money speculation. There was no Raskob around to devise stock schemes. Nor would he have tolerated him. In the midst of the 1920–21 recession, Ford fired Frank Klingensmith, his treasurer, for suggesting borrowing. Ford angrily turned away representatives of J. P. Morgan and forced the car dealers to carry the company. Joe Galamb, a mechanic who played a major role in the development of the model T and shared many of his boss's prejudices, including his well-known anti-Semitism, described in an interview the reasons behind Ford's lone wolf attitude: "Mr. Ford didn't like Wall Street because there were Jews in it. In 1919 the finance capitalists in Wall Street were trying to take over his company. . . . Mr. Ford didn't like the du Ponts. . . . One reason why Mr. Ford was against du Pont was because he was so interested in General Motors. . . . He didn't like the Mellons either. . . . Mr. Ford didn't like anybody who had anything to do with the stockmarket."[50]

Ford felt no particular obligation toward stockholders. Making cars was more important to him than making money. Indeed, he reinvested all profits in the company and bought off the Dodge brothers and other shareholders to maintain his independence.[51] Nor did Ford have any interest in "appropriate" rates of return—the magical 15 percent at Du Pont. He practically gave away the Model T by constantly reducing its price.

Ford also had no social aspirations. Rejection by the denizens of Grosse Pointe meant nothing to him. The fact is that his success resulted, in part, from his sustained rejection of what a historian aptly called "conspicuous production," that is, the temptation to build a car to appeal to the social group to which one aspires, a bug that had infected most other car manufacturers.[52] The Model T was essentially a farmer's car that did not require good roads and for which replacement parts could be found in any rural hardware store.[53]

It is no surprise, then, that Ford's social and political views were hardly representative of other major corporate heads. Ford did get involved in politics, but there was little obvious connection between his political activities—the Senate race against wealthy patrician Truman Newberry or his involvment in the peace movement—and the interests of corporate America. Infected with a late-blooming variant of utopianism, he wanted to create a life for his men. But Henry Ford, the birdwatcher and fan of Emerson's poetry—the only writer he ever read—the tinkerer turned industrialist, also fought hard to prevent unionism at all cost while some corporations began to integrate unions as part of a larger vision of managerial strategies.[54]

Ford's hard and successful business maneuvers—whether fighting the Selden patent (the attempt by the Association of Licensed Automobile Manufacturers together with lawyer-inventor George Selden to monopolize the development of the internal combustion engine), buying Lincoln, letting the dealers carry the company during the postwar recession, or intuitively choosing the right advertising slogan ("Spend the Difference" rather than "Save the Difference")—show a mind with keen commercial sense.[55] Ford had a system unequaled in America: the best product on the market, the best way to produce it, and able managers to make the most of these advantages. As the company proclamation for Thanksgiving of 1911 read, the Ford Motor

Company voiced special thanks "for the fact . . . that satisfaction and good fortune in motoring has been freely vouchsafed to our 100,000 Ford users. That we have been guided in effecting such economies as have enabled us to reduce the price of the Model T for 1912, so that the motor car is now a possibility to thousands who found it beyond their reach before. For the hastening of the construction of new Ford buildings made necessary by the demand for 75,000 Model T's."[56]

The reality that should be stressed, however, is this: In the years of the company's unchallenged success, when the number of cars sold went from a mere 6,000 in 1908 to over 775,000 in 1919 and the workforce jumped from 690 people to over 44,000, Ford's managerial style, if at odds with that of other giant enterprises, was perfectly in tune with the attitudes of the men he hired, the machinists and draftsmen who helped build his assembly line and design his Model T.[57]

The men who surrounded Ford were of a radically different sort than those who surrounded Pierre du Pont not only at Du Pont but also later at G.M. The Ford men did not come from the college-educated elites and manufacturing establishment of the Gilded Age. At Du Pont, the Development Department, as soon as it was created, hired young Ph.D.s from Johns Hopkins and soon drew on a large network of scientists. But Ford called on talents found in other social strata. A gifted tinkerer, he surrounded himself with other tinkerers, twenty years younger than he was, but like Ford without formal education. They were representative of the diversity of the industrial population of the Midwest in the Gilded Age. Although some came from rural America, some from other towns and cities, and others from abroad (especially from Canada, Germany, and Ireland), most had spent some time in the northern industrial belt that stretched from Pittsburgh to the Great Lakes before they moved to Detroit.

These self-made men made up the elite of a new industry where there was much to gain and little to lose. Alfred P. Sloan, who had been educated at M.I.T. and became the organizational wizard who succeeded Pierre du Pont at G.M., corroborates this observation. He vividly recalls that the men who worked in the budding automobile industry were "in the main, rather simple people on the surface."[58] Yet these men rightly attributed to themselves some of the major innovations of our century. In the metals lab or in the machine shop, they tinkered. Technical men, they acquired their engineering expertise on the job and took no part in the corporate synthesis of science, management, finance, and consumption that characterized other large corporations. As tinkerers and production men, they were Thorstein Veblen's heroes. What Veblen missed, however, in concluding that engineers and entrepreneurs are necessarily antagonistic, is that these ingenious individuals, stimulated as they were by an expanding market, combined their ingenuity with entrepreneurial skills.[59] A collective portrait of these men reveals the diversity of the emerging corporate world.

Some tinkerers concentrated on technological innovation, others on testing, others on running the growing shops. But no matter what their area of expertise, they shared the same background and the same youthful enthusiasm. First among the tinkerers was C. Harold Wills, who actually built the first Ford cars. Wills, in turn, recruited John F. Wandersee, a chronicler of the early days at Ford. Wandersee was born on a farm near Milford, Wisconsin, in 1877. His parents were German immigrants who had moved to Jefferson County, where the young man received his schooling. Wandersee came to Detroit in 1900 at the age twenty-three to join his brother, who happened to be Wills's friend. Ford and Wills sent Wandersee to United Alloy Steel to learn how to manage a steel laboratory. Wandersee's knowledge of vanadium steel, in particular, played an important role in the success of the Model T. When the decade closed, Wandersee was only thirty-three, his Canadian wife twenty-four. They lived in Detroit with their two-year-old daughter.[60]

Wandersee recalled other men whom Ford hired: "After I had been there alone about a week, more people were hired. Frederick K. Strauss was one. He was put in charge of the machine shop. Then they hired a pattern maker by the name of Dick Kettlewell. He was making patterns for the designs. After that in the latter part of October, August Degener came there. I think he came direct from the Nageborn Machine Company."[61] Degener was the son of a German cigarmaker. His brother also worked on automobiles while their sister was a dressmaker. Though adults, the three siblings, like the children of many immigrants still lived with their parents in the Detroit East side. Another important figure, Charlie Mitchell, who came a little later, was a blacksmith.

These mechanically minded men without formal education flourished in the loose organization that initially characterized the Ford enterprise. They lived for cars. When they were not working—and they worked hard—they went together to Chicago to support the car racers, Barney Oldfield, who raced the Old 999, and Frank Kulick, known for his daredevil temperament.[62]

The reminiscences of some of them are particularly helpful in delimiting the social milieus from which they came, milieus that are rarely associated with the development of giant enterprises. Bill Klann was born in 1884 in Detroit to a family of German immigrants. His father, a tailor, sent him to parochial school for three years, then to public schools. In 1898, while still in high school, he worked on Saturdays in a blacksmith shop. Klann remained in high school, however, for just six months. He served a six-year apprenticeship at the Detroit Shipbuilding Company (as engine room oiler, tool crib boy), at the same time taking International Correspondence School courses in drafting as well as pattern, foundry, and machine shop practice. Like Wandersee, he was brought into Ford by the network of employees who were on the lookout for promising men. He started working at Ford in 1905 at the suggestion of Gus Degener, who had graduated from the same primary school. At that time Klann was "capable of making parts from the blue prints and could do tool room work."[63] He impressed his fellow workers by his "ability to operate machine tools at exceptionally high rate of speed" and, before the creation of the Time Study Department, soon defined work standards.[64] His ideas about the progressive assembly also proved instrumental.

Ernest Pederson, born in 1888 in Iron Mountain, Michigan, graduated from high school in Duluth, Minnesota, and went to the University of Michigan. He dropped out after two years and took a job in a construction company back home in Iron Mountain. He was hired by John Henkle, the employment manager at Ford, to be a car tester. Soon, his job expanded to driving cars for whatever purpose the company needed, both testing cars and chauffering executives. The turning point in his career came when the company began sending unassembled cars to dealers to save space on railroad loads. He was sent to Milwaukee, Des Moines, Sioux City, and New York to help with assembly work, which he seemed to have a knack for. He set up a "progressive" preassembly line device. Because he was working on the same idea, Ford put Pederson in for a big promotion. In May 1913, Plant Superintendent Charles E. Sorensen promoted him again, this time to head the final assembly department. There he worked closely with Billy Klann of the motor department and Alex Sparks of the rear axle department. The following year, Ford and Sorensen gave Pederson a complete education in car making by sending him to all the departments, including tool room, the cylinder production, the foundry, and others. That same year, perhaps to complete his sense of having arrived, he got married.[65]

Immigrants also became mechanical executives like Klann and

Pederson. National origin and level of education mattered little compared to individual ingenuity. Joe Galamb, Carl Emde, and Richard Kroll were immigrants who bypassed much of the ethnic community experience to work directly in what would rapidly become a giant American enterprise. Joe Galamb joined Ford in 1905 at age twenty-four. Born in Hungary in 1881, he studied at the school of Industrial Technology in Budapest, worked in an automobile plant in Dusseldorf, Germany, then traveled to the U.S. with two friends to see the St. Louis World's Fair of 1904. Galamb worked first in New York in a paper-box factory, then moved to Pittsburgh to work at Westinghouse as a toolmaker. He went to Detroit where Wills hired him. Galamb became the principal draftsman on the Model T. Carl Emde, a German "from the old stock," who spoke broken English, was known in the tool design department as a brilliant man though rough and tough, who insisted on precision and accuracy. As Walter Wagner, another tool designer, recalls, "there was no half-way with him." Emde joined Ford in 1906, helped with advances in machine tools and by 1912 headed a tool design department of twenty-five designers and draftsmen. Richard Kroll, born in Prussia in 1884, had spent his teen-aged years in Detroit, where his father, a brickmason, had moved. Kroll started out as an apprentice in the Brass Iron Works. At twenty-one, he got a job at Ford as a toolmaker and a machinist through Paul Neinas, who sang in the same church choir. Neinas was in charge of the experimental room on Piquette Avenue, where the Ford factory was located before the move to Highland Park. Kroll finished his career as director of quality control.[66]

In the case of these men, innovation was not the product of a new corporate synthesis but instead of raw aptitude, ingenuity, on-the-job experience compounded by hard work and the excitement of discovery. As Sorensen recalls in what is otherwise an exercise in self-aggrandizing: "We proved we could develop our own workers into foremen and superintendents. In the six years from 1908 to 1914 [Clarence] Avery was the only outsider that broke through the barrier of the basic organization."[67] Sorensen goes on to celebrate Henry Ford and Edison's lack of formal education. To these men, degrees gave only the pretense of knowledge. Typically, the Ford executives who contributed both to technological innovation and industrial organization had no formal training and were quite young when they assumed positions of responsibility.[68]

It was not that these men did not want to learn, but they had their own ways of doing so. Thus Charles Morgana, who had come from

Keim Mills in Buffalo after Ford purchased it and who was in charge of procuring new machine tools would, according to Wandersee, "go around and pick up ideas from other companies making production machines and bring them back to Carl Emde."[69] Typically, the tinkerers embraced ad hoc training and pursued knowledge informally, outside the educational establishment. But despite Sorensen's claim, a few "college men" did contribute to the tinkerers' knowledge. Klann recalls that a school was started in his basement around 1912 and 1913. Clifford Herbert, a twenty-four-year-old graduate of Cornell, had just come to the shop as a mechanical engineer to learn the automobile business. Klann notes, "I was teaching them [the college men] the practical side and they were teaching us the theory. That went on for about three years."[70]

This constant noninstitutional exchange of ideas led to innovation. Thus, Pederson's clerk, Al Hussey, who had graduated from the University of Illinois in engineering, started time-cost studies after having penetrated the ranks of the tinkerers. Hussey's book, showing how many man-hours it took to produce a car, was the beginning of the Ford minute-cost system.[71] Thus the celebrated Ford standardization as surveyed by *Scientific American* in 1914 and described in detail by Arnold and Faurote's *Ford Methods and the Ford Shops* a year later, had been put in place by men who were atypical only in another corporate context.[72] They were actually representative of a special blend of tinkering and entrepeneurship that characterized the automobile industry.

As Ford grew, the company needed people who could drive men as well as design cars. Typically the executives who ran the shops rose from the ranks of the tinkerers. Ed Martin was a "burly, stodgy" French Canadian. When hired in 1904, he was put in charge of spare parts used for repairs. Only four years later, at age twenty-six, he became plant superintendent and tested the first assembly line.[73] Charles Sorensen, a Dane, came to the company in the spring of 1905 as an assistant pattern-maker. In 1907, at twenty-five, he became head of that department. He gained Ford's notice by quickly producing models of ideas introduced by the design group, for Ford understood models better than diagrams. Sorensen became assistant plant superintendent in April 1908 and played a major role in installing continuous conveyor belts to bring material to the assembly line.[74]

The ability to mold this diverse group of men—united only by their technical aptitude and enthusiasm—into first-class production executives is one reason for Ford's extraordinary success. Another is that Ford attracted first-rate men to build the bureaucracy necessary to run the company despite his legendary distrust of nonmechanical executives and record keeping. Georgia E. Boyer, one of the first women clerks, recalls a day at the Piquette plant when "during lunch hour, Mr. Ford went into the Accounting Department and picking up all the ledgers and other books pertaining to bookkeeping, he threw them out of the window onto the street. When the accountants returned from lunch they were amazed to find their books gone. Mr. Ford told them that he saw no reason for keeping a set of books. He said, 'Put all the money we take in in a big barrel, and when a shipment of material comes in, reach into the barrel and take out enough money to pay for it.'"[75] But for all the legendary stories about his antipathy to bureaucracy, Ford admitted the necessity of maintaining a total of over 500 clerks to process the ever increasing paperwork the automobile industry generated. There was a bureaucratic system at Ford (see chap. 5). Furthermore, Ford developed an elaborate sales program to distribute as many of his low-priced cars to the masses as possible.

Those nonmechanical executives that Ford hired were distinct from those who ran the shops, but they shared with them an outlook on life. James Couzens was a counterpart of Wills; both left Ford later in the teens—Couzens to a political career, Wills to his own car company. Wills had not gone beyond high school; he had no drafting education but had been trained by his father, a Welsh immigrant and master mechanic. Couzens, on the other hand, was the only member of the Ford organization with clearly a middle-class background. Born in Canada in 1872, Couzens was the son of an English grocery clerk who later owned a small soap factory in Ontario. Couzens nonetheless received his training on the job. He went to Detroit at age eighteen and got a job as car-checker for the Michigan Central. He later became the freight office director of the railroad, excellent training for running a large organization. He then became clerk, office manager, and business adviser to coal merchant Alexander T. Malcomson, Ford's original partner. From 1902 on, Couzens oversaw finance, bookkeeping, purchases, shipments, advertising, and sales at Ford. He set up the branch house system. Irked by Ford's pacifist tirades, Couzens resigned in 1915 to begin a successful political career that would take him to the mayoralty of Detroit and the U.S. Senate.[76]

In 1907, Couzens hired Norval A. Hawkins as commercial manager. If Couzens was a counterpart of Wills in the Ford organization, Hawkins was a counterpart of Bill Knudsen, who was production manager during the First World War. Both men, as it turned out, ended up at G.M. in the twenties, and their departure from Ford signaled the decline of the pioneering firm as Henry Ford clung obstinately to his Model T instead of adjusting to new market conditions. Born in Ypsilanti, Michigan, where his father was in the hotel business, Hawkins came to Detroit in 1888.[77] Hawkins's accounting firm advised large industries on better business methods and labor-saving systems. Hawkins also regularly contributed to the new business magazine *System*, which was published in Chicago. Hawkins's rise to prominence is especially noteworthy because thirteen years prior to his appointment at Ford, he had been jailed for embezzling $8,000 from Standard Oil in Detroit, where he had been employed as an accountant. According to Georgia E. Boyer, "the Standard Oil Company told Mr. Hawkins that if he would tell and show them how he had manipulated the records, they would guarantee his release."[78] Once at Ford, Hawkins proved indispensable. He revolutionized the sales division. He started *Ford Times*, which included updates on car design and production, on dealerships, and on ways to increase business. *Ford Times* appeared monthly, then twice a month. The new commercial manager understood mechanics well enough to bureaucratize them. He helped set production schedules on the basis of sales estimates. He helped with departmentalization. He insisted on cost accounting efficiency and proper allowances for depreciation and reserves. His sometimes rigid auditing of all branch accounts and elaborate body of forms for accounts and reports adapted to various departments generated resentment from Sorensen and others who argued that record-keeping took too much time.[79] But clearly, both Hawkins and Couzens were successful precisely because they could relate well to mechanics. They may not have been tinkerers, but they partook of the same vision of industrial life. They too learned on the job as they created an organization capable of supporting large-scale production and distribution. Like the tinkerers turned executives, they wanted efficiency but were not concerned with developing a managerial ladder in tune with the organizational theories that characterized other segments of the emerging world of big business.

Other major figures of the Ford sales and accounting organization were also closer to the tinkerers than we have been led to believe. Either they shared social origins or at some point in their lives were exposed to mechanical work. Frank L. Klingensmith, the chief accountant who was forced to resign in 1921 after arguing that Ford should borrow, not cut prices, to get out of financial trouble, was, like

CHAPTER THREE

Bill Klann, the Michigan-born son of German immigrants. He attended Ypsilanti Business College in 1900 and was working at a low-level clerical position in the wholesale hardware business before being hired at Ford in 1905. F. H. Diehl, the head of purchasing, was born in Akron, Ohio, in 1877, of a good mercantile family. He went to high school but also acquired mechanical training with the Goodrich Tire Company of Akron. These men and others, such as John R. Lee, head of the Keim Mills and later head of the sociological department[80] (the department instituted to insure that Ford workers lived decent "American" lives and could be paid five dollar a day; see chap. 5), followed different career paths and had different goals.[81] But they all sought to bureaucratize mechanical executives only to the extent required by their own specialized administrative and commercial function and without alienating them. For these mechanical and paper executives shared much in common. They created the organization inductively and intuitively as opposed to the more theoretical and self-conscious brand of capitalism typical of the Du Pont synthesis.

REFORMING

Other parts of the corporate world were far from both the Du Pont managerial synthesis and the Ford inductive approach to the creation of large-scale organizations. New sectors of the insurance industry embraced the reform movement that swept turn-of-the-century America. The life insurance companies offer a striking contrast with the two models we have seen so far.

As in the case of the automobile industry, the du Ponts played a role in the insurance industry, but in this instance, only a circumstantial one. Coleman du Pont, tired of living in Wilmington and eager to let cousin Pierre run the expanded powder company, launched several real estate ventures in Manhattan. After building the McAlpin Hotel, whose organizational chart had given Pierre pause, he became the prime mover behind the rebuilding of the home office of the Equitable Insurance Company after fire destroyed its headquarters in 1912.[82] Du Pont built the skyscraper at the behest of Paul Morton, Equitable's president. Morton had a successful career as a business executive or, as he liked to put it, as "an organizer, a systematizer and a master of men,"[83] first with the railroads at C. B. & Q. (see chap. 2), then at the Santa Fe. After a brief term as secretary of the navy in the Roosevelt administration, he was brought in as president of the Equitable Life Assurance Society in New York City in July 1905.

Morton's appointment came at a critical time when the life insurance business needed to overcome the adverse publicity generated by a 1905 investigation chaired by New York State Senator William Armstrong. The very success of the insurance industry had brought to the large companies like Equitable, New York Life, and Mutual, huge sums of money, hence numerous opportunities for investments of all kinds. Investments ranged from loans to real estate developers, subscriptions to the large municipal bond issues, United States government securities, railroad securities, and other stocks as the market for industrial securities expanded. Not all these investments were safe. The Armstrong investigation was precipitated when Wall Street speculator-turned-muckraker Thomas W. Lawson exposed the men of "frenzied finance," Standard Oil Vice-President William Rockefeller, Morgan partner George W. Perkins, and other trustees of large insurance companies. He accused them of blatantly violating the guaranties of sound investment that policyholders had a right to expect "in the placing of loans, in the purchase of properties and securities, and in the underwiting of enterprises." In the process, they pocketed money "never shown on the books of the corporation."[84] The fear of unrestrained speculation combined with the publicity surrounding the conspicuously extravagant life-style of men like James Hazen Hyde, heir to the controlling stock of the Equitable, culminated in the state probe of the life insurance business. This legislative investigation, under Counsel Charles Evans Hughes's scrutiny (soon-to-be governor of New York, and later Chief Justice of the Supreme Court), led to major reforms, including abolishing lucrative policies with deferred payments (the infamous tontines) and placing limits on investments. The investigation, in historian Morton Keller's words, steered the insurance business toward "the ideology of public responsibility."[85] With new executives, and soon a new building, Morton pledged to make Equitable "the safest and most conservative life insurance institution" and to make it known "not only as the strongest financially but the strongest morally."[86]

The need to clean house, however, does not account for the particular character of the insurance industry after the Hughes investigation. Life insurance had remained beyond the reach of most nineteenth-century workers, who had traditionally turned to voluntary associations to insure a decent burial and to provide a minimum for their family in case of untimely death. Beginning in the 1870s, industrial insurance—a new field—assumed this function and penetrated the homes of millions of workers in the form of dime-a-week policies.[87] The company that developed this business in the United States, closely following the British model, was Metropolitan Life. In 1869, a voluntary association of German-American workers, the Hildise Bund, approached the newly formed Metropolitan to underwrite life insurance for members of the society. The Bund continued to collect weekly premiums from its members, but it turned them over to the Metropolitan four times a year, employing the collecting technique that became the hallmark of industrial insurance.[88] This early relationship with a German-American, working-class, voluntary association, perhaps facilitated by the German origins of some of the well-established businessmen and professionals from Brooklyn who founded the company, helped give Metropolitan a reputation for fair dealing and also encouraged it to develop industrial insurance on its own. It was the incentive of increasing this sort of business that led life insurance companies to advocate reform in the public interest.

Taking a close look at the work of Metropolitan Life (with Prudential the largest company in the field of industrial insurance), in the first two decades of the century, then, provides a view of the critical relationship between some corporate organizations and the reform movement. While concerns for employee welfare were not new, they were never at the center of corporate activity. The railroads' efforts had been partly defined as a countermeasure to programs advanced by the labor movement; Du Pont's employee programs were directed toward the managerial ladder; Ford's welfare programs were closely tied to the Americanization efforts of the World War I era.[89] With Metropolitan, promoting social welfare became a business. Metropolitan and companies like it actively worked to improve the living conditions of its clients as well as its employees.

Ultimately exonerated because it did not engage in the potentially ruinous practice of deferred payment policies, Metropolitan is a particularly good example of the way in which big business could coopt the reformers' program. As we have seen, engineers, industrialists, financiers, professionals, and tinkerers took part in the building of corporate America. In the case of industrial insurance, corporations, by taking over the work heretofore left to voluntary associations, encouraged social activists to join its ranks.

Corporate America participated in social reform in ways that are much more central than the well-documented exchange of philanthropy or corporate welfare for social control. Taking a cue from the progressive movement, insurance officials began involving the company itself in welfare reforms. In 1909, under the auspices of the Charity Organization Society, Haley Fiske, the most important man behind Metropolitan's expansion, met Lee K. Frankel and hired him to organize the Metropolitan welfare program. Frankel, a chemist by training who had become director of United Hebrew Charities, was reporting to the society the results of his study of workingmen's insurance companies in Germany. He was in the process of proposing to the Russell Sage Foundation—the pioneering institution that was funding the massive Pittsburgh Survey the idea of organizing a social insurance bureau when Fiske lured him to Metropolitan.[90]

Frankel, in turn, hired a young biologist, Louis Israel Dublin, as his assistant to fulfill his mandate of making the Metropolitan "a social institution." Dublin (which was the immigration officer's understanding of "from Dubilna," near Kovno, Lithuania) was born in 1882 to a family of well-educated Jews who migrated to the United States when he was a child. Dublin spent his teenage years in New York tenements and knew the Jewish East Side well: he understood the infant mortality, tuberculosis, early widowhood, and other social ills of the slums. The young man who contributed to the family income by selling newspapers was recognized as a mathematical prodigy and entered C.C.N.Y. at fourteen. Later on, he studied biology at Columbia while teaching mathematics at City College. He received his Ph.D. from Columbia in 1904 when he was twenty-two. After a brief stint as an actuary at New York Life, young Dublin embarked with Frankel in an ambitious health campaign on behalf of Metropolitan. This was coupled with a scientific program of gathering and tabulating health data. His efforts were rewarded by the larger academic community almost twenty years later when he became president of the American Statistical Association in 1924.[91]

Dublin's upbringing in the Lower East Side, his education at City College and Columbia, and his personal commitment to improving the living conditions of New York should have brought him to social work rather than to the corporate world. Louis's wife, Augusta Salik, had been a social worker in Philadelphia after graduating from Barnard College, where she had known Elizabeth Beardsley Butler, another social worker and author of the landmark volume *Women in the Trades*, which was written for the Russell Sage Pittsburgh Survey. The Dublins so admired Elizabeth Butler that they named their first daughter after her.[92]

The men like Dublin and Frankel who helped make life insurance a socially responsible business emerged from the same institutional background as the leaders of the settlement movement. To take but one example, when Mary Kingsbury Simkhovitch opened the Greenwich Settlement House in 1902 (with the sponsorship of such pioneers of the settlement movement as Felix Adler and Jacob Riis), several of her companions who served on the board of directors (a few were even residents at the house in the early years) also came from Columbia University, the Charity Organization Society, and the Russell Sage Foundation. Among them were her Russian-born husband Wladimir, associate professor of economic history at Columbia, and Edwin R. A. Seligman, who held a chair in political economy also at Columbia. Others were part of an educated elite involved in immigrant life such as New York-born, Harvard-educated, vice-president of the Society for Italian Immigrants Walter Brush, and Edward T. Devine, general secretary of the Charity Organization Society, where Metropolitan Vice-President Fiske had first met sociologist Frankel. Paul Kellogg, who had directed the Pittsburgh Survey, joined the board of managers of Greenwich House two years later, in 1903.[93]

Not only did Frankel and Dublin come from this educated milieu of reformers, they shared in the goals of the progressive crusade and phrased the company program in terms typical of the settlement movement. Under Frankel and Dublin's leadership, contracts were made with local visiting nurse associations in various parts of the country to care for sick policyholders. Frankel had been close to Lillian Wald when he worked for the United Hebrew Charities. Wald, in turn, in her capacity as the director of the Henry Street Settlement House, was most anxious to develop the integrity and independence of the emerging nursing profession.[94] Having nurses working for an insurance company was a new route to explore, and the two struck a deal. Metropolitan nursing program was not a mere professionalization of the "friendly visitor," the middle-class woman who volunteered not only to visit the needy families but also to work toward their moral regeneration. Rather, it became a significant contribution to public health.

Metropolitan also launched major educational campaigns. Dublin and his staff prepared a vast library of health and safety information.[95] In the preparation of pamphlets, the company cooperated with those reform associations, institutions, professional associations, and religious groups that pursued related goals. It prepared a volume on water (and its superiority over alcohol) under the auspices of the Scientific Temperance Federation of Boston. It prepared another devoted to the playground with the help of the Playground Association of America. With the cooperation of the National Association for the Study and Prevention of Tuberculosis, it distributed pamphlets about the prevention and treatment of tuberculosis, a disease that accounted for 17 percent of the deaths of its premium policyholders.[96] At the request of the Brooklyn Branch of the Young Men's Christian Association, 10,000 copies of the company's circulars were distributed in moving-picture theaters, the most popular form of family entertainment among working-class communities, as G. Stanley Hall, the founder of the American Psychological Association, correctly observed. The company also distributed disposable drinking cups: 100,000 were sent with the traveling exhibit of the Committee for the Prevention of Tuberculosis, and in 1913 and 1914, twenty million were placed in the cars on the New York Central and big four railroad lines.[97]

In cooperation with the Boy Scouts of America, the company organized the Health and Happiness League for young policyholders between the ages of six and eighteen. Membership allowed young people the opportunities of competing in essay contests and going on field trips and other outings. To join, young people had to sign the following pledge:

> I promise: First—I will wash my hands and face before each meal, and my mouth and teeth each morning and evening. Second—As spitting is unclean and helps to spread consumption and other dangerous diseases, I will not spit upon the public streets nor in public places. Third—I will not use a public drinking cup. I will use only paper ones, or carry my own cup. Fourth—I will destroy every house-fly I possibly can. Fifth—I will never throw rubbish in the streets, as dirty streets make sick people. Sixth—I will do something to help my mother every day. Seventh—I will try and do at least one kind act to some one every day. Eight—I will permit no rude or offensive word to pass my mouth, even when provoked.[98]

The company also prepared large exhibits for international expositions. Here again a major part of the corporate activity echoed the effort of reformers such as the great show on tenement houses organized by Robert DeForest (president of the Charity Organization Society, trustee of the Russell Sage Foundation, and the man who brought Frankel and Fiske together) and Lawrence Veiller that stimulated the revision of building codes in New York City and other communities.[99]

Like reformers, the company sought cooperation with public

agencies as well. Its publication, *The Child*—printed in English, German, French, Polish, and Yiddish editions—was distributed by many cities to new mothers and through school systems. Metropolitan worked with the New York City Health Department, New York State, and neighboring states for distribution of health-related literature and lobbied for improved health conditions in factories. The company's physicians investigated the effect of white phosphorous on workers in match factories, and the company employed its network of agents to lobby congressmen to limit its use. Lobbying was also aggressively conducted at the state and local level for municipal improvements as well as better recording of vital statistics.[100]

It is important to see the extent to which the activities of prospective customers shaped the image the corporation wanted to project, that is, being the friend of the working class. The company took pride in its willingness to help policyholders during the depression of 1893, the Pennsylvania coal strike in 1902, the Fall River strike in 1905, and the San Francisco earthquake of 1906 by paying claims for lapsed policies and allowing delinquent policyholders to reactivate their policies without medical examination. The inclusion of strikers among victims was a revolutionary move for a corporation. Yet it was justified in the most neutral way possible. Strikes were considered a form of hardship akin to a natural disaster. Ties with labor leaders would intensify over the years. When, in 1924, Lee K. Frankel, by then second vice-president of Metropolitan, published a small volume on workers' health under the auspices of the National Health Council, which he chaired, Samuel Gompers wrote the foreword.[101]

To be sure, these activities were self-serving, for it was in the insurance companies' interest to help lengthen life. Their investment income came from the nickels and dimes millions of workers turned over every week for their life insurance. Much more, however, was at stake than mere financial gain. Initially, Metropolitan had been chartered as a public, profit-making enterprise, but it became a mutual in 1915 when the company bought back its stock on behalf of the policyholders. This prevented the possibility of any large stockholder ever gaining control of the stock and reversing the course set out by the directors.[102] Transformation of the corporate structure through mutualization brought the company closer to the goals of the fraternal organizations. Having taken away the economic raison d'être of thousands of fraternal associations, Metropolitan now held its enormous assets in trust of policyholders. Thus the company projected itself as the enlightened "sum" of its policyholders, able to guide them toward new, more satisfying levels of health and a more fruitful life. In this sense, it shared fully in the goals of the reform movement that swept turn-of-the-century America. The search for scientific information about health and disease and the attempt at prevention were animated not only by the search for profit but also by reform for the collective good. Men like Dublin saw in the resources of large corporations a means to achieve some of their goals. They diagnosed needs and took on real causes. In attacking these problems, these corporations put their financial power behind social change. Interest and ideology make for a powerful combination.

The first industrial policy was issued on November 17, 1879. By 1920, Metropolitan and other companies such as Prudential had enrolled over 46 million individuals for industrial insurance in the country, often several in the same family. A little over a third of Metropolitan's death benefit of about $150 was sufficient to cover the cost of a decent funeral and the balance provided additional subsidy. It was not much but it was enough to provoke a complete change in "the management of death in America."[103]

By 1883, Metropolitan had more than 1,600 men operating from nearly fifty district offices, canvassing houses week after week to collect the fixed weekly premium (ranging from 5¢ to 70¢).[104] The company relied on as many as 10,000 agents in the late 1890s. In the process of recruiting these agents, the Metropolitan and other similar corporations turned many social workers, charity workers, members of voluntary associations, and middle-class members of ethnic communities into representatives of the corporation. These agents were part of a larger selling hierarchy consisting of assistant superintendents, superintendents, and chief supervisors. In the 1890s the top positions were still held by Englishmen, whose experience with industrial insurance was indispensable to the new American business. Seven superintendents came from Great Britain under contract as did the two chief supervisors. These supervisors had been agents of the English Prudential Company at the time of their hiring, a job to which they had come from positions in English friendly societies.[105]

The supervisors and the special agents insured uniformity of methods across all agencies. About 60 percent of the assistant superintendents had been promoted from positions as agents while practically all the remaining superintendents themselves were promoted from their previous positions in the agency division. Overall, these middle-level managers were a homogeneous group. Only 32 percent of them had started their career as workers. Most had acquired a high school education and experience in white-collar positions before their entry into the insurance world. The group was also homogeneous ethnically: 73 percent of the assistant superintendents were born either in the U.S. or in England. That left, however, a sizable fraction of middle-level managers of diverse origins, often educated members of the ethnic middle class who could render special services. A substantial percentage of Metropolitan agents were also of quite diverse origins. In the 1890s, the most successful of these agents canvassed about 900 households a week collecting 10¢ from each, and many among them came from the very immigrant communities they targeted. Only a third of them were born in the U.S. (some of immigrant families). Of the total, 24 percent came from Germany, 12 percent from England; the others were born in English Canada, French Canada, Ireland, Italy, Bohemia, Russia, Austria, and Hungary. These agents were carefully selected, and the most successful knew their territory well. Several had already been collecting for the company in the same community for over sixteen years in 1896, twice the average length of service. None had formal education beyond grade school; none graduated from a high school but many of them, because of their origins, spoke three or four languages. One Bohemian, who spoke Russian, Bohemian, and Polish attended night school to perfect his English. His success as an agent, however, was among the fellow members of his ethnic community. Districts of Brooklyn were explored by Russian-Jewish agents. Parts of Worcester and other New England textile towns were canvassed by French-Canadian agents. And parts of the Boston Irish district were canvassed by a former American-Irish policeman. Such men acted as brokers between the corporate order from whom they were taking their directives and the semiautonomous communities of their fellow immigrants. Only about 10 percent of the agents had experience with paperwork, most of them as store clerks; only one among the successful agents had been a traveling salesman. Most had been employed as industrial workers or skilled artisans, sometimes working on their own account, before embarking on an insurance career.

As these agents entered working-class communities, they projected a complex image. Representatives of financial interests, they were also priers. As were the British practitioners, agents who collected the money from housewives week after week became regular observers of the family's welfare. Their judgments and possibly gossip were feared by women who would rather pay than give overt signs of difficulties.[106] However, the agents had other roles. As representatives of a new ethnic middle class, they were intermediaries and assimilators; as representatives of the reform movement, they were also a cross between the traditional friendly visitor and the scientific advocate of health reform. Altogether, they were salesmen and apostles of a corporate order that projected itself as a public service.

The days in which corporations such as the railroads stood accused by William Dean Howells of being blind to their public service obligations were partly over. A segment of the corporate world had made it its business to take on exactly those responsibilities. While most big business organizations had little to do with immigrant communities other than tapping them as customers, those corporations that dovetailed with the reform movement were successful in attracting an educated immigrant middle class. While some middle-class members of ethnic communities worked hard at building and preserving community institutions that provided their members with a margin of security, others joined those progressive governmental and business organizations that provided an alternative to community institutions. Men like Frankel and Dublin were community leaders whose talents and particular expertise could not find an outlet in the Jewish Lower East Side. Louis Dublin was a contemporary of Abraham Cahan. But he could hardly find in the Jewish community an outlet for his skills in applied mathematics the way the great Jewish writer and journalist found one for his talent.[107] Yet both men were ethnic leaders who worked toward easing the assimilation of their fellow immigrants and who served as role models to all who knew them. Working for a progressive organization and helping shape it as a progressive organization provided educated members of ethnic communities the means to gain status, to assimilate, and also to care for their own. Thus part of the ethnic middle class consciously moved out of the ethnic community by joining those large-scale organizations to which they had affinities. Such moves were critical, for each one of them created a new bridge between otherwise separate parts of society.

These men, who were committed to social betterment, helped keep the corporations they had joined socially responsible. At the 1923 convention of the Metropolitan attended by Herbert Hoover, then secretary of commerce, and Al Smith, governor of New York, President Fiske described his company as a great public institution. After underscoring the significance of mutualization, he moved on to claim that corporations like his represented the true interest of the workers: "Take the entire population of the United States and Canada and one-sixth of them are members of the Metropolitan. And for the most part they are working men and their families. Sovietism, Socialism, pretend to represent the working classes. Not Americans!" [108]

As the Metropolitan president delivered his speech, the company agent at Muncie, Indiana, Charles A. Langdon, had a radio set placed in a church eight miles south of the town and acted as host to a number of guests to reinforce the message transmitted over the waves. [109] That was the very time when Helen and Robert Lynd were conducting their landmark survey of Muncie—Middletown. As the Lynds, who had a different conception of socialism than Haley Fiske, yearned for a golden past of local participatory democracy they had partly imagined, they underscored Metropolitan Life's role—especially through the nurses' program (12,217 visits by seven nurses in Middletown alone in 1924) in "breaking down one of the most cherished regions of 'ancestor wisdom,' " through the "diffusion of modern health habits of pregnancy and childbirth"—perhaps bringing about a desired outcome but, unfortunately, at the expense of local autonomy. The Lynds saw "in operation the sprawled process of cultural diffusion by which Middletown [was] inching along in the business of keeping healthy." [110]

By mid-century, life insurance companies were the largest recipients of personal savings and, in turn, the largest institutional investors. This did not mean, however, that their executives, who had been at the forefront of the corporate "quest for security," had unduly profited. As Morton Keller has made a point of noting, when C. Wright Mills posited the concept of an American power elite in 1956, he virtually ignored the large insurance companies. [111]

The pervasive influence of big business in today's economic life reinforces our tendency to look back at corporate America as a monolith—a kind of self-contained, uniform bureaucracy sensitive only to market criteria. Furthermore, as all corporations eventually submitted to a partnership with government and labor, [112] much that was unique to any one organization has faded over the years.

In looking at the characteristics of Du Pont, Ford, and Metropolitan, I have tried to underscore the diversity that has marked the origins of big business, for we too often lose sight of it. Du Pont shows us an organization composed of well-educated managers with a theoretical bent who placed a premium on internal organizational matters and on science. Creators of giant organizations, these men took it for granted that their work was of necessity for the public good. Ford gives us a very different picture. At Ford, self-taught managers substituted an inductive approach for their counterparts' theories. Although Ford's managers equally believed that what *they* were doing would serve society best, profit was secondary, and they endowed the upper reaches of the corporate world for a time with a democratic and popular legitimacy. At Metropolitan, we saw a third trend that would soon extend to a vast business sector of social services: managers utilizing their expertise to diagnose society's needs. Like other reformers, businessmen in such organizations displayed a significant consciousness of social problems and a willingness to cooperate with other agencies to solve them.

Both celebrations and condemnations of the capitalist system mask the heterogeneity of its origins and the plurality of its vision. It is in part because of this very diversity that budding corporations came to dominate our economic and social landscape. They recruited specialized talents from across the generation that reached adulthood in the Gilded Age and eventually brought its scattered elements together. In the process, vastly different types of individuals endowed each organization with a particular meaning, purpose, and subculture.

FOUR

INSIDE
THE
SKYSCRAPER

That form of lofty construction called the "modern office building" . . . has come in answer to a call, for in it a new grouping of social conditions has found a habitation and a name.

Louis Sullivan, "The Tall Office Building Artistically Considered," 1896.

In New York, it is by a thousand feet of height that the game is played, the sport of skyscrapers. Those mad Americans, how they have enjoyed themselves!

Le Corbusier, *When the Cathedrals Were White*, 1937.

CHAPTER FOUR

Threadfirst tall office buildings were designed in the late nineteenth
century both as headquarters of rapidly growing corporations
and as speculative ventures.[1] By World War I, the large brick
structures of the masonry era had given way to the massive, steel-
framed skyscrapers serviced by powerful elevators. The design of tall
office buildings reflected not only the work requirements of managers
and clerical workers, who processed the ever increasing amount of
information and paperwork required by corporate business practices,
but the social conventions of these groups. The skyscraper came to
represent not only the administrative face of the corporation but the
administrators themselves. Seen from this perspective, skyscrapers are
emblematic of simultaneous and related creations: a new vertical universe at the heart of American cities and a new work culture. We can
say that corporate architecture was not a mere symbol of corporate
culture but rather a part of a larger process of social construction.

DOWNTOWN

The demand for floor space in a limited, central area, coupled with
new construction technology, provoked a rapid rise in downtown land
values in the late 1880s. Speculators were quick to estimate land values on the basis of the income city lots would generate if covered with
skyscrapers, not only taking into account gains in floor space relative
to ground area, but also the more intensive use of ground areas by
shoppers. For instance, land values in the central business district of
Chicago shot up. In 1873, they represented 12.5 percent of the aggregate property base for the entire city; in 1910, they represented
40 percent.[2] The increasing separation of administrative and production tasks in American industry and the importance of proximity for
decision-making among managers of different industrial sectors created this boom.[3] Administration was now systematically relocated in
city centers, in close proximity to financial services, while factories,
with their greater requirement for horizontal space, were rebuilt in
production suburbs.

The growing distance of administrative from productive tasks did
not in itself transform tall buildings into corporate symbols. The administrative enterprise that these buildings were meant to house was
not initially equated with corporate power. Although McCormick
had transferred all administrative functions from its works on the Chicago River to new headquarters in the Loop by 1879, the company
chose to print a view of its works—a traditional emblem of corporate
might—rather than its headquarters on its stationery until well into

the 1880s. The view, complete with smokestacks—symbol of "coke-town" capitalism [4]—represented the company's contribution to the mechanization of American agriculture. Smokestacks were a symbol of a company's productive power. But as the nineteenth century progressed, the emblem of the smokestack became ambiguous. When Cyrus McCormick shut down the works in 1886, and the great lockout made the nation's headlines, factories and chimneys became a reminder of class conflict. They were replaced on McCormick's stationery by a rendering of a reaper in a bucolic setting on the Great Plains. [5]

Although McCormick did not view its downtown headquarters as the best representation of its mission, neither McCormick nor the public were oblivious to the symbolic potential of tall office buildings. In the late 1800s, new downtown office buildings were increasingly represented in guidebooks as typical of the audacious edifices the corporations clustered through the Loop. [6] In other words, the construction of single large office buildings did not in itself suffice to make such structures corporate symbols. Rather it was their agglomeration that pushed them into American consciousness as symbols of the corporations' financial strength and standing.

FROM MERCANTILE TO CORPORATE OFFICE

The need both to concentrate and isolate large numbers of clerks according to their specialized function was just one sign of the end of the mercantile culture that had dominated office work. In mid-century mercantile offices, scriveners, bookkeepers, and clerks still associated frequently with merchants. And clerical work was still the most common avenue to a business career in America as well as in Europe. The clerks' aspirations gave them the special appearance that Edgar Allan Poe recounted in "The Man of the Crowd," which supposedly was set in the London of the 1840s, but more likely reflects sights Poe observed in the streets of New York or Philadelphia. [7] Poe divided "the tribe of clerks" crowding the streets downtown between young men who could look ahead and older clerks. The "young gentlemen with tight coats, bright boots, well-oiled hair and supercilious lips" marked their hopes by adopting manners that were "an exact fac-simile of what had been the perfection of *bon ton* about twelve or eighteen months before." In Poe's words, the British clerks "wore the castoff graces of the gentry" they emulated. On the North American side of the Atlantic, clerks emulated not gentlemen but businessmen. [8] Not all were to reach lofty business altitudes, and the older clerks, who never achieved moneyed positions, naturally bore all the signs of a life in the office, from "coats and pantaloons of black or brown, made to sit comfortably" to "slightly bald heads, from which the right ears, long used to pen holding, had an odd habit of standing off on end." In lieu of hopes, these older men were left with "the affectation of respectability."[9]

In countinghouses on both sides of the Atlantic, the relationship between clerk and employer was often a personal and particular one. British black-coated workers "mixed" with the sons of gentlemen and were expected to behave accordingly.[10] American clerks were fewer in number, and they expected to become businessmen themselves. Merchants encouraged them in their hopes and thought it worthwhile to foster their sense of identification with mercantile goals. American advice books routinely encouraged young clerks to show initiative by performing tasks without direct remuneration.[11] As *Hunt's Merchants' Magazine* put it in 1841,

> The majority of clerks are young men who have hopes and
> prospects of business before them. . . . A good clerk feels
> that he has an interest in the credit and success of his em-
> ployer beyond the amount of his salary; and with the close of
> every successful year, he feels that he too, by his assiduity
> and fidelity has added something to his capital—something
> to his future prospects, and something to his support if over-
> taken with adversity; and a good merchant encourages and
> reciprocates all these feelings.[12]

This text embodies some of the characteristics often invoked to contrast the American scene with that of the Continent: initiative, hope of mobility, and simultaneously, recognition of a possibility of downward mobility ("if overtaken with adversity"). Starting out as a clerk in a store was a typical entry-level job in a mercantile economy.[13]

With the rise of large-scale business organizations, the nature of clerical work changed drastically. The sheer amount of work exploded, and the number of clerks required by corporations gradually subjected the everyday interplay between those who ran the corporation and the clerks to bureaucratic rule and hierarchy. Long before Taylor's disciples were redesigning factory production lines, middle-level managers redesigned offices to serve a new, highly differentiated system. The construction of large office buildings of the masonry era (1870s and 1880s) was the first step. These new buildings symbolized an irreversible break with older forms of capitalism.

McCormick, as we have seen, recognized the separation between factory work and clerical work early. So did the railroads—the first American bureaucracies—which built administrative hubs well separated from stations and shops. The growing realization of the importance of administrative rule can be seen in the case of the C. B. & Q headquarters. The C. B. & Q. started modestly in downtown Chicago. From 1852 to 1871, it rented the second and third floors of the Michigan Central, near the river and the railroad terminal. After the 1871 fire, the Michigan Central renovated and occupied the entire building. The C. B. & Q. moved the records that survived the blaze first to its freight office and box cars and then from 1871 to 1873 to a three-story building on South Michigan Avenue. As its space requirements continued to increase, the company moved its headquarters to a larger, five-story brick building on the northeast corner of Michigan Avenue and Randolph in 1873. Finally, the C. B. & Q. commissioned the architectural firm of Daniel H. Burnham and John W. Root to build a new headquarters at Adams and Franklin Street. The building was ready in 1883. Thirty years later the company left its masonry home for a new, thirteen-story skyscraper across from the new Union Station.[14]

The 1883 office was a large, 124 foot by 178 foot, six-story building occupying about a quarter of a city block.[15] It had an interior court with a giant skylight. The court was surrounded on each floor by open galleries, and the approximately three hundred employees, 93 percent of them male, worked in offices and large rooms which opened on to them.[16] Employees could leave the office for one hour at lunch, yet most brought their lunch from home, ate it in the building, and then did their smoking out in the galleries.

The Chicago office, with its combination of public and private spaces, would be taken as a model for regional headquarters. Under Albert Touzalin's general management, the B. & M. had built a three-story headquarters in Omaha in 1879, a brick structure in Italianate style. It had a flat roof and a heavy ornamental cornice. The road's offices were located in the upper floors, while the first floor was still rented to wholesale grocers and wholesale notions dealers. As it grew, the B. & M. took over the first floor and, in 1886, added a fourth floor. Ten years later, the building was completely renovated and remodeled after the Chicago headquarters. It featured a central court topped by a pyramidal skylight and surrounded by galleries. The first floor held a reception area and general office space. The second floor comprised the conference room, the mail clerk's and paymaster's offices, and the general office. The tasks conducted on the third floor were supervisory. There were offices for the superintendent of transportation, master carpenter, roadmaster, signal and water service, division superintendent, chief dispatcher, dispatcher, resident engineer, and master mechanic. There was also a telegraph office. The fourth floor was used by the American Railway Express Company as well as the B. & M.'s general baggage agent, tax collector, train master, and medical examiner. The telephone room was located here. Each floor was equipped with fireproof and burglarproof vaults.[17]

As can be seen in the cases of the C. B. & Q. and B. & M., access to light was a crucial consideration in the design of the early large office buildings. The need for abundant natural light to reduce the use of gas burners (Edison patented the first electric light bulb only in 1879)[18] and limit the terrifying risk of fire, especially in offices where clerks spent so much time recording data and keeping books, was imperative. The interior court was one solution to this problem, for it provided a central source of light. Such a design encouraged the use of large rooms with interior as well as exterior windows. But the nature of these spaces changed the social relations occurring within them. In such rooms, individuals could not escape the scrutiny of others, both their superiors and their peers. Any transgressions in accepted behavior were immediately visible to all. Only upper-level executives were rewarded with a private source of light, an enviable sign of status, and could remove themselves from the public eye.

Frank Lloyd Wright took the concept of the light court to its logical extreme in the Larkin Building in Buffalo by making the court itself a large office space. There, about one hundred clerks, in addition to those in large rooms throughout the building, processed some of the paperwork generated by that company's mail-order business in soap and other toiletries. Occasionally, the court was transformed into an auditorium, as when the company invited Billy Sunday to preach his prohibition campaign to its employees.[19]

Some of the features of the mercantile office were still in force in the large bureaucratic structures of the masonry era such as the C. B. & Q. headquarters: They were still male preserves and managers and clerks still worked in close proximity in some of the divisions. Nonetheless, these early tall office buildings lent themselves to the spread of a hierarchical work environment and were conducive to elaborate systems of communication within the office hierarchy and between the company and the public.[20]

Very few descriptions of office interiors have survived from the late nineteenth century, but an incident at the new C. B. & Q. headquarters in March 1884 offers an unusual opportunity for a detailed view of how work space was distributed among the office workers. After the company safe was broken into at lunch, the company first dismissed and later sued paymaster Charles Bartlett for negligence.[21] Through the records the suit generated, we can reconstruct the organization of that division and trace the interplay beween old and new features of office culture.

The paymaster, cashier, and general bookkeeper, with their assistants all under the control of the treasurer, occupied one large room on the second floor off the west gallery. They were separated by two rooms from the private room that Peasley, the treasurer, occupied. Like executives today, Peasley enjoyed a corner suite at the southwest corner of the building, thus benefiting from an abundance of light and a commanding view. The private domain of the paymaster, cashier, bookkeeper, and their assistants was protected from the general office traffic in order to function smoothly. Indeed, in 1884, the three middle-level executives who worked hidden from the public eye at the business of receiving, accounting for, and paying out the revenues of the company had ample time to perfect their operations. They had shared space at C. B. & Q. for about seventeen years. These veterans of the C. B. & Q. were Fred. C. Smith (annual salary $3300, twenty-four years with C. B. & Q., nineteen years as cashier), Frank S. Bagg, the general bookkeeper (annual salary $1800, about twenty years with C. B. & Q., seventeen years as general bookkeeper); and Charles S. Bartlett, the paymaster (annual salary, $3300, twenty years with C. B. & Q., seventeen as paymaster).

These middle-level managers were assisted by young clerks—still all men—who were entering the office hierarchy: Thomas White, assistant cashier (three or four years at C. B. & Q.); Fred C. Farrington, clerk for the cashier (two to three years); R. F. Maxwell, assistant general bookkeeper (an errand boy for three years, bookkeeper for the purchasing department for four years, cashier for the general passenger office for three years, and then for the last two years employed in the treasurer's room, first as a clerk to the paymaster); T. M. Garrett, assistant paymaster (a year and a half of service at C. B. & Q. and several years with Peasley's bank at Burlington, Iowa); Robert Maher, clerk to the paymaster (in that position for about a year and a half and in the company's service at Galesburg off and on since 1878); and lastly William Broadbeck, porter and bank messenger (eighteen years with C. B. & Q.). Broadbeck was the only one among the employees in the treasurer's office who was older than the clerks and who had not experienced promotion within the hierarchy.

The isolation of the paymaster's office from the larger office environment was deliberate. It was achieved by a public anteroom that served as buffer between the gallery and the division. Because of the need for light, there was no solid wall between the anteroom and the paymaster's office. Rather, separating the anteroom and paymaster's room was a wooden partition four to five feet in height. The partition, which was punctuated by a series of tellers' windows, was surmounted by glass panels that let in light from the central court. Along the inside of the partition was a counter and a standing desk, at which the paymaster's assistants transacted their business with company employees and the public through the open windows. The public anteroom, the wooden partition, and other features of the interior design of the treasurer's suite were conceived not only to keep the payroll division isolated but also to hide from view the three safes it contained. The office design, then, reflected the needs of the paymasters' group, with its complementary requirements for isolation from and interaction with a larger bureaucratic structure. Each section of the building was similarly designed according to its primary function and its relation to the whole.

Ordering the work environment soon became the object of much professional attention. From Chicago, a group of enterprising editors appropriately entitled the journal they founded in 1900 *System* and devoted articles in every issue under the rubric "battlefields of business" to problems of interior design. Reporting on the Oliver Typewriting Company of Chicago, *System* insisted on the need to centralize some departments such as stenography and filing, for everybody needed access to them. It was equally important to isolate others such as accounting. In between these two extremes was the office of the traveling salesmen. Salesmen required access to secretarial services and to the offices of the middle-level executives to whom they reported. Elsewhere in the journal, the editors discussed not only the way a boss and a secretary should interact, but also how the secretary could utilize office space so that she could present her boss with relevant information at precisely the most appropriate time![22]

THE ARCHITECTURAL IMAGERY OF THE VERTICAL CITY

Office buildings of the masonry era were still modest in size. The change permitted by the development of steel-frame construction and the multiplication of tall office buildings became apparent around the turn of the century. In 1896, the well-known architectural critic Montgomery Schuyler described the Chicago business quarter as the "heart of Chicago," which seemed, in his mind's eye, to rise from the suburbs. "It is indeed curious," he wrote, "how the composite image of Chicago that remains in one's memory as the sum of his innumerable individual expressions is made up exclusively of the sky-scraper of the city and the dwellings of the suburbs. Not a church enters into it . . . . Scarcely a public building enters into it."[23] As for Chicago factories, yards, and railroad terminals, Schuyler did not even mention them. It was as if they had already disappeared from the urban scene. Schuyler was of course presenting an idealized view, for the Loop was still jammed with factories and sweatshops, and streets were congested with large wagons carrying lumber.[24]

Interestingly, Schuyler's view is a fair description of the world of most executives and white-collar workers at the end of the masonry era and in the early days of steel-frame construction. These men were our protocommuters shuttling back and forth from the downtown to the new suburbs. Already by 1880, a third of the C. B. & Q. middle-level executives and clerks (counting only heads of households among the latter) had settled along that road's line between Chicago and Aurora, that is, toward the west, in Clyde, Riverside, Western Springs, Hinsdale, and Downer's Grove. As company employees, they took advantage of the privilege of commuting free.[25] Among the middle-level executives, only one lived on Prairie Avenue, close to the home of bosses Amos T. Hall and James Walker and to Chicago's "upper stratum." Some settled in the good streets of the Loop and on the South Side. One lived as a bachelor in a very good downtown hotel (the Tremont), and only one in a boardinghouse. Younger clerks, on the other hand, crowded the Loop's boardinghouses.[26]

Edward Ripley, a freight agent, had a large house in Riverside, the wealthy suburb created by Frederick Law Olmsted and Calvert Vaux. Like other Riverside residents, Ripley supported a family and employed two servants in his household. As a Riverside resident, Ripley had cause to appreciate Schuyler's perception of the architectural symbiosis between skyscraper and suburb. William Le Baron Jenney, the architect who pioneered the first "skeleton" skyscraper with the construction in 1885 of the nine-story Home Insurance Company Building in downtown Chicago, had designed the hotel and water tower adjoining the C. B. & Q. railroad station in Riverside, two landmarks of American suburban architecture.[27]

Schuyler's two-tiered city took many years to become common-place, for many industrialists resisted the trend to separate administrative functions until well into the twentieth century. In Detroit, Henry Ford, who despised accountants, never built a separate headquarters for his paper types. When Ford commissioned Albert Kahn to design the Highland Park factory, the automaker had in mind a facility where he and a dozen other tinkerers could develop and perfect the technique of assembly-line production.[28] Clerks, who had to process the huge flow of paper work required to control the booming automobile and parts business, were placed in a wing attached to the massive concrete structure.

Ford's competitors took a different approach. After World War I, when corporate executives finally perceived the potential of the automobile industry, they quite literally made it over. Just a few years after Ford's Highland Park factory was completed in 1918, John Raskob, Pierre du Pont's right-hand man, and Alfred P. Sloan, who later succeeded du Pont as president of General Motors, conceived of a gigantic office complex on Grand Boulevard in Detroit. They envisioned an administrative center removed from all production sites, designed entirely to manage the diverse divisions of General Motors. The recognition of the importance of nonproduction processes fits well within the philosophy that governed all of G.M.'s operations. As we have already noted, G.M.'s aggressive marketing, especially the introduction of a "full line" of cars to match every pocketbook and the annual model, set the industry standard and also forced Ford, totally infatuated with his Model T, to follow suit and diversify his production.[29] Thus, the building of the G.M. headquarters marked not only the coming of age of the automobile industry but also the ascendency of the financial and administrative functions over the technical and productive.

The transformation came early to Chicago, late to Detroit. No city, however, escaped the transformation in the urban landscape Schuyler had sensed. New York architects took a different approach from their Chicago brethren. When Daniel Burnham called them to design large sections of the World's Columbian Exposition, they had already challenged the geometric commercial architecture of Adler, Sullivan, and their Chicago colleagues.[30] The movement for a horizontal civic architecture was championed by the architects of Chicago's White City and, later, by the advocates of the City Beautiful movement. It is exemplified in such buildings as New York's Metropolitan Museum of Art, Public Library, or the Brooklyn Museum and is often seen as characteristic of an emerging effort at reordering cities around a few focal points on monumental axes. But New York also saw an extraordinary burst of tall buildings as corporations promoted a vertical architecture and chose architects who designed office buildings in a variety of historical styles.[31] Clearly, the precision of the historicism these New York architects espoused—Ernest Flagg's Beaux-Arts style for the Singer Tower, the Gothic revival of Cass Gilbert's Woolworth Building, or the Italian Renaissance that inspired N. Le Brun's Metropolitan Life Building—was not as important as the resonance it was designed to evoke.[32]

When Frank W. Woolworth asked Cass Gilbert to build a skyscraper in New York, he wanted a replica of the Parliament in London. Instead, Gilbert built him a Gothic cathedral adapted to commercial circumstances, for "just as religion monopolized art and architecture during the Medieval epoch, so commerce has engrossed the United States since 1865." On the evening of April 24, 1913, "President Wilson pressed a tiny button in the White House and 80,000 brilliant lights instantly flashed throughout the Woolworth building."[33] Thus was inaugurated a "Cathedral of Commerce" built with a fortune amassed in dime stores.

With the multiplication of tall buildings, the symbolic contrast between horizontal and vertical architecture faded rapidly. The Woolworth Building is a case in point. Shortly after its construction, the Woolworth tower occupied a key space in New York skyline. It marked for all who entered the city from the Brooklyn Bridge the location of both New York civic and business centers. By the time Woolworth died in 1919, his tower was more associated with New York the city than with the man or his business. Soon, civic art manuals suggested building public monuments modeled after the Woolworth Building, for the tower offered significant advantages over the traditional dome.[34]

THE CORPORATE SYMBIOSIS

The Metropolitan Life building, designed by N. Le Brun & Sons for the life insurance company and the tallest building in New York until the construction of the Woolworth Building six years later, is a good example of the corporate symbiosis of image and function. The company erected several adjacent buildings in the 1890s between 23d and 24th streets with the main company entrance at One Madison Avenue. By 1901, the company, having practically filled a block, sought to create harmony among these buildings by emphasizing their horizontal lines and carrying them around the block at the same level.

The crowning cornices stood 165 feet above sidewalk level. Soon, however, "the mounting price of real estate, combined with the demand for more floor space" compelled the Metropolitan "to overcome the serious disadvantage of prodigious land costs, by piling floor upon floor."[35] In 1907 the company broke ground for a 45-story tower on the northwest side of the block, where the Madison Square Presbyterian Church once stood.

The Metropolitan Tower projected an image quite different from the Woolworth Building. Architect Le Brun and Metropolitan officials found the campanile of the Italian republics, a symbol of civic responsibility and public service, representative of the aspirations of an insurance corporation. Their choice also emphasized Metropolitan Life's commitment to responsible business practices at a time when so many other New York insurance companies—but not Metropolitan Life— had come under the indictment of the Armstrong commission, whose findings prompted New York State to regulate the insurance industry (see chap. 3).

Metropolitan officials were anxious to demonstrate their allegiance to the reform movement, to participate in public health campaigns, to work toward lengthening life. Actuaries not only made up life tables and computed insurance premiums, they also developed the new field of social statistics. Given this evident commitment, it was natural that the company, in conjunction with the New York Charity Organization Society, organized regular visits to the Metropolitan Tower for graduates from Vassar, Smith, Bryn Mawr, and other women's colleges. These women, who were selected because of their leadership in their respective institutions and their interest in social work, were taken to the top of the Metropolitan Tower where they could look down as Metropolitan Life officials at the tenements and appraise the field of their future work.[36]

They stood at the apex of an edifice that was radically different from its masonry predecessors and which represented new efficiencies in commerce and social work. The tall office buildings of the masonry era housed about three hundred workers, the new skycrapers over four thousand. The Metropolitan, whose successes signaled the decline of working-class voluntary associations, actively built a bureaucratic organization within the walls of its skyscraper and contributed to the creation of a new white-collar universe in downtown New York. The extent of Metropolitan's activity in this regard can be gauged by Remington's claim that there were 1,170 typewriters in use in the Metropolitan building in 1915. The Remington copywriter felt compelled to add that if all these typewriting machines were piled on top of one another, they would reach an altitude of 975 feet, or 300 feet higher than the Metropolitan campanile![37]

The need for efficiency was reflected on a grand scale in the head-quarters of large organizations like Metropolitan Life. If architects designed the outside envelope, managers devised the workspaces. The process of sorting and processing insurance applications, collecting premiums, and disbursing payments was carefully worked out, and each division specialized in one or several related steps of the job. In the medical division, twenty-seven employees maintained a correspondence with 2,200 doctors who had established medical reports on applicants. They transferred individual files either directly to the policy division or to their supervisors if they doubted an applicant's eligibility. In the policy division, several hundred employees inspected the applications anew and sorted them according to the applicants' age, job, geographic area, desired level of coverage, and so on. Once this sorting was done, the individual files were numbered and sent to the audit division where, in 1896, auditors supervised 156 accountants and 395 clerks, including 18 stenographers. The audit division, distributed through four stories, prepared 77,000 insurance policies a week and also wrote all rejection letters.[38]

Actuaries occupied two floors. Another floor was reserved for the filing division. Metropolitan had a gigantic filing system maintained by sixty-one employees and comprising twenty million insurance applications filed in 20,000 boxes. There were also 700,000 accounting books, half-a-million death certificates, and, necessarily, an alphabetical index. Other divisions such as the agency division, purchasing, and specialized insurance programs were located on other floors.[39]

Additional gains in efficiency were made by applying new technology. Visitors were shown a variety of technological advances in information processing throughout the building. By 1914, actuaries were using a new Peirce system of punched cards that represented a significant improvement over Hollerith's.[40] They used other sorting and tabulating machines that could read 200 cards a minute. Each piece of equipment, the company estimated, could do the work of fifteen clerks.

The allocation of space in the building balanced the efficiency requirement with that of prestige and public relations. Thus, one of the foremost rooms in the insurance building was the cashiers' office on the first floor. There, thirty-two cashiers, all men (naturally, as their position put them in constant interaction with the public), worked in a central, elaborately decorated room. That room was directly connected to the marble court and a marble stairway modeled after that of the Paris Opera. The stairway led to the executive suite, finished in dark mahagony, handsomely carved, with furniture to match. The cashiers' office had a high, two-story, ceiling which was surrounded by a gallery.[41]

In these surroundings, the cashiers outdid themselves, as Metropolitan reported in booklets that induced statistical vertigo. In 1896, those thirty-two clerks processed 55,000 checks to superintendents, assistants, agents, and other employees; over 50,000 checks to policyholders—a payment to policyholders every eight minutes—and over 5,000 checks to medical examiners across the country.[42]

In a sense, the Metropolitan Life building was an administrative marvel, an enormous machine dedicated to processing insurance claims. By 1914, five years after the completion of the tower, over 20,000 occupants and visitors entered the building daily, including 3,659 white-collar workers (2,371 women and 1,288 men), 600 blue-collar technicians who worked in the printing shop, kitchen, and so on, and employees of firms that rented sections of the tower. The systems supporting this workforce were a feat of engineering. The building contained forty-eight elevators that traveled a combined 124,090 miles a year. The offices were connected to each other and to the outside world by 2,462 miles of telephone wire. The Metropolitan building was "a city in itself."[43] Visitors who encountered it for the first time had difficulty believing that so many employees worked for a single company.

MEN AND WOMEN

The interior organization of skyscrapers, then, represents a culmination of changes begun in the large office buildings of the masonry era and a continuing preoccupation with flow charts and the cult of efficiency that business flaunted to deflect criticism during the progressive era. If the famous "organization man" was born with the tall office building, the organization woman appeared on the scene at the same time as well.[44] The bureaucratic, hierarchical, and somewhat futuristic work environment at Metropolitan Life was increasingly feminized, a factor that had as much effect on the organization of interior space and on corporate culture as the need for efficiency. As early as the 1890s, Metropolitan employed more women than men.[45] The Miss Remington who worked for Metropolitan Life was most often a foreman's or a craftsman's daughter, born in the United States of American-born parents (as we will see in chap. 5). When she married, she stopped working immediately. If for Lily Bart, Edith Wharton's aristocratic heroine, the young women who worked in downtown offices "lived a life in which achievement seemed as squalid as failure,"[46] the young women themselves saw it differently. They perceived their employment as a means of gaining at least partial independence from their families. The typical corporate stenographer did not make enough money to live on her own but contributed significantly to the family budget.

Lower middle-class families, who would not let their daughters work in factories, saw the office world as a respectable environment. Families counted on employers to enforce a strict code of behavior for their daughters as well as impose a safe separation between men and women in the workplace. The company, in turn, strove to discourage all but the most formal relationships between men and women, avoiding the situations that created so much controversy within the growing federal bureaucracy.[47] Only such segregation could insure the respectability of women's employment. Furthermore, the dress code was strict and proper behavior enforced. Women normally wore a long dark skirt covered with a white apron and a white blouse animated only by a black bow tie. Women clerks were not allowed to take down their hair in the office or even in the lavatories.[48] We see in the early twentieth century a modern version of what had happened in Lowell at the beginning of the nineteenth, when the Boston associates hired matrons to oversee the young farmers' daughters who had left the countryside to work in the cotton manufacture.[49] In this respect, the world of business became considerably more rigid and regimented than that of government. Lack of money (or the reluctance to use Treasury surpluses to build a bureaucracy), the persistence of the spoils system, and the slowness of administrative, meritocratic reform combined to make the federal administration in Washington a rather informal world in the late nineteenth and early twentieth century.[50]

The company was consciously involved in the complex process of feminization of the office work. Entire divisions were staffed primarily by one sex or the other. Some divisions were fully segregated. The mail room had only male employees. The central tube room, "one end of the pneumatic system with its arms of brass reaching to every part of the building," handling 5,000 messages a day, was also staffed by men. This was no doubt a holdover from the days of messenger boys. The telephone switchboard, however, was staffed entirely by women. The telephone operator was one of the first occupations to be feminized in offices, for men had too quick a tendency to swear on the phone! The insurance application numbering room also had only women. The stenographic pool comprised about two-hundred women but only a few women stenographers were stationed among executives in the larger divisions.[51]

In all divisions where men and women did work together, women were confined to well-defined tasks usually that did not involve expert knowledge or the use of advanced technology. Typing was the only technology women at Metropolitan learned to use. This allotment by difficulty of work was clear in the actuarial division. In 1914, the actuarial division had about 490 clerks—70 male and 420 female. Most of the female clerks had for their principal work the cataloguing of the cards recording the details of each policy.[52] The male clerks, on the other hand, performed the actual computations on the calculating machines, thirty-five machines for multiplication and division, and seventy-five for addition. The contrast with the looser, emerging Washington bureaucracy is again striking here. Women employed by the Census Bureau were often more ambitious and capable than their poorly qualified male counterparts. Consequently, they had been hailed by their supervisors as better fitted than men to operate the Hollerith machines. In the insurance world, however, women were kept away from the calculating machines.[53] Women's work was to record, compare, classify, recount, arrange, and file, but not to calculate. That was the work of male clerks who could become certified actuaries, a profession women had not yet penetrated.

The division of labor by sex also existed in the audit division, which comprised 300 male clerks and 700 female clerks. The male clerks of the division were accountants and bookkeepers, attending to "the keeping of more than 10,000 accounts with the Company's agents and Field Representatives and also a complete accounting with each branch office." Here again, these men monopolized statistical work. Only when their task was completed did women in the policy division attend to "the issue, lapse, revival and transfer of industrial policies."[54] In these departments, the subordination of women in the office hierarchy was reflected by the physical organization of the office. In the large, unpartitioned workrooms, male clerks sat at desks; women at tables. By 1914, when telephones were made available for use by subordinate clerks, only male clerks had them on their desks. The reports of all medical examinations, for instance, were handed to women clerks who read the doctors' diagnoses. Following strict guidelines,

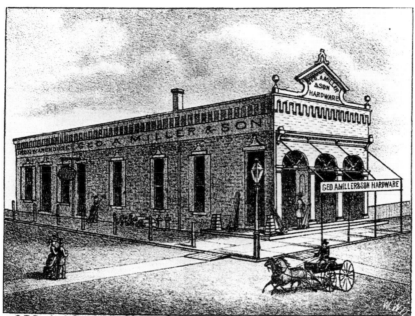

GEO. A MILLER & SON'S HARDWARE STORE, COR MAIN & QUEEN STS.
LENGTH 106 FT. WIDTH 23 FT. STORE ROOM 79 FT. 9 IN. X 20 F. 4 IN. WARE HOUSE 26 X 20 FT 4 IN.

1. Geo. A. Miller & Son's hardware store in Chambersburg, Pennsylvania, 1878. (From I. H. M'Cauley, *Historical Sketch of Franklin County, Pennsylvania,* 1878.)

2. George M. Steinman, merchant in Lancaster, Pennsylvania, 1883.
(From Franklin Ellis and Samuel Evans, *History of Lancaster County, with Biographical Sketches of Many of its Pioneers and Prominent Men,* 1883.)

3. Interior view of the Omaha headquarters of the Burlington & Missouri River Road in Nebraska, remodeled as it was in 1886. (Courtesy of the Nebraska State Historical Society.)

4. The executive, engineering, and office forces of the Ford Motor Company, 1913. These are the people who are helping Henry Ford and James Couzens make the Ford "the Universal Car." There are five hundred and seventy-two people shown in the picture—yet not all of the factory executives are included. Were we to show all the workers at the factory the picture would be more than twenty-five times as large as this—for it would include more than 16,000 faces. Mr. Ford and Mr. Couzens are indicated by X. (This photograph appeared in *Ford Times* 6 (July 1913): 411–14; from the collections of Henry Ford Museum & Greenfield Village.)

5. The tallest spire of New York: detail of the Woolworth Building, completed in 1913. (From Edwin A. Cochran, *The Cathedral of Commerce*, 1917.)

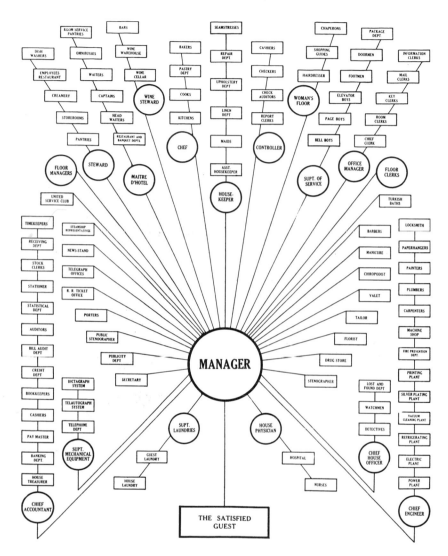

The Above Sketch Shows in Diagrammatic Form the Various Departments
Comprising the Organization of the Hotel McAlpin

6. The organizational chart of the
McAlpin Hotel in New York City,
c. 1911. (Longwood Manuscripts,
Group 10, Series A, File 418, Box
4; courtesy of the Hagley Museum
and Library.)

7. The Metropolitan Life Insurance Company tower at the end of its
construction, 1908. (Courtesy of the Metropolitan Life Insurance
Company Archives.)

INDUSTRIAL or BURIAL FUND INSURANCE.
BY THE
METROPOLITAN
LIFE INSURANCE COMPANY OF NEW YORK.

ESPECIALLY ADAPTED TO PERSONS OF MODERATE MEANS.

Ages from 1 to 65 taken.
Dues collected weekly at the houses of members.
No initiation fee charged.
Cost 5 cents per week and upwards.
Males and Females taken at same Premium.
Claims payable promptly at death.
No increase of payments.
Benefits from $14 to $1000 in ca.

SECURITY TO MEMBERS, $2,000,000
Surplus, $400,000.

OVER TWO MILLION DOLLARS
ALREADY PAID TO MEMBERS FOR CLAIMS.

"No effort spared to protect the interests of policy-holders."
"Careful and painstaking management."
"In no instance has a flaw in the title, or a deficiency in value been found."
"Too much cannot be said in praise of the Company's investments."
"Every step taken has been to render the security of the insured beyond question."—*From Official Report New York Insurance Dept.*

❦ ILLUSTRATIONS. ❦

5 Cents a week (less than 1 cent a day,) will insure a Child aged from 1 to 12 for **$14** to **$123.**

10 cents a week (less than 1½ Cents a Day) will insure a Person aged 20 for **$210.**

25 Cents a Week (less than 4 Cents a Day,) will insure a person aged 30 for **$410.**

50 Cents a Week (about 7 Cents a Day,) will insure a Person aged 35 for **$710.**

ACTIVE AND EXPERIENCED AGENTS WANTED.
Apply to **ALLEN L. BASSETT,** Supt.
191 Market Street, Newark, N. J.
OVER. ❦

8. What is Industrial Insurance? n.d. (Trade card collection, courtesy of the Baker Library, Harvard Business School.)

9. "Metropolitan Belles," 1896.
(Courtesy of the Metropolitan Life
Insurance Company Archives.)

10. The filing section at Metropolitan Life, 1890s. (From the Byron collection, courtesy of the Museum of the City of New York.)

11. The filing section at Metropolitan Life, c. 1920. (Courtesy of the Metropolitan Life Insurance Company Archives.)

12. The telephone exchange at Metropolitan Life, 1890s. (Courtesy of the Metropolitan Life Insurance Company Archives.)

13. The telephone exchange and information desk, 1890s. (Courtesy of the Metropolitan Life Insurance Company Archives.)

Lunch Room, for Girls Only—1896. (Tea and Coffee Served)

14. Lunch room in the Metropolitan Life building, 1896. (Courtesy of the Metropolitan Life Insurance Company Archives.)

15. Stenographer taking dictation in an executive's office at Metropolitan Life. (Courtesy of the Metropolitan Life Insurance Company Archives.)

16. Young men and women on the roof of the Metropolitan Life building. (Courtesy of the Metropolitan Life Insurance Company Archives).

17. Miss Remington, c. 1907. (Courtesy of the Hagley Museum and Library.)

Remington opened to women
the doors of business life

18. Young "typewriters" en route
to New York, c. 1911. (From *Remington Notes*, 4 no. 11, courtesy of
the Hagley Museum and Library.)

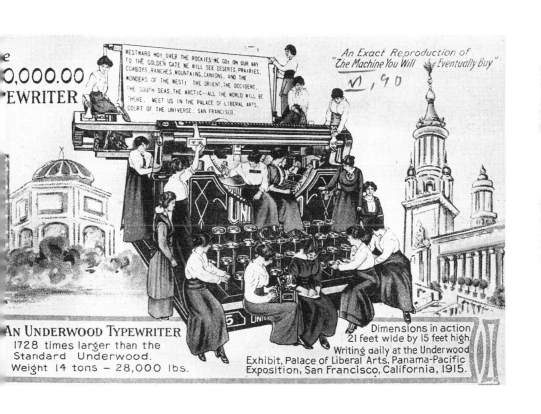

19. The Underwood typewriter, 1915. (Trade card collection, courtesy of the Baker Library, Harvard Business School).

20. Young women from Vassar College, Smith, and Bryn Mawr, observing New York City from the top of the Metropolitan Life Insurance Company tower, c. 1910. (Courtesy of the Metropolitan Life Insurance Company Archives.)

21. Der Drummer, c. 1900. (Trade card collection, courtesy of the Baker Library, Harvard Business School.)

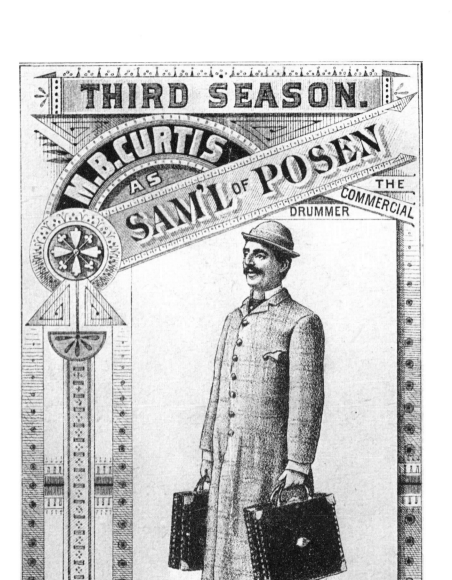

THIRD SEASON.

M.B.CURTIS AS SAM'L OF POSEN

THE COMMERCIAL DRUMMER

DER DRUMMER IS THE MOST INNOCENT MAN ON THE ROAD, REBECCA

22. Smoking Tobacco, c. 1900.
(Trade card collection, courtesy of
the Baker Library, Harvard Business School.)

23. The Eureka Mower, c. 1900.
(Trade card collection, courtesy of
the Baker Library, Harvard Business School.)

24. The Plano Harvester, c. 1900. (Trade card collection, courtesy of the Baker Library, Harvard Business School.)

25. Third convention of the sales department, E. I. Du Pont de Nemours Co., Washington, D.C., October 15–20, 1906. (Courtesy of the Hagley Museum and Library.)

26. Challenge Cleanable Collars, store advertising card, E. I. Du Pont de Nemours Co., c. 1919. (Courtesy of the Hagley Museum and Library.)

these women referred all cases beyond their limited knowledge to a section head, a man, and then to a medical examiner, also a man.

This is not to say that women could not experience a degree of advancement. Women clerks, who made $9 a week in 1915, could be promoted to stenographers, who made $11, significantly more.[55] The company, in fact, encouraged women to develop their skills, within limits, by offering several levels of typing classes. Men, however, were coached under the direction of the actuarial staff. The purpose of the course they took was to prepare them for the various examinations of the Actuarial Society. There was the two-tier system at work. Men had a career ahead of them. Women dominated the office numerically and most of the work rules revolved around them. But they were women, and their true vocation was considered to be marriage and childbearing.

Although women were not allowed in positions of substantial authority, rules that deferred to the gentility of women were enforced. The Metropolitan offices were tightly run. No cuspidors were provided, chewing tobacco was strictly prohibited, and smoking was permitted only in restricted areas and during the lunch break. Compared to the male culture of office work prevalent in the masonry era, this new feminized office culture provided a model of domestic cleanliness. The vice-president in charge of the building enforced this appearance by making sure that the custodial staff kept the office spotless.[56]

In spatial terms, the supervision of female employees at Metropolitan was achieved by cloistering them. Male and female employees entered the building through different doors, followed different hallways, and took different stairways and separate elevators. Men and women could go up and down throughout the building, but they could see each other only through the grills of otherwise segregated elevators. Furthermore, the bureau of information, the primary source of information for visitors, was located at the men's entrance because it was assumed that only men from outside the company would visit the building. In 1914, when the entrance to the building had been transformed into a vast arcade joining two New York avenues, the use of separate entrances from the outside was no longer feasible. Nonetheless, within the building, men and women still used separate hallways, elevators, and entrances.[57]

In the work regime itself, the company maintained as much segregation as it could in its efforts to bolster its ideal of respectability.

Strict discipline was enforced. The work routine was planned exactly so that clerks had "little time to accomplish more than the regular weekly work that [came] to them."[58] Electric clocks, centrally regulated, were distributed throughout the building.[59] An electrical "call system" for interviews was also a great time-saver. Clerks were expected to work quietly, without carrying on personal conversation, loud talking, or laughing. The room arrangements were such that few conversations could take place between men and women.

The gender division was reinforced in other ways throughout the building. Men and women ate in different dining rooms, and while men were free to walk about the city during their lunch break, women had to stay in the building. They could take a stroll only on the rooftop, a few at a time, where they could enjoy a splendid but distant view of New York and its harbor. This roof had been especially tiled to make "a fine promenade" for the clerks.[60]

But let us not confuse rules and regulations with real life. The bureaucratic processes within the skyscrapers required some contact between the sexes. If some departments were segregated, men and women worked together in many others. Paradoxically, the segregation of women was undermined by their exclusion from the ranks of management and their relegation to a limited number of jobs. Although women stenographers reported to some women supervisors, in most instances women were in a subordinate position to men. It was common to see male supervisors in all-female divisions. In filing, for instance, two men supervised an all-female staff. A male clerk desiring to dictate applied to the head of the stenographic division, and a stenographer was sent at once. In all male divisions, one often saw a few women taking dictation.[61]

Despite elaborate company rules, informal interaction between workers of both sexes also took place everyday. Sexual mores in the society itself were changing, and the skyscraper proved to be a locus for change rather than a fortress against it. The company wanted to provide a generally pleasant work environment. As dance was a favorite pastime—there were no fewer than 500 popular dance halls in New York City in 1910[62]—the company established a dance program. Musicians were engaged by the company on Mondays and Thursdays for this purpose. The company even paid for the dance teacher. To be sure "Metropolitan belles" were allowed to dance only among themselves in the company hall at lunchtime. But Metropolitan officials, in effect, permitted their employees to train in the office for their Saturday outings to the less predictable dance halls around Manhattan or on Coney Island.[63] Furthermore, Metropolitan could not altogether prevent the sexes from mixing. Small groups of male and female clerks could and did meet each other on the building roof, where they occasionally danced. Such informal contacts between the sexes at work had never existed before,[64] and individuals pursued them outside the office in the new world of commercialized leisure. The office became a safe, regulated environment in which young men and women could practice the social skills valued in the outside world.

Many a Miss Remington found a husband in the new vertical, bureaucratic universe of downtown New York, Chicago, and other metropolises. The revolution in mores was expressed through the design of skyscrapers in city centers just as it was, beyond them, in the development of a new world of amusement: the dance hall, the attraction park, and the new movie palaces where G. Stanley Hall, William James's student and founder of the American Psychological Association, liked to send his students to observe moviegoers.[65] These were the places, at work and at play, where men and women of a new generation learned to know each other.

BACK TO THE PUBLIC ARENA

While a silent revolution in work culture and mores was taking place inside the skyscraper, its outside envelope drew the rage of reformers and merchants. Many New York merchants lobbied to limit the height of buildings in downtown New York. Their complaint—if not the rationale for their complaint—struck a responsive chord in the progressive city government. At stake was the old issue of saving Ladies' Mile.[66]

Fifth Avenue merchants for years had complained of tall loft buildings crammed with workers. "Many of these [lofts] are cheap in construction and appearance and are at the same time of considerable height, the highest reaching about eighteen stories. . . . These buildings are crowded with their hundreds and thousands of garment workers who swarm down upon the avenue for the lunch hour between twelve and one o' clock. . . . Women shoppers tend to avoid the section in question at this hour. Ordinary business is practically at a standstill until one o' clock, and shopkeepers complain bitterly of financial losses."[67] The Fifth Avenue Association also attacked taller skyscrapers when corporations joined garment manufacturers in pushing the city upward.

Others complained of a loss of light. Downtown bankers such as the Fourth National and Chase National, whose offices were flooded with light after a fire destroyed the old Equitable building, campaigned for a city park on its site in lieu of "the thirty-six story building, covering the entire block, which the Du Pont Company is preparing to put up."[68] Coleman du Pont, Pierre's cousin and his predecessor at the presidency of the family business, went ahead with the infamous Equitable Life Assurance Society building anyway. Completed in 1915, it was so massive that it darkened all four surrounding streets and set a record for usable office space.[69]

Because of such abuses, the architectural community was equally concerned with regulating skyscraper construction. Ernest Flagg, architect of the Singer Tower and prime spokesman for architectural reform, advocated that no building should exceed 75 percent of its plot area with a height not exceeding "once and a half the width of the street on which it faces, with a maximum of one hundred feet" and that unrestricted towers built above such structures should not exceed 25 percent of the plot area.[70] In the end, the Board of Estimate and Apportionment of the City of New York adopted an alternative scheme of setbacks put forth by architect D. Knickerbacker Boyd of Philadelphia.[71] With the setback and zoning law of 1916, new buildings could not be solidly constructed with a height of more than two and a half times the width of the street on which they fronted. A tower or series of towers could be erected on this base, the floor space diminishing in proportion to the increase in height.[72]

What is remarkable is that the argument at the heart of the debate was framed again—one more time—around the concept of efficiency.[73] No matter the organizational revolution inside the skyscraper and the resulting advance in managerial techniques, New York City Committee Chairman Ed Bassett argued the majority opinion that skyscrapers were inefficient, for they imposed unmanageable congestion on the surrounding streets and were bad investments. As he put it: "If a hundred more buildings the size of the Woolworth Building and the new Equitable Building should be erected and filled with tenants, the streets would not hold the traffic, to say nothing of the danger of panic conditions."[74] He continued, "If all the workers capable of being housed in the new Equitable Building should go to the subway at once, it would take twenty minutes for all trains, express and local, to transport them if directed exclusively to their service."[75] Even more to the point, Bassett argued the committee opinion that skyscrapers did not pay, that is, they cost more to erect than they generate in revenue; smaller buildings, the committee argued, did pay.

Notwithstanding plentiful evidence that undermined their position, Bassett and his committee members reiterated the line Brandeis had taken at the ICC hearing four years earlier (see chap. 1). Bassett actually made the case that there was a natural limit to height for a building to be profitable, just as Brandeis had argued that there was a naturally efficient size for business firms. Giant firms, Brandeis maintained, must inherently resort to unethical practices to avoid competition.

The businessmen and the architects who designed their tall buildings knew better. They had realized that tall buildings were actually the only paying solution to rising land values. In addition, towers had great drawing power. From the still uncompleted Metropolitan spire, *The New York Herald* flashed a search light to the north to announce Taft's election to the presidency in October 1908; the light would have gone south had Bryan been elected. And towers paid for themselves. Vice-President Haley Fiske of Metropolitan Life insisted that "the tower was built as a proper investment of the funds of the company."[76] Tenants occupied about 40 percent of the Metropolitan complex, and the tower naturally took its place in their advertising logo.[77] In the year 1910, over 25,000 visitors looked at New York from the top of the Metropolitan tower.[78]

In his turn, F. W. Woolworth spared no effort to make the facilities attractive to tenants when designing his own tower and instructed architect Cass Gilbert accordingly.[79] While corporations reserved as much as half of the available space for rental in order to finance their headquarters, developers also built skyscrapers for the exclusive purpose of renting to hundreds of small firms that needed to be close to one another to conduct business in the new vertical city centers.[80] The du Ponts continued to invest in New York. It is Pierre du Pont and his lifelong associate John Raskob, no longer active in either the chemical or automobile industry, who conceived of the Empire State Building, this time a financial failure but only because of the Great Depression.[81] As skyscrapers grew larger and extended over entire city blocks, the first floor naturally became an interior extension of the city street, connecting streets and avenues. In that connecting space were created arcades with banks and stores, yet another way to capitalize on the real estate investment.

Bassett sounded like Brandeis in other ways, and his protest was another aspect of the movement against bigness Brandeis championed. Bassett noted that although natural limits ought to stop builders from constructing excessively high structures, those laws apparently had failed to operate in the case of certain areas of downtown Manhattan. The community, guided by his committee of concerned citizens and public figures must now seek to protect itself "against the new experimenter who is determined to put up a building higher yet."[82] Like Brandeis, who had sided with shippers against the railroads, Bassett sided with Fifth Avenue retailers against factory owners and corporation builders. With its pecular vision of efficiency, the progressive crusade, against bigness and for fairness, was now directed to the heart of the city's landscape.

Yet, turn-of-the-century skyscrapers were much more than "cathedrals of commerce," vertical expressions of corporate power that contrasted with the horizontal, irenic architecture of civic buildings favored by reformers. While most critics were concerned primarily with the skyscrapers' outside envelope, only a few became aware of the change corporate bureaucracies were implementing inside the buildings. In 1904, one wrote in the *Atlantic Monthly* that "for generations the small business, that is, the business house as it was before the advent of the Great Corporation and the Trust, was a school of character second in importance only to the Church." Such opportunities, if not for advancement, but for gaining knowledge of the world was absent in the new world of corporations: "There are thousands of all grades of capacity who now have no other feeling than that of the clerk, or the servant." And his prediction, that "men who have grown up simply as clerks . . . will become more and more men of detail,"[83] preceded by some fifty years C. Wright Mills's analysis of the white-collar man. Was managerial power already dependent on the routinization of clerical work? What is sure is that the new world of offices—exemplified by the modern skyscraper—was the locus of a complex social and cultural change that resulted from the combined effects of the creation of a bureaucratic universe and of the growing emancipation of young women from the traditional mold of "true" womanhood. What is less sure is how clerks, both men and women, actually perceived their new work and the significance of a rapidly growing "petite bourgeoisie" of white-collar workers on the makeup of the American middle class.

FIVE

THE
COLLAR
LINE

In every city, town, and farmhouse, were myriads of new types,—or type-writers,—telephone and telegraph-girls, shop clerks, factory hands, running into millions on millions, and, as classes, unknown to themselves as to historians.

Henry Adams, *The Education of Henry Adams*, 1907

Mrs. Zero to Zero: I should think after pushin' a pen for twenty-five years, you'd learn how to do it without gettin' ink on your collar.

Elmer Rice, *The Adding Machine*, 1965

CHAPTER FIVE

B y the turn of the century, the large corporations had begun to require great concentrations of office workers. The historical trend can be roughly summed up in the following figures. In 1870, no more than 1 percent of the United States' workforce was employed in clerical occupations. By 1900 this group had grown to over 3 percent. Forty years later, clerical workers comprised 10 percent of the working population—enough to make it a large transitional group in the social structure. But it was in the first decade of the century that the growth in the number of clerks reached its highest level for any ten-year period: 127 percent. If we add sales employees, managers, and professionals to these figures, the white-collar group as a whole grew to 37 percent of all U.S. workers by mid-century. Furthermore, women, who were virtually absent from the clerical workforce in 1870, made up a quarter of clerical jobs in 1900 and 62 percent in 1950. While at the turn of the century, most working women were still employed as domestics, farm laborers, unskilled factory operatives, and teachers, clerical work had emerged as the dominant category for women's work by 1950.[1]

Clerical workers also swelled the ranks of the federal bureaucracy in the late nineteenth century, but their numbers remained small by comparison to corporations. And their careers were still subject to political patronage as popular feelings supported the control of civil service jobs by national political parties long after the introduction of the merit system.[2] Yet the bureaucratic spheres would eventually merge. By the middle of the twentieth century, both private and public sectors had generated those complex organizations that made America "modern" in the eyes of social scientists and that stimulated economists, sociologists, and psychologists.[3]

The expansion of the clerical force was more than an enlargement of the opportunity structure. The availability of so many new white-collar jobs actually fostered the expansion of the American middle class and set in motion a complex process of class redefinition. This is not a universally accepted proposition. Using contradictory evidence, several historians have argued that the growth of white-collar occupations generated instead a swelling of the working class. Others have pointed to the division of white-collar tasks into series of standardized procedures, such as in mail order houses like Sears, to support Harry Braverman's thesis of clerical proletarianization.[4] Still others have directed attention to low salaries and absence of social protection as an indication that white-collar workers in corporations had not attained middle-class status.[5]

There is little doubt, however, that during this period in which the demand for white-collar workers expanded sharply, white-collar employment was widely perceived as middle class. Although the range of jobs and aspirations that comprised the heading "white collar" was large, and the line of division between blue-collar worker and white-collar employee remained admittedly diffuse in some areas,[6] the tradition of white-collar jobs as the appropriate reward of an education and as a first step to a commercial career (chap. 1) accounts for the standing that clerical work enjoyed even after it became standardized. White-collar work represented a well-tested avenue of training and mobility, and this conception was ingrained in the American middle class. Indeed promoters of vocational education during the second half of the nineteenth century found themselves fighting this perception. They lamented the fact that native-white American boys preferred low-paid clerkships to honest manual labor.[7]

White-collar occupations were also seen as a path to upward mobility. The prerequisites for corporate clerical work were a solid foundation in English grammar and proficiency in writing as well as the ability to comport oneself in accordance with the rules of conduct that were then defined in offices. In a country that drew its working class mostly through immigration, these prerequisites for office work limited applicants to educated, native-born Americans. This simple fact is of overriding importance. Immigrants could readily see that this expanding sector of the economy would be available to them only if they developed a better than working knowledge of their new country's language, in itself an act of assimilation. Securing a job in this sector, in turn, meant even further assimilation, for the rules were set entirely by and for native white workers. While the required skills could be easily acquired by children of immigrants, a mode of life, not a mere job, was at stake in the transition to white-collar work.

THE OFFICE WORKERS OF THE C. B. & Q. RAILROAD

Although office workers comprised only 2 percent of their workforce in 1880, the railroads were ahead of other industrial sectors in instituting a new hierarchical work culture for thousands of white-collar employees under the close supervision of the middle-level managers whose ideas and activities we examined in chapter 2.[8] The clerical workers who applied for work with the Burlington Railroad in the late 1800s and those who were actually employed in the Chicago office as of June 1880 provide a representative grouping. The form and content of the letters of application, combined with the socioeconomic and demographic characteristics of the existing clerical employees who, no doubt, passed through a similar process of solicitation, reinforce our vision of a distinct, homogeneous clerical culture.[9]

Most applicants were young, native-born Americans; 90 percent were below twenty-five years of age.[10] The letters these young men and women wrote (the latter making up less than 10 percent of all applicants) emphasized common themes. They believed in their own potential for upward mobility and in the individual's quest for betterment. Many mentioned that they were willing to accept a low salary to start with because they were confident that their talent would lead to rapid promotion.

The applicants, who attended high school in the 1880s and 1890s, also stressed their education, know-how, and desire to further their training. A young woman applicant claimed five years of "general education" at Northwestern Academy and University. Many pointed to additional specialized training in the small business colleges sprouting up throughout the country. They professed to look at such jobs as a means of furthering their education. A nineteen-year-old graduate of the Chicago public schools and the Chicago Business College sought his first job at a C. B. & Q. station because he wished to fulfill his "notion" to learn telegraphy.[11]

Most handwritten notes, which made up about half of the letters, showed a fine hand, the sign of a good education, while the typewritten ones had a very professional look. All showed a sense of the proper etiquette and a working knowledge of the standard formulae of business letters, a knowledge that was practiced as a form of art. These letters clearly reflect a distinct ideal of conduct, which was modeled after that of their prospective employers. It is certainly true that applicants designed their letters to appeal to their employers' tastes, but their expression of business values is too enthusiastic and too pervasive to be dismissed as simple opportunism.

The applicants believed that character was almost as strong a qualification as experience. Lester Taylor, a former stenographic and typewriter instructor from Milwaukee, a self-proclaimed master of "phonology" who could "write blindfolded on Remington typewriting machines," had worked for Deering Harvester in Kansas. But even such a well-qualified applicant as Taylor took care to assure C. B. & Q. officials of his "character and ability." One twenty-year-old applicant who worked for the Queen and Crescent Route of the Cincinnati, New Orleans & Texas Pacific Railway proclaimed that he had held the "responsible position" of cashier for two years and had even been in charge of the "entire management" of the office during the treasurer's absence. He too declared his "honesty, integrity, and reliability." Another young man, nineteen years of age, who lived with his parents, pointed to his previous experience as bookkeeper and bill clerk, but also emphasized that he did not smoke cigarettes and gave several references for his "character, habits, and ability." Another applicant of about the same age said, "I have no bad habits such as smoking, chewing, drinking or swearing." And a young bank clerk vouched to "being temperate (neither smoke, chew, drink, nor carouse) and competent (as the bank officials will attest)."[12]

The voices that emerge from this correspondence give us an idea of these applicants as a group. Most were youthful, though there were some exceptions. Two formerly well-paid executives of the railroad who had fallen from their managerial positions—sobering reminders of the possibility of downward mobility—wrote to their former colleagues in the hope of obtaining low-level clerical positions for which they were clearly overqualified. Only one veteran of the Spanish-American war—the kind of man who persistently searched for jobs in the federal government—applied to the railroad. Only two applicants stressed family poverty. Of the handful of letters from immigrants, all were fluent in English and evinced socialization into the white-collar world. One of them reminded the railroad of the usefulness of bilingualism for writing instructions for foreign labor. And finally, there were a few rearguard applications from scriveners who complained that "typewriters" (i.e., young female typists) had displaced them from their jobs. But as a former employer told the railroad, these men had been supplanted because their only value to their previous company was that "their 'n's' could be distinguished from their 'u's' and their 'm's' from their 'w's'."[13]

These letters show frequent movement of workers from firm to firm. Several, as we have seen, were already employed by railroads. One applicant from the auditor's office of the Chicago and Alton Railroad Company wrote to the C. B. & Q. when a change of ownership leading to restructuring forced him to look for another position. Others held positions in insurance companies, banks, or other large employers of white-collar workers when they applied. This sort of horizontal exchange is evidence of the growing number of clerical workers and the establishment of these workers as a recognized group with well-known skills and aptitudes.[14]

The 1880 payroll books of the C. B. & Q. provide additional information about this group and further distinguish them from blue-collar workers. The line listed a total of 271 clerical workers employed in the Chicago office as of June 1880. About 32 percent of these workers were heads of households who lived in the city and its immediate suburbs.[15] Generally speaking, the men in this group were native-born Americans (or immigrants from Great Britain), over twenty-five years of age, and had been married only recently. Most earned enough to pursue a middle-class life. They typically made $800 a year ($67 a month) and supported small nuclear families. By comparison, unskilled workers in 1880 usually made less than $300 per year, while few skilled workers brought home $500.[16]

The better paid could afford to employ servants. Thomas Jackson, for example, was a claims clerk in the general freight department. Thirty years old, he made over $100 a month and lived in Evanston with his wife (also native born) and four children. Mrs. Jackson, who stayed home, was helped by a cook. Seven other clerks who were heads of households also employed servants. In other families, despite the relatively high salaries of these clerks, family economy was practiced. For instance, Jacob Wilson, a passenger agent making $90 a month, lived with his wife and five children. His oldest daughter, who was nineteen and still lived at home, was a school teacher. These families, however, did not practice the complex pooling of incomes from several skilled and unskilled occupations that characterized the immigrant working-class family of the period. Occupations usually pursued by other members of the household, whether family members or boarders, were clerkships (in stores or for the board of trade), law, medicine, and teaching. Only in one case did members of a C. B. & Q. employee's household (a daughter and a boarder) practice dressmaking, typically an immigrant occupation. As it turns out, this lone case came from the household of one of the few immigrants in the office.

Only rarely did C. B. & Q. clerks set up house in blue-collar neighborhoods. About half of the clerks who were heads of households lived in Chicago's newly created suburbs (see chap. 4). Among suburbanites, only three lived north of Chicago, one in Waukegan, off the Chicago, Milwaukee and St. Paul Railroad, and two in Evanston. Just like the executives, most located their households along the C. B. & Q. line that stretched west between Chicago and Aurora. While only one clerk lived in Riverside, eight families headed by a C. B. & Q. clerical worker had located farther down the C. B. & Q. line in Downer's Grove, a quiet commuting suburb incorporated in 1873, with streets shaded by growing maple trees the first inhabitants had planted in hope of obtaining a sugar supply.[17]

Most clerks at C. B. & Q., however, had not yet established a household of their own. About 22 percent were young men only beginning their careers and still lived with their parents. These C. B. & Q. employees were generally the sons of clerical workers, merchants, or manufacturers with a distinct white-collar life-style. In some instances, their families' earnings were comfortable enough to allow them to employ a servant, as in the family of C. B. & Q. clerk Delbert Rodgers, the son of Theodore Rodgers, a lumber and hardware dealer who lived in Downer's Grove. In other families, one or two sons working for the C. B. & Q. supported a widowed mother; in a few instances, both fathers and sons clerked in the same office.[18]

The sisters of these clerks rarely worked, although there were a few exceptions. In one household where the two brothers worked for the C. B. & Q., a sister worked as a railroad clerk (although not at C. B. & Q.) and helped them support their mother and younger brothers and sisters. In another household where the father was also a C. B. & Q. clerical worker, one sister was a school teacher and the other was employed in a book bindery. Altogether only a handful of sons clerking at C. B. & Q. in 1880 came from blue-collar families. In one instance, the father was a carpenter, while in another he was a piano tuner. In a *unique* case of intra-railroad/intra-familial crossing of the collar line, the father of one clerk was a railroad fireman. Even though the railroad had been in operation long enough for the offspring of their blue-collar workers to have reached working age, none of the clerical employees were sons or daughters of that elite blue-collar group—the engineers.[19]

The largest group of clerks, ranked by domicile, were boarders. They were a part of the large urban population that had left their families, but had yet to establish their own. The boarders and lodgers, constituting 34 percent of the total, can be roughly divided into two groups, boarding either with families or in rooming houses. Here again, the clerks held themselves aloof from their blue-collar contemporaries. Boarders sharing space with a family usually chose a middle-class family and if there were other boarders, they were middle-class boarders. In short, boarders usually lived in families headed by someone of the same or of a superior occupational status. In one case, a Riverside doctor housed a C. B. & Q. worker; in another case, also in Riverside, a C. B. & Q. clerk who was head of a household rented a room to a fellow office worker. A similar arrangement in Chicago proper comprised three C. B. & Q. clerks. Sometimes a widow rented rooms to her son's C. B. & Q. colleagues. In yet another instance, the head of household was an executive of the C. B. & Q. and his brother, who lived with him, a clerk in the same department. Two other boarders in this household were a merchant and an architect. Out of fifteen "familial" arrangements, only in three instances did a clerical employee board in the home of a blue-collar worker.[20]

The situation was somewhat more complex for the slightly smaller number of clerks living in boardinghouses near their offices in the city center. Here residential mixtures of blue- and white-collar workers were more prominent. In one instance, railroad brakemen, railroad machinists, telegraph operators, engineers, conductors, and C. B. & Q. clerks were among the twenty-six lodgers in a large boardinghouse. This association by industry reflects the specialization so well described in an earlier era by Thomas Butler Gunn in *Physiology of New York Boarding Houses*.[21] Yet other boardinghouses in which C. B. & Q. clerks lived were occupied by people of the same occupation but from a variety of industries and commercial ventures, as well as members of the teaching profession, a new ordering reflecting the changing times.

In short, it is hard to imagine a better drawn "collar line" than at C. B. & Q. The absence of occupational traditions or a widely recognized institutional separation between blue- and white-collar workers (a separation reinforced in Germany by the state and in Britain by the gentlemanly tradition)[22] did not mean that blue- and white-collar workers mingled easily in America in the early days of bureaucratic growth. There is some evidence of fluidity, but overwhelmingly the white-collar world seemed well separated, whether one looks at the living arrangements of C. B. & Q. clerks or at the organization of neighborhoods, family organization, intergenerational career patterns, schooling, moral codes, or technical culture.

CLERICAL WORK AT FORD

As clerical occupations multiplied in the decades following the 1880s, the middle class and working class changed and so did the boundaries between them. In the manufacturing industries, in particular, the working class split along lines of skill, and skilled workers began crossing the collar line in an attempt to maintain their prerogatives. To understand the process of middle-class extension, one needs to explore further the split within the working class that accompanied the burgeoning of corporate bureaucracies. Eric Hobsbawm, reflecting on British social history, argues that the emergence of a new and mainly white-collar lower-middle class largely explains the proletarization of the labor aristocracy in England during the Edwardian period. For the British labor historian, the labor aristocracy's fate was tied to the increasing proletariat, not with *embourgeoisement* as the Leninists would have it. The American case, muddled as it was by the multiethnic character of the working class, lends itself to a different and more complex interpretation.[23]

As the demand for clerks rose in the decades following the 1880s, the offspring of skilled workers began to seek clerkships. In Pittsburgh, the combination of new technology, the employer's drive against unions, and the growing number of new immigrants undercut the labor aristocracy's security as well as its working-class consciousness. At the same time, the traditional responsibilities of skilled workers were now, at least in part, overtaken by managers, trained technicians, and even scientists. Skilled workers looked for ways to improve their positions by entering the managerial hierarchy and in effect crossing the collar line.[24] In Detroit, the old working class, with its craft hierarchy, rapidly disintegrated as semiskilled/unskilled assembly-line workers regrouped around the largest factories in small mill towns segregated by ethnicity.[25] We have seen in chapter 1 that the managerial revolution had divided the existing educated middle class. It also contributed to splitting the traditional working class.

Ford Motor Company between 1908 and 1912 provides a second case study thirty to forty years after the first bureaucratic experiments of the railroad. At Ford, we can see the solidification of white-collar workers into a distinct group, as well as the movement of skilled workers across the collar line to management posts. Whereas the railroad embraced the bureaucracy, the quixotic Henry Ford was legendary for decrying bureaucratic complications (see chap. 3). But for all the stories about his antipathy to bureaucracy, Ford, with James Couzens, actively created a large pool of clerical employees subdivided into a variety of departments to process the ever increasing paperwork the booming automobile industry generated. Ford's strict enforcement of the rule that prevented married women from working contributed to significant turnover. The company hired over 1,200 clerical workers between 1908 and 1912 to maintain a constant pool of about 500 employees. In 1910, 446 white-collar employees were on Ford's payroll. Almost 30 percent of them were women. While about a third of the clerks were heads of households or single people living by themselves, about half were sons and daughters still living with their parents, and the rest boarded somewhere in the city.[26]

Although the collar line was not the barrier it was in the 1880s, it represented a sharp demarcation in attitudes, especially as the gap between skill levels required for white- and blue-collar work widened. Detroit was a city of tinkerers, but it was also a city of assembly-line workers. The distinction between white- and blue-collar workers can be seen in the standards of personal conduct that members of the Ford sociology department expected from their subjects. As part of his plan to institute the then unheard of $5 a day wage, Ford drew two hundred men from his white-collar workforce and placed them in what he called his sociology department. They investigated the private lives of Ford employees to see if they were deserving of the new pay. The investigators were usually selected from the clerical workforce, and the best of them were later rewarded with a Ford agency.[27]

Regardless their own level of schooling, the investigators did not hide their feeling of condescension toward their blue-collar colleagues, the men on the assembly line. The reminiscences of one of them, George Brown, provide an accurate measure of the clerks' view of unskilled workers. They lived like "hillbillies," he said. "I think that Mr. Ford personally, from his heart, did a wonderful thing to show these people how to live, and to teach them the American way of life. . . . A lot of them used to use their bath tubs for coalbins. A lot of them didn't know what a bathtub was, a lot of the foreign element from Europe. Those investigators taught those foreigners an awful lot. They, what you'd call, Americanized them." Investigating work was very "interesting" to Mrs. Brown, who seemed to view her husband's subjects as unreconstructed pagans. She remarked of the workers: "A lot of them were living together as man and wife, but they weren't married at all. The investigator would make them show their marriage certificate and they didn't have any."[28] The Browns' testimony matches that of C. R. Smith, Sr., a record clerk at the office of the Highland Park Plant in 1912. Smith drove members of the sociology department to the employee's homes and reported that "the foreign born were living like cattle."[29]

White-collar workers such as these investigators saw themselves as living in quite a different sphere. Although their opinions are no doubt self-serving, they clearly derived considerable pride from their rise in the bureaucracy. George Brown exemplifies this attitude. Considered fairly, his rise to the white-collar world took hard work and determination. Born in Detroit in 1881, he went to public school and started to work at age eleven as a shoe worker, then as a bellhop on the Detroit and Mackinac boat. He eventually took two years of bookkeeping classes at a YMCA night school, which he jocularly called his college. Later, Brown moved on to a wholesale hardware company at the foot of Woodward Avenue. He was about eighteen then and bought material throughout the city for the hardware company stock department before being transferred to the credit desk. At this point in his career the only possibility of advancement was to go on the road, but Brown had just gotten married and did not want to become a salesman.[30]

A young city salesman who had been talking to Treasurer Frank Klingensmith tipped him off that there was an office opening in the accounting department at Ford. Klingensmith had just fired an office worker because of irregularities. In 1907, the Ford accounting department had a staff of about ten and given the work that needed to be done, Ford could not allow it to be shorthanded. Klingensmith, who had been a bookkeeper at Standard Brothers, knew the hardware store Brown worked in. Furthermore, Henry Ford had been one of its customers. Klingensmith hired Brown, whose new duties were to check all the invoices ready for payment. The job, Brown felt, placed him in a position of importance where his word "was law."[31]

Brown, the newly minted white-collar man, made heroes of his superiors. Quite naturally he especially admired James Couzens. At that time "Mr. Couzens was what you'd call 'the man who pulled the trigger.' He was *everything*. Whatever was to go, had to pass him. . . . Then they brought Hawkins in as the sales manager. Oh, boy, he was a crackerjack! . . . When Hawkins came in and took over the sales position, it just seemed to revolutionize the handling of the sales end of it. God, that man had a wonderful set of brains!"[32]

Clerks at Ford were not alone in keeping a distance from workers. Foremen and skilled workers who held supervisory positions in the factory also held themselves aloof from the semiskilled and unskilled workers. Perhaps the ultimate recognition of their special position was that the foremen won virtual exemption from the sociology department's investigations. Although they had no objections to their work being investigated, they resented being subject to the inquiries of the investigators, whom they considered their equals. When John Lee sent Jack Smith to investigate his brother-in-law, Klann simply refused to let his relative proceed with the investigation. As Klann put it, "we were trying to teach other fellows how to live and they wanted to investigate us at the same time."[33] The matter was settled by putting Klann on the sociology department honor roll, together with Ed Harper, Charlie Hartner, Avery, Perini, and other foremen, where they helped the department investigate other men.[34]

In short, the foremen shared the prejudices of white-collar management and the clerks toward unskilled workers. Klann lumped Italians and blacks together in his patronizing assessment: "A lot of the colored fellows and the Italian fellows were the same way. They came from the old country and they had their wives and kids over there. 'Why don't you send for them?' I asked. Well, they had no money and we'd draw their pay for them and put it in the bank. 'Now, you send for your wife and kids and bring them over.' It did a lot of good in some cases."[35]

Company policy further reinforced the difference between foremen and assembly-line workers. Foremen were placed on the salaried roll together with the office workers. Although it may seem illogical to conflate in the same payroll top executives, foremen, and clerks, this classification reflected their elevated status, even though status sometimes turned out to be costly. Klann remembers how much he resented being paid a salary, for he used to make more by the hour: "Your pay went down. I cried when I got $100 a month. Boy, did I cry! I used to earn $125, $140, and $145 a month before, when I got time and a half for Sundays. You still worked the overtime, but you didn't get paid for it."[36]

As a rule, however, such men could expect to prosper and many did. Oscar Snow, foreman in the cylinder line, retired to his farm outside Detroit in 1926. He had purchased the farm and the machinery, valued at $1,000, necessary to place fifty-five of the eighty acres under cultivation. Although Snow had supported his mother and his sick wife for some time, which had cut significantly into his savings, he still had $700 in the bank and $472 in Ford investments when he retired. He continued to be paid at least half pay until 1932, a special arrangement granted only to salaried employees.[37]

Foremen and white-collar workers not only removed themselves socially and culturally from assembly-line workers, they joined forces to fight the labor movement. Klann remembered that he carried a gun during the 1919 strike. "I shot two fellows in the foot . . . . I was driving a Ford car and one night two of them followed me home and they jumped on the running board. . . . The purchasing agent at that time was hurt so bad he never came back to work at all. They were tough babies in those days."[38]

The ability of skilled workers to penetrate the collar line in this city of tinkerers created unusual patterns of mobility for those who wished to succeed in the white-collar world of work. It was not uncommon for ambitious clerks to leave their jobs in the hope of eventual promotion to mechanical executive. Such was the case of Ernest Grimshaw. He was born in Detroit in 1889 to a family of twelve children and left school early. Employed by Leland and Faulconer in 1903, he became an office boy at Ford in 1906, attended business college at night, and was promoted to the purchasing department. Grimshaw's first duty there was as a filing clerk. In 1908 Grimshaw was moved to the claims department to handle orders for parts, an important source of company revenue, and later became receiving clerk in the claims receiving department. But in 1911, he gave up his office career for one on the shop floor and became an apprentice toolmaker. Grimshaw's further promotion hinged on his move out of office work. He wanted, as he said, to learn "a trade," and plant superintendent Martin had him trained by Max P. Friedrich, the foreman of the toolroom at Highland Park. The Ford Motor Company did not have an apprentice school at that time, and Grimshaw took private courses in the mathematics required for toolmaking. His experience as a clerk helped him in the toolroom, where he was assigned to ordering stock. At the same time, he familiarized himself with blueprints, tools, and procedures. Apprenticeship in this manner took four years. Grimshaw was employed in supervisory positions in various tool- and die-making departments of the company until his retirement in 1957; he also became an instructor in the Ford Trade School for two years after working on the Model A tooling.[39]

Although Ford's skilled and white-collar workers showed distinctly different work preferences, the sense of privilege they both shared and their attitude toward assembly-line workers derived from their common social origins. Ethnically these Ford families were either "native" whites or of old immigrant stock, and they lived in the new peripheral lots near the Grand Boulevard, not in the immigrant neighborhoods.[40] While semiskilled and unskilled workers who worked on the assembly line invested much of the income earned by pooling family resources in order to buy homes in their tight, working-class, ethnic communities, the class of young people working in the lower managerial and clerical positions of new large organizations lived in more cosmopolitan parts of town and were not in such a hurry. Acquiring a home was just one of several priorities. It would come in due course.[41]

Furthermore, an examination of Ford's clerks and foremen reveal the development of familial traditions of white-collar work. For instance, parents of male clerks either held skilled jobs or followed clerical pursuits. Fathers were pattern makers, foremen, salesmen, teachers, and bookkeepers. Conversely, half of the working sons of Ford clerks were employed at skilled occupations and the other half in offices, while all working daughters followed office or commercial pursuits.

This last fact, the number of women who found work in offices, points to the most significant difference between the corporate bureaucracy of the 1880s and the 1910s. The feminization of clerical work in itself stimulated the enlargement of the middle class. In the 1880s, the railroad workers' office was still a male preserve. Thirty years later many young female clerks worked alongside their male counterparts, not only in the insurance industry (as we have seen in chap. 4), but also in the automobile industry. With men and women now working side by side, gender roles and career patterns had to be adjusted.

At Ford, the feminization of the office itself was reinforced by Henry Ford's health campaigns. Ford was a health faddist. As tinkerer and manager Joe Galamb recalls, "Many times [Ford] experimented with soybean bread on us. He often said he was going to develop a perfect food sometime that we would not have to eat anything else with. . . . He changed his ideas on diet all the time."[42] Tobacco was also an object of Ford's ire. George Brown recalled what the office environment was like in the days of tobacco chewing. "In the office every man had a white-enameled cuspidor beside his desk. I don't know why, but it seems as though everybody chewed, even the young fellows. I don't think that Couzens chewed. . . . I often used to think, 'How can these girls stand that?'"[43] The women did not have to put up with it for long, however. Ford replaced tobacco with chewing gum. Even Fred Diehl, the purchasing agent who was a heavy tobacco chewer, replaced his wad of tobacco with a wad of gum.[44] Smoking was allowed only in the lunchroom. Although Ford's reform failed on the shop floor, the plan succeeded in the offices, where it contributed to the domestication of the workplace. There the growing presence of female workers began to be felt.

Corporations constantly adjusted values to the aspirations of a rapidly expanding white-collar workforce. And increasingly, white-collar workers were native, white women, recruited from the same milieu that provided both Ford's tinkerers and male clerks.[45] Their fathers were native-born Americans of native parents or native-born

Americans of German or Canadian parentage. Half worked at skilled occupations, while half were employed in clerical occupations.

These women often exercised considerable responsibility despite the restrictions Ford imposed on them as a group. Such was the case of Georgia E. Boyer, the first woman to be hired at Ford. Born in Detroit in 1887, Georgia Boyer worked at a temporary position for Dun and Bradstreet for a short time after high school. She joined the service department at Ford in March 1907 when she was twenty. Her brother, William E. Boyer, was a draftsman who had worked for Ford in the early years.[46] In the midst of redrawing Ford's rough sketches to scale, he moved on to Cleveland to make more money, thus missing the opportunity to cash in on Ford's later success. Georgia was not hired, however, because of her brother's connection with the firm (as Sorensen's sister later was), but because a friend had mentioned an opening. She was interviewed by the manager of the parts department and was trained to operate the billing machine by the cashier of the accounting department. After this, she learned to use the typewriter and was employed to type orders. Finally she was promoted to what was considered a man's job, preparing these orders. She recalled: "I had studied the parts catalogue showing pictures of all the parts of the cars and had learned to some extent their use and part numbers. At that time we had very few branches and I don't think any dealers, so when an individual needed a part for his car, he had to order mostly by description rather than by part number. It was my job to place the correct part number of the article wanted and determine the manner of shipment before turning the order to be written up for shipment. Many times I made trips to the factory to look at a car to be sure I was sending the correct part."[47] The part business soon became a very lucrative component of Ford's business and a major source of office work as farmers throughout the country began to repair their cars themselves.

It is, nonetheless, hard to generalize about the work experience that women had before entering Ford or about their achievement once in the company. Some like Elsie Currie in 1913 were hired out of high school. Others like Mary Harper, who had been file clerk with the Hudson Motor Car Company before being hired at Ford in 1912, already had experience in the work place. A few like Georgia Boyer achieved positions of responsibility. Lillian Donohue, who was hired as a stenographer in 1912, showed exceptional skills at handling the billing machine. By 1925, when she quit to get married, she was responsible for all the foreign billing. Other billing clerks such as Irma Wallace operated a comptometer, an early calculator. No matter the rank they attained, they were all carefully drilled in their tasks and subject to Ford's unbending policy on errors. In 1913, Katherine Nurse lost a half-day's vacation for incorrectly handling a parts order as did Fay Floody, a stenographer, for another mistake.[48]

In 1910, the largest single group of women at Ford were employed as stenographers, and over half of these stenographers still lived with their parents.[49] This is not surprising, as it was a matter of policy that Ford jobs were reserved for unmarried women. Some who supported their elderly parents or widowed mothers were usually helped by several brothers and sisters, and their siblings' jobs reflected the mix of occupations characteristic of the new white-collar grouping of skilled and clerical jobs. Of the four children of a dependent older couple from the Netherlands, two were in automobile factories (a son as a draftsman, a daughter as a stenographer at Ford). The second daughter was a bookkeeper in a shoe company, and the third was a shipping clerk for a cheese company. In the case of a German widow, one daughter was an embroiderer and another a stenographer, while her sixteen-year-old son was a helper in a plumbing firm. In the case of an American family, one daughter was a stenographer and the other a bookkeeper, while an eighteen-year old son clerked in a factory.

A similar mix of skilled and clerical occupations typical of the new lower middle class also prevailed among the complete households with working fathers. In all cases the fathers were evenly divided between skilled occupations and white-collar clerical occupations. There were also a few farmers. But no stenographers in this group (where we know the father's occupation) were the daughters of assembly-line workers. The closest we come are the daughters of two machinists. These women's fathers were most frequently salesmen, teachers, store owners, and accountants.[50]

When looking at the younger generation only, we can see even more clearly that these women together with their brothers were representative of the more homogeneized white-collar workforce that was beginning to emerge in corporate America. Of all working brothers only about 24 percent had blue-collar jobs (electricians, machinists, and plumbers). The rest were invariably clerks, bookkeepers, and salesmen. Of the working sisters, only about 14 percent were dressmakers or machine operators in the garment industry. The overwhelming majority were employed as bookkeepers, clerks, stenographers, and salesladies.[51]

Only a few among Ford's female workers lived on their own. One young woman, Mary Borland, appeared to have rented a room in the home of a single automobile tester, an arrangement that would have undoubtedly appeared suspicious to investigators if they had discovered it. The other, Gladys Cross, lived with her grandmother and her sister, also a "typewriter."[52] Most of the rest who did not live with their families lived as boarders. Of the young stenographers in this category, only a few boarded in a family, however. The others lived in boardinghouses of the city center.[53] Some were extremely homogeneous, housing only clerical workers. In a large boarding house at 365 St. Aubin Avenue, twenty-three of the twenty-seven boarders were women office workers, including a secretary at the Detroit YWCA. The middle-class working women's boardinghouses, openly turning down factory operatives, acted as one historian put it, as a shield between the city and the "domestic ideology."[54] Although these women were gainfully employed, they still behaved as if they lived with their families and were concerned with protecting their reputation and status.

No matter where they lived, however, Ford's women workers were subject to scrutiny by the sociology department. Many significant features of white-collar behavior and life-styles on savings, on consumption, on private lives show up in the few investigations that have survived. This is the case with Elsie Bruggeman, who started with accounting in 1910, was a comptometor operator in the audit department when she left in 1923 to marry. She was investigated in 1915, and the investigator approved her for $5/day:

> I am satisfied that her mother, a widow, is dependent upon
> her support. They live alone at this address. Mrs. Bruggeman
> has $800 in savings and $700.00 due her on a land contract
> for four lots sold, but no income aside from interest on that,
> except the daughter's. Both mother and daughter carry insurance, the mother's costing $24.80 per year and the daughter's
> $8.16. Miss Bruggeman's present bank account is Highland
> Park State Bank, Book number 4294, $88.00, $210.00 having
> been withdrawn to invest in furniture. A brother, recently
> married, took most of their furniture which he owned, so it
> became necessary to refurnish. The furniture is not yet in

the house. They live frugal, spending only $16.00 per month for rent, though their flat is cosy and comfortable. Being of German extraction, there is no doubt they will take good care of what they get, as is indicated by the savings of the mother and daughter.[55]

Because they had to quit Ford when they married, most women left after seven or eight years. Some women, however, tried to outwit the system. Bessie Smith, who had been hired in 1912, was dismissed in 1918 when it was discovered that she had kept her maiden name even though she had become Mrs. Ben R. Slesnick.[56] That her husband had just enlisted in the navy made no difference. When the company suspected that a woman had married, an investigation was ordered. This happened in the case of Florence Cunningham, who lived at 3005 West Grand Boulevard when she was investigated in 1923.[57] The investigator made an exhaustive inquiry. Such a thorough investigation is worth citing in full, for it reveals much about the internal rivalries among young women clerks and lower middle-class life, in addition to what it tells us about Ford's internal policies. The story also suggests that young women delayed marriage to keep their job. The investigator wrote:

> Regarding rumor that employee is married to Mr. Blair Replogle, writer found that employee, her mother and father, and Mr. Replogle, lived at lower flat Colburn Avenue. The flat contains 7 rooms, 3 bedrooms and sleeping porch. County records do not show marriage. Mr. Cunningham, her father, is working at the Burroughs Adding Machine Company. Mr. Replogle is a salesman for the Deyo Ford dealer. They occupied the flat at Colburn Avenue for about a year, paying $75/month. Mrs. Epstein, wife of the owner of the building, living upstairs, stated that she was not on very friendly terms with employee or her parents and that everything was all right while they paid such reasonable rent but when she raised the rent to $85/month, Mrs. Cunningham found fault and decided to move. She disposed of the furnishing to the present occupants. That Mr. and Mrs. Cunningham are now at a furnished 5 room apartment, a friend's now visiting east or abroad and that Mr. Replogle is rooming and boarding on Palmer Avenue. Writer followed employee three different times. Each time she met her mother at the Boulevard. Once on Saturday, they went to the Gen-

eral Motors Building where they had luncheon and then boarded the streetcar for downtown. On other occasions, they went to a restaurant on Woodward Avenue and their apt, the Lorenzo, corner of Grand Boulevard and 7th Avenue. Mrs. Epstein stated that to the best of her knowledge, Miss Cunningham and Mr. Replogle were not married, that Replogle and Miss Cunningham are good friends and that Miss Cunningham told her that she felt too *independent* (my underscore) to get married. She liked Mr. Replogle and had given up her girlfriends as there is too much jealousy among girls. Replogle, Mrs. Epstein stated, paid $5/week room rent and that he very seldomly had a meal with the Cunninghams, that he often stayed on the porch while they were having their meals. She heard Mrs. Cunningham ask Miss Cunningham and Mr. Replogle in a joking way why they did not get married. Mr. Replogle replied laughingly that he had asked her twice now and he was going to ask her just once more. Mrs. Epstein said their actions did not indicate that they were married. She stated that recently she heard Miss Cunningham crying and sobbing in her room and her mother told Mrs. Epstein that the weeping was caused by the talk in the office concerning Miss Cunningham and Mr. Replogle, that she must choose between being married to him and retaining her position. Mr. Replogle is known as single at the Deyo office. He and Miss Cunningham have been seen in each other's company frequently and he has also introduced her as his fiancée. Mrs. Epstein says that Mr. Cunningham's health is not good, that he suffers from some chronic kidney ailment. He has been offered a job in Chicago by the Burroughs Co. but he had not definitely decided to accept it. Mrs. Epstein says that he is a strawboss outdoors. Mrs. Cunningham was planning on going east in a short time to visit a married daughter in New York State. Mrs. Epstein thinks that Miss Cunningham has a fair size bank account because they are very careful with their money. That her mother was a dress maker and makes all their dresses. Also in things around the home they were very economical. The Ford investment department shows deposit of $1897 by Miss Cunningham. Mrs. Epstein also says that the family are selfish and they never entertained. They lived by themselves and that Miss Cunningham chummed with her mother. Mrs.

Epstein appears sincere in her statement. She feels hurt because Mrs. Cunningham told the new tenants that the Ep-
steins were noisy people to live under. I do not believe that
Mrs. Epstein was shielding Miss Cunningham.[58]

No records of action taken on this case have survived.

Women who passed their investigations showed themselves models of respectability. Mildred Baxter, typical of this group, was about
twenty-five in 1918 when she worked in the commercial department.
Baxter, who wore glasses, was always demurely dressed, with a white
blouse, a bow tie, necklace, and dark skirt. She worked until her marriage. Women who refused to submit to a routine investigation were
automatically considered suspect and were immediately discharged.
This happened to Miss Chadwick, who had been hired as a stenographer in 1914 at only $2.00 a day. She was dismissed the very day she
insisted on her privacy.[59]

Ford's emphasis on preserving the office environment for unmarried women might have reflected his own idiosyncrasies, but it also
served the traditional view of women. Their true vocation was marriage and childrearing. This is one reason that the new lower middle
class of Detroit, just like that of New York (chap. 4), sent their unmarried daughters into the office. Firms reassured middle-class families
that their daughters were well chaperoned in the new office environ-
ments, and their work thus acquired the status of respectability. The
workplace was a fitting shelter until they had the opportunity to become wives. Although women benefited from this development in certain respects, the real winners were male clerks. Men had traditionally
looked to clerical work as an entry into business. The growth of the
bureaucracy with its many low-level positions, however, had made advancement less certain. With feminization of many clerical tasks, men
were bumped up to those positions offering the prospect of advancement. The middle-class cultural taboos that effectively limited wom-
en's jobs to unmarried women cushioned the effects of routinization
for men and effectively retarded the creation of a large white-collar
proletariat.

GOLDEY COLLEGE AND DU PONT

By 1910, the demand for clerks had become so pressing that more
women than men were hired as clerks in corporate offices. It is not
surprising that women outnumbered men among the graduates of
the new business colleges. At the same time that educators discussed

integrating business classes in the high school curriculum, special-ized institutions continued to spring up across the country.[60] Because courses in most of those institutions had no fixed length, students were able to enter the class at any point throughout the school year. If needed, they took an English preparatory course. In an effort to attract good students, some business colleges tried to attract experi-enced teachers. "Do you object to doubling your salary?" read a Pierce College pamphlet addressed to teachers in the Philadelphia area in 1905.[61] The tract also stressed the regular employment throughout the full year and the potential for career mobility teachers would find in a school run on business principles.

Goldey College, founded in 1886 in Wilmington, Delaware, was one of many such local enterprises. It bore the name of its founder and offered a business program designed to prepare its students for jobs as clerks. In 1910, it had an enrollment of seven hundred in day and evening classes. The courses included arithmetic, banking, book-keeping, business forms, business practice, commercial law, composi-tion and rhetoric, correspondence, English grammar, penmanship, rapid calculation, shorthand, spelling, and stenography. The instruc-tion was practical: students in the bookkeeping class were asked to keep bank accounts, make out trial balances and statements, and, in effect, do the work of a practicing bookkeeper. Courses were designed to reproduce the actual office. Instruction on such relatively esoteric topics as commercial law was limited to basic concepts appropriate for a good clerk.[62]

While most had not graduated from high school, all had received some common or high school education before entering the business college. The college drew most of its students locally. Those students from outside Wilmington lived as boarders in Wilmington families. Goldey maintained an employment bureau to place its graduates. By 1910, it had found jobs for 150 of them with Du Pont.[63]

In 1910 alone, Du Pont hired 63 graduates from Goldey College, 27 men and 36 women to work in the company's newly constructed office building on Rodney Square, a structure that accommodated more than 500 employees, most in sales and in accounting.[64] Turning to the men first, less than half had a household of their own and the others were boarders or lived with their families. Most were young (only three were above forty) and without adult children. In the case of the few older clerks, one had a daughter who was a stenographer at Du Pont and the other a daughter working in the public library. None of the wives of married clerks worked. All were born in the

United States, most of native-born parents. As we can see by comparison to Ford, these bookeepers and clerks of Wilmington were representative of the new lower-middle-class world that coalesced so dramatically in the period.[65]

The universe of our group, however, does not look quite as homogeneous when we turn to the larger group, the women. Rather, it resembles even closer the picture we encountered in Detroit. While two-thirds of the fathers of women who lived at home were born in the United States, three were born in Ireland and two in Great Britain; there was also one Russian Jewish family. At least one native-born father was an iron worker and one father, from Ireland, was a laborer in a cotton mill. All others were evenly divided between skilled occupations, supervisory positions, and clerical and commercial pursuits, thus exhibiting the mixed characteristic of a lower middle class from which corporations now drew heavily.[66] None of the mothers of these young women worked outside the home, and the overwhelming majority of their working brothers were engaged in clerical occupations (as clerks, telegraph operators, and so on). The graduates' sisters were in bookkeeping or stenography. The lone exception was a dressmaker.

A brief look at young women working in four large department stores on Market Street in Wilmington (E. H. Brennan, Crosby and Hill, Kennard and Co., and Lippincott and Co.) adds another dimension to these findings.[67] Department stores were concerned with projecting an image of decorous service but had to hire young, lower-middle-class women to work behind the counter. Like the office clerks, these women were native-born of native parents; very few daughters of Wilmington's immigrant unskilled workers entered the department stores any more than the office.[68] The salesgirls' fathers were also equally divided among skilled occupations (plumber, electrician, harnessmaker) and white-collar jobs (clerks, bookkeepers, dry goods merchants, salesmen). It was no accident that these young women came from the same lower-middle-class milieu as office workers, for salesgirls and stenographers were often sisters. Almost all of the salesgirls' working sisters were employed as teachers, bookkeepers, or stenographers.

Some historians have suggested that the saleswomen hired by department stores felt uncertain about their place in society, as they were simultaneously "driven by the social relations of the workplace" to view themselves as belonging to the working class and "cajoled by the rewards of mass consumption" to identify with the middle-class.[69] The low wages paid to salesgirls in particular, and the fact that some of them occasionally resorted to prostitution in case of need, have also prompted historians to point to the destructive effects of white-collar work on young working women. But treating these mostly young and single women as creations of the workplace alone hardly gives a realistic picture of their lives and aspirations. In the end, what may have attracted one sister to the more demanding office environment and the other to the counter was a mixture of personal inclination and academic achievement. The more ambitious and better trained young women went to the office.

The vast change wrought by the feminization of office work between 1880 and 1920 can be judged from the famous Remington ads of the period. In 1919, the Remington Company claimed proudly that it had introduced more than two million women since 1874 "to paying positions and the means to a bigger life. Each year this number is increased by about 75,000."[70] Miss Remington became a model for many young women. "Is 'Miss Remington' simply an idealized character, or is she real?" asked the manufacturer in its promotional literature. The answer he provided was very much to the point: "She is an idealized character, and that makes her real."[71]

What was important for the Remington Company was that Miss Remington typified "not only the operator but also the machine." However, from a sociological viewpoint, Miss Remington's aura of beauty and perpetual youth was largely the result of the corporations' policy of hiring only young, unmarried "typewriters." A stint in the domesticated corporate office had become a rite of passage for young women before marriage and motherhood.

The social organization of office work, then, suggests two interrelated propositions. First, the collar line was significant in American society, not just in the office but also outside. Although the nature of white-collar work changed drastically in the period studied, the growing lower middle class that swelled the ranks of clerical positions continued to take their cues from business values. Wearing a white-collar was a distinctive mark of belonging to the middle class. The working-class origins of white-collar workers and their frequent crossings of the collar line only underscore the process of middle-class reformation and the concomitant separation of skilled work, clerical work, and sales work from unskilled factory production. White-collar work was indeed standardized and subjected to scientific management just as blue-collar work was. But while routine tasks on the assembly line were for unskilled immigrants with limited knowledge of English,

CHAPTER FIVE

white-collar work became the preserve of a more educated, native-born, lower middle class that sought respectability.

Second, the common belief that feminization signals both the systemization of office work and consequently the "de-skilling" of white-collar workers, to return to Braverman's phrase, is misleading. "The degradation of work"[72] means little unless understood within a social dynamic. For women's work was to be transitory. In other words, the middle-class taboos that centered around marriage and childrearing effectively set a time limit on the business positions women held. Systemization of tasks and discrimination were therefore made bearable because they were temporary. In the meantime, families benefited from combined incomes, and men were not threatened in their life-long careers. Furthermore, the presence of large numbers of women in the offices led to refined mores and the rapid disappearance of a typically male work culture, at least among clerks. In both processes, the corporations acted in tacit understanding with the young women's families. The new woman was not just a creation of the workplace but instead the convergence of ideas held by employers and families. The lower-middle-class families who most benefited from the enlarged household income agreed to supply the ready, useful, and cheap labor the corporations desired but only under proven conditions of respectability.

The corporate world divided the working class and in effect granted middle-class status to part of it.[73] Yet the rapid multiplication of clerks employed at routine tasks had long-term negative consequences. If clerical workers of the mid-nineteenth century, small in number as they were, could hope for a business career for themselves, the redefinition of tasks on the scale of the corporate revolution eventually changed that outlook altogether. White-collar employment, a major consequence of the formation of bureaucracies, ceased to be an obvious avenue of mobility and contributed instead to the imposition of a homogeneous work culture.

SIX

ON
THE
FARM

*The greatest division of material and mental labour is the
separation of town and country.*

Karl Marx, *The German Ideology*, 1845–46

*The Americans never use the word "peasant," because they
have no idea of the peculiar class which that term denotes.*

Alexis de Tocqueville, *Democracy in America*, 1835

CHAPTER SIX

William Jennings Bryan died in 1925 only a few days after the trial of John T. Scopes. Bryan had spoken for the prosecution against the Dayton public school teacher at the trial that focused on the issue of "whether human beings are descended from monkeys or were made from clay and Adam's rib." [1] Seizing on Bryan's death as an occasion to identify fundamentalism with rural backwardness, H. L. Mencken took a parting swipe at the lawyer from Lincoln, Nebraska, by sardonically assuring his readers that Bryan loved all country people, including the "gaping primates of the upland valleys." Bryan, Mencken insinuated, was himself a bit of a bumpkin. "What moved him at bottom was simply hatred of the city men who had laughed at him . . . if not at his baroque theology, then at least at his alpaca pantaloons." [2] For a city-smart critic like Mencken, Bryan, who had risen to prominence by embracing the farmers' search for agrarian democracy, was an obvious target.

Behind Mencken's equation of the farmer as hick was his distaste for farm life, with its glaring lack of basic amenities and the rawness of farmers who had become inured to it. Farmers struggling with the weather and the unpredictable swings of the market toiled endlessly up Hamlin Garland's *Main-Travelled Roads* (1891). Yet not all observers saw farm life as necessarily degrading. The reports of the progressive country life movement drew attention to rural backwardness only to affirm the reformers' confidence in the self-reliant, educated farmer. Ambivalent progressive agriculturalists asserted that rural isolation built character rather than bred ignorance and advocated government programs to keep the best and the brightest on the farm. [3] Support to land-grant colleges, experimental stations, and county agents, however, did not offset the shift in population and activity from the country to the city. The fortitude and determination that their ideal farmer displayed did not guarantee a good profit; increasingly farmers required capital and business sense.

As an increasing majority of Americans relocated in cities, the popular disdain for the farm only hardened. These new attitudes found their voice in the work of historians as well as in the scathing commentary of Mencken. Arthur Meier Schlesinger, Sr., who began conceptualizing his *Rise of the City, 1878–1898* in the mid-twenties, openly sided with the city smarts. [4] Schlesinger attacked the Turnerian notion of frontier democracy by describing the city as the "cradle of progress." Within the city "all the new economic forces" that transformed America in the late nineteenth century were focused: "the vast accumulation of capital, the business and financial institutions, the spreading railway yards, the gaunt smoky mills, the white-collar middle classes, the motley wage-earning population. By the same token the city inevitably became the generating center for social and intellectual progress. To dwell in the midst of great affairs is stimulating and broadening. . . . The person of ability, starved in his rural isolation, might by going there find sympathy, encouragement and that criticism which often refines talent into genius."[5] If there had ever been a rural contribution to modernity, city dwellers like Schlesinger and Mencken had already forgotten it.

MECHANIZATION

It is striking that while intellectuals stressed the dichotomy between urban and rural life and reformers tacitly admitted it, big business did just the opposite. Large corporations never dwelled on urban-rural differences. Instead, they sought to blend the city and the country into one producing and selling mechanism. Corporations penetrated the farm and fostered an integrated world dependent on an unceasing stream of communication between big city headquarters and rural agencies.

The corporations' influence on isolated rural communities was not evenly felt. By the turn of the century, the American farmscape was clearly divided into four large regions. There was the old diversified farm land in the northeast; the newly conquered, rich, soil of the midwestern wheat and corn belts (the old northwest); the poor, labor-intensive, cotton and tobacco south; and the ranching west, which had not yet benefited from the great modern irrigation projects. Although eastern capital reorganized western ranching early on, big business had the greatest influence in the midwest, where first wheat and then corn crops lent themselves to mechanization.[6] Between 1869 and 1909, the portion of the nation's farm output produced west of the 95th meridian (the western part of Minnesota and Iowa and the states further west) grew from 6 percent to 30 percent.[7]

As it turned out, developing a high-yield, mechanized agriculture required the concerted effort of only one generation. In this expanding midwestern region, a host of American-born or immigrant entrepreneurs (more than half of all farmers in Wisconsin, Minnesota, and Dakota Territory were foreign born by 1880),[8] devoted their working lives to creating the corn and wheat belts. They were blessed by geography and stimulated by an expanding urban market. But no sooner had these farmers plowed under the short grass prairie, than they encountered the emissaries of big business.

Willa Cather captured the corporation's presence, its impact on the rural landscape, and its penetration of rural life in her many descriptions of Nebraska. Cather understood that the corporations altered not only the basics—modes of communication, production techniques, means of economic exchange—but also social hierarchies and cultural references.

Eleven-year-old Willa and her family had stepped off a train in Red Cloud, Nebraska, in 1883 after a long journey from Winchester, Virginia.[9] Red Cloud—one of the market towns geographers call central places—was, with its 1,839 inhabitants in 1890,[10] the rural seat for the surrounding farming community. It became the Black Hawk "buried in wheat and corn" of *My Ántonia* (1918), the story of a young Bohemian girl who grew up on a nearby farm. Cather pitched her novel to reflect faithfully the average person's emotions and experiences.[11] She saw big business shaping life early on in this "clean, well planted little prairie town, with white fences and good green yards about the dwellings."[12]

The neatly laid out town was itself the product of the large corporations. The young executives and technicians who worked for the railroads organized many such towns (see chap. 2).[13] They drew the master plans, devised land policies, and brought in settlers of various national origins. They created a landscape and an organizational framework that was to shape the political economy and that would justify their outlay. In *My Ántonia*, Cather notes more subtle but no less pervasive influences. In Cather's Black Hawk, the railroad had already imposed its own social hierarchy on the rural community. Thus, Larry Donovan, Ántonia's first love, who would later abandon her with their child, was a passenger conductor, who saw his position as a source of prestige. He was "one of those train-crew aristocrats who are always afraid that someone may ask them to put up a car window, and who, if requested to perform such a menial service, silently points to the button that calls the porter. Larry wore this air of official aloofness even on the street, where there were no car windows to compromise his dignity." Confident of the importance of the hierarchical world he lived in, Donovan confided in his female companions that he should have become a clerical worker and made his career in the office branch, "and how much better fitted he was to fill the post of General Passenger Agent in Denver than the roughshod man who then bore that title." As a consequence, Ántonia talked of her lover as if he were already the president of the railroad.[14]

The influence of other corporations besides the railroads was also evident. Large corporations went out to the countryside and sold mass-produced tools and machinery. Here and there along Black Hawk's horizon, one could see "black puffs of smoke from the steam thrashing machines" after the wheat harvest season. Sewing machines also made their way into the homes of the better-off farmers. Young Ántonia, whose family could not afford one, used the neighbor's, "pedaling the life out of it" while "singing . . . queer Bohemian songs." [15]

The price of mechanization was increased isolation. Mechanization required large acreage. As farms grew larger, the number of farmers decreased and the distance between surviving farmers increased. By the time a system of rural free delivery became operative at the turn of the century, farmers in the United States lived more than a half mile from their nearest neighbor and several miles from the closest town. [16]

But simply by going to town, the farmer could break his seclusion. Although mail-order houses distributed consumer goods to outlying areas, in small rural centers the farm population had access not only to services but also to a variety of urban amenities. There, department stores and large commercial houses sold goods through local merchants. Black Hawk, on the main Burlington line, was a stop for salesmen from Chicago. Urban salesmen "used to assemble in the parlor" in the Black Hawk hotel on Saturday nights. The Marshall Field's man from Chicago "played the piano and sang all the latest sentimental songs." [17] Then on Sunday, all the travelers—the Marshall Field's man, a furniture salesman from Kansas City, a drugman, a representative from a jewelry house who also sold musical instruments—displayed their goods in an old store building behind the hotel and took orders from town merchants.

That big business should pay special attention to the country should be no suprise. Sixty percent of Marshall Field's profit in 1900—based on 75 percent of its sales—came from its wholesale trade, which was still primarily conducted in the rural market. [18]

Consequently, although the corporations intensified rural isolation, they also counteracted it. They brought people closer together in other ways as well. Henry Ford built his cars for farmers. By the time Ántonia became a grandmother, one of her daughters had acquired a Ford, and Ántonia observed that with the Ford "she don't seem so far away from me as she used to." [19] Norval Hawkins, Ford's marketing manager who would later join G.M., described farmers who bought Fords as "practical people" who want "efficiency," "economy," and the means to break free from rural isolation. By 1920, some 30.7 percent of the farmers nationwide had cars while only 3.6 percent had tractors. The two states with the highest percentage of farms with automobiles were Iowa and Nebraska, 73.1 percent and 75.6 percent respectively.[20]

Most importantly, corporations influenced large numbers of farmers by sending scores of new representatives to live in farming communities. They also hired some agents away from the local implement manufacturers and recruited others among country merchants, crossroad blacksmiths, and rural postmasters.[21] The transformation of the countryside resulted not merely from the consequences of technological innovation but also from the close relationships agents of large corporations developed with farmers. The specialized nature of the farm implement business required the agents of McCormick and later of International Harvester—the company that formed from the fusion in 1903 of McCormick, Deering and other companies—to develop enduring contacts among farmers.[22]

As a result, by examining the lives, ideas, and work of corporate agents, we can understand how the incorporation of American society affected farmers' lives, their daily routine, and also their larger commitments and vision. Conversely, we can appreciate the farmers' contribution to corporate success, for farmers—and farmers' wives like Ántonia—were not passive recipients of corporate-induced change but used the corporation to reorganize their own lives.

Technical innovation, for instance, involved a constant dialogue between implement manufacturers and their rural customers. A farmer normally served as his own mechanic, and he quite often turned to the salesman for advice and instruction. The salesmen in turn represented the farmers to the engineers and corporate tinkerers who designed the tools. When farmers complained, McCormick agents listened. R. B. Swift, the general agent at Carbondale, Illinois, understood the importance of addressing the farmers' complaints about deficient designs. In 1886, he informed the company, "I am here making settlement and attending the fair with machines. You have had quite a dropper business here and a paying one. Unless the machine is improved for another year, you will lose it. The machine is not right if you let the farmers tell the story and they are the ones who buy the machine."[23]

Farmers, who customarily tinkered with equipment and parts, sometimes took a direct approach. They not only identified problems with the machinery, but engineered solutions, which they were eager to share with the corporations. When Swift was promoted to the patent office at headquarters, he maintained a voluminous correspondence with farmers. From Algona, Iowa, John Lamuth offered to sell the company his patented four-horse equalizer, which "has been thoroughly tested and works to perfection. I have not disposed of it yet and am not prepared to manufacture them myself. I thought it would be a nice thing for your Harvester and perhaps you would like to buy the patent!"[24] From Gorham, Maine, Ansel Stevens hoped the company would show his proposed guard finger at the World's Columbian Exposition: "Should you want to use it and put it in the world fair you can have it cheap."[25]

The cornhusker was long in coming and proved a long-term design project for farmers as well as corporate engineers. While the reaper business was booming, corn was still cut by hand, "with the same hacking knife and in the same slow laborious manner than it was forty years ago," agent E. C. Beardsley wrote from Aurora, Illinois, in 1874. Beardsley pushed the company to move into the cornhusker business, pointing out that one of the farmers he was in touch with, George Burk of Sycamon, had "a machine fully protected by patents for cutting cornfodder and dropping it in gavels on the ground and also has patented the implements for picking up and shocking these gavels—by which an acre of corn fodder can be secured as easily as an acre of grass. . . . Your agents would follow up the grain harvest with the corn as they now follow up the grass with grain."[26] But it would take another twenty years for the cornhusker to be perfected. Swift, in the 1890s, still corresponded with various inventors about it. From Fayetteville, New York, in 1892, Darwin H. Van Histyne, more tinkerer than scholar, wrote that he had "found how to inprove the machine to cut corn fodder to six or eight feet high with out widing the aprons and have found how to improve the machine in seven difent places wich is of important. I would like to know what you will do. inside of a week. so that i may know wether it is best about seeing some other comppany we have too of them in this State."[27]

Tinkerer-inventor-farmers not only participated in the development of agricultural machinery, they often acted as unpaid agents. When agents missed a community, the tinkerers went after them. In reporting his progress in the design of a cornhusker to the company patent agent in 1888, Baleslav Karvan, a Hungarian "inventor" from Linwood, Nebraska, added: "Many citizens here asked me of your machines, so please send me your catalogue of them, in two languages—Bohemian and English."[28] As Robert Ostergren has noted about the Swedes in the Upper Middle West, the immigrants' willingness to innovate was expressed in the speed with which they mechanized their farm operations. While their homes may have been built to conform to traditional patterns, the layout of the farms was dictated by the requirements of the new machines rather than the farms of their fathers. Acquiring a new piece of machinery was an event important enough to be reported in the local newspapers. And the new machines often found more than one user, for the less fortunate farmers who could not afford the equipment resorted to hire or shared machines with their neighbors.[29]

This continuous exchange of information between business firms and the farming communities is important in understanding the process of innovation. Farmers could not afford to act as passive recipients of engineering innovations. They recognized that their chances of survival depended not merely on machines but on carefully designed machines. They formed a conscious community of users who participated in innovation and, in some cases, in the profits that it brought. Many found in the corporation the competitive advantage they sought.

REBELLION OR BUSINESS AS USUAL?

Historians, however, have emphasized not cooperation but rebellion—the farmers' resentment not of technology but of the businesses that produced it. The vast grain exchanges and trusts were the "focal points of capitalism" that farmers fought in their efforts to champion their version of economic justice.[30] A look at McCormick agents' observations as they expressed them in their letters and reports from the field during the 1870s, when the Grange movement reached its climax, and again in the 1890s, when populism was most deeply felt, reveals that agents enjoyed significant support among farmers, although the agents themselves were not particularly sympathetic to the Grange's goals. The agents' reports actually confirm what economic historians have shown, that is, the struggling farmer—with a high debt-to-asset ratio—was atypical and concentrated only in some areas.[31] Although agents faced a difficult situation, they did not feel seriously threatened by the waves of rural rebellion, at least not in the areas of staple agriculture where they were most actively involved. There, rural contentiousness seems to have coexisted with business as usual.

The Granges, as is well known, made significant headway in developing cooperative grain elevators and in enforcing maximum rates for grain storage. Yet the more radical Granger laws were abandoned by midwestern states before their constitutionality was upheld by the Supreme Court in 1876.[32] The Granges also stimulated the growth of mail-order houses, which sold products directly, without markup by intermediaries,[33] but were not effective in their attempts to purchase the technologically advanced, expensive farm machinery produced by large corporations.

E. C. Beardsley, a McCormick agent, who had established an extensive network of customers among Illinois farmers from his base in Aurora, reported that the better-off farmers were not overly concerned with equipment costs. While trying to establish his trade around Sycamore on the Great Western route, he requested *"the selectest lot of mowers* on that road that you ever sent out of your factory" for farmers "of old standing—wealthy—independent and hard to please." In the past they had demanded not only good and practical equipment but also a high quality of workmanship. "Say what you will in favor of plain machines *for work*," the agent wrote from Sycamore, Illinois, in 1868, "in nine cases out of ten if you find a piano in a farmers house and a silverplated carriage in his barn just so often does a farmer buy a mower because it is polished, burnished and painted fancifully."[34] E. C Beardsley observed the Granges closely and reached the conclusion that they would not affect his business. In describing his customers in January 1874, Beardsley was moved to argue that "the farmers' movement—so far as it undertakes to regulate other peoples business—is a thing of the past. The Granges have got so intermixed with politics and railroads that they have lost sight of the original ridiculous cry of 'extermination to middle men' and the majority—in fact I think all sensible thinking farmers—have come to see the absurdity of the notion that they can purchase any or all their supplies at 'first hands.'"[35]

Despite his disparaging attitude toward the Grange, Agent Beardsley was well aware of how sensitive farmers could be toward middlemen like himself and the large concentration of capital they represented. Thus, in 1874, he advocated a more conservative approach to marketing. He advised headquarters to give agents "this year plain practical printed matter and lots of it without any mention of the Grange. Your usually perfect machines with a *brilliant finish* and every part carefully made and adjusted and guarantee everything to run smoothly and I'll guarantee that the agents will not permit the Grangers to subject you to any annoyance."[36] His strategy was to desensitize the issues by hewing closely to the technical and practical matters of mechanization. His sales supported his contention. In 1874, Beardsley sold a total of 284 pieces of equipment in his district (including 79 single-frame mowers, 2 large reliable self-rakers, 18 regular mowers, 179 advances and 6 single reapers).[37] He estimated that he could sell up to 355 pieces of equipment (10 reliable, 120 mowers, 175 advances and 50 harvesters) the following year should both price and crop be fair. Should the company build a corn harvester, he would sell one hundred of these.[38]

Agent H. C. Addis also advised moderation in dealing with the Grange. Based in Omaha, he reported in August 1873 that while the Granges had done no harm in Iowa, they had "almost ruined our sale in some localities of Nebraska." In January 1874, he cautioned headquarters about the Grangers:

> Should I be called upon to advise Reaper Manufacturers I would most emphatically say *let them alone*, donot fear them, donot run after them, treat them *as an organization* with perfect indifference, treat them kindly as you would all other farmers, and donot displease them, there is no necessity for that. Make one price on machines, not one price to farmers and another to Grangers. do business entirely through your agents, and should a Grange want a quantity of machines, I would instruct my agents to sell to them a little below my retail prices, and should they want time I would require *each member* to become personally responsible for *each* and every machine.[39]

Addis was himself quite creative in working out deals with the Granges. While traveling through Wyoming and Colorado at the end of January 1874, he wrote from Denver: "I happened here in a most excellent time the State Legislature and State Grange are both in session at this place. I am waiting to see what is best to do. The Granges have elected a man who is in the implement business here for their *state agent*. I have some hope of being able to make an arrangement with him. . . . I may let him have the agency at Denver and we appoint agents at other points."[40]

By March 1874, Addis believed the movement was spent. Back in Omaha, he reported that "the Grangers are making grand pretensions but they have no money and must have credit, and when the pinch comes they must buy machines as normal. I have less faith in their ability to harm us, and fear them less than I have at any time."[41] And by April: "I look upon the Grange move as a complete fizzle already. They are about discouraged in the west and I think will abandon the idea of doing away with middle men for in most instances the *middle men* they appoint have improved upon them so that they are ashamed of themselves. They will buy machines that suit them and on such terms as they can. I have no fears whatever."[42]

Addis was no doubt wise in fearing grasshoppers a great deal more than the Grange. In the spring of 1873, he adopted a wait-and-see attitude toward Grange activity: "The Granges are playing hob, cant tell what the outcome will be though I think no harm to us."[43] But in the face of an invasion of grasshoppers he recommended immediate action. A few days later, he telegraphed headquarters to stop any shipment to Nebraska because grasshoppers were "sweeping over the interior of this state."[44] When the grasshoppers went north, the company resumed delivery. The following summer, Addis stopped shipments to parts of Iowa because of a new attack of grasshoppers. As H. R. Gould, the Omaha agent, put it, the "hoppers" made the prospect "look *blue*" for money. "You well know what hard work it is to make [the farmers] think they have made any thing, when 25 percent of their crop that they depend on to pay debts with 'corn' is eaten up."[45]

One reason that agents did well was McCormick's insistence that agents deal fairly with farmers, no matter what their circumstances and avoid any activity that might tarnish their image. In the late sixties, Addis, based in Omaha, had been admonished by the company to return a free railroad pass and to terminate his affiliation with a dubious detective association. It was acceptable for a McCormick representative to be an officer of the state agricultural society, to serve as worshipful master of a lodge of Free Masons, or officiate in a Good Templars Society, but not to enter any agreement that could excite suspicion among farmers. After Addis claimed that every act of his life was "*Open* and above board and with the *fear of God*" before him and that he tried to "act just and upright with all men" and to do his "duty as a Christian," he was allowed to keep his job.[46]

McCormick agents again strove to avoid controversy in the 1890s, when indebted farmers fought against the gold standard—a boon to moneylenders, be they Eastern capitalists or British investors—and against the tariff that protected industrialists. They continued to stress the technological sophistication of their wares and reported business almost as usual during the great wave of populist unrest. Once again, they noted the different reactions among farmers. Shortly after William Jennings Bryan had become his party's nominee for the presidency by exhorting Americans not to "press down upon the brow of labor" a "crown of thorns," and not to "crucify mankind upon a cross of gold,"[47] Angus Stewart, a McCormick agent from Minnesota, wrote that most men in small rural townships were not in favor of bimetallism.[48] His reports again lend credence to the economic historians' contention that the more vocal farmers were those who faced long hauls and difficult access to silos and railroad lines.[49] In 1896, Stewart correctly predicted McKinley's victory and argued that there were "spots where the Populistic craze is not dormant where silver is yet the rage, but these spots are mainly where poor crops have been the rule for two or three years."[50] Discontented farmers, who fought the railroads and other growing corporations tooth and nail, were more likely to reside on the outskirts of the corporate network and benefit little or not at all from it.

It would be wrong, however, to dismiss the rural rebellion against business, even in rich areas of staple agriculture, by merely pointing to the movement's decline when agricultural prices rose after a long period of deflation. The economic historians' point seems to be that a few cents difference in the price of wheat was enough to quell the sentiment behind this great mobilization. They argue that farmers should have behaved rationally in the first place, that is, realized that not only wheat but other prices were also declining in a deflationary situation and that their purchasing power was therefore less affected than they claimed it to be.[51] Economists sometimes expect too much of human nature. Stewart took a more cautious approach and sought not to alienate the populists in his area even after the price rise. Although he correctly predicted the Republican victory in 1896, he also thought that governor and congressmen would be former Republicans turned silverites. Nonetheless, he realized that the tide had turned against the populists. Still, immediately after McKinley's election, he wrote, "Look out for $100,000 from this end of the line this month, provided there are no more snow storms or elections."[52]

COLLECTING

A perennial source of conflict was collecting. Implement companies were as careful to avoid unnecessary disagreements with farmers over credit as they were to avoid disputes about the Grange and populism. The likelihood of such disputes was mitigated by the farmers' experience with credit. Farmers, like other entrepreneurs in American society, were deeply involved with credit long before the advent of consumer credit on a large scale. Credit, in fact, overshadowed all other forms of economic transactions. Eastern capitalists and their agents, servicing the mortgage mania of the 1880s, poured into the Great Plains ready to loan money for land purchases. Sources of credit were also near at hand. Midwestern farmers had long formed claim clubs or squatters associations in order to make payments on land they had settled prior to its offering at public auction. These clubs were used to protect farmers from claim-jumpers. They were also used for purpose of speculation, allowing farmers to purchase land with credit borrowed from the club in order to sell for a profit later. Mortgages, no matter who the lender, were a very common way of raising money for a variety of purposes.[53]

Manufacturers of farm implements knew that their best chance of receiving full payment for their equipment was to wait for good weather and growing conditions. When crops failed, they had little to gain by taking farmers to court.[54] McCormick followed the farm markets closely and revised its stategies accordingly. In February 1869, Addis wrote from Omaha: "I find money matters very tight indeed through out my district wont be able to collect much until after another crop I find it wont do to push farmers for they cant pay. Grass hoppers took most of crop and what is left wont bring much. I am doing some hard*drumming*. and I believe we will have to be content with what we can get and wait for the ballance."[55] Yet trust, as well as prudence, shaped the attitudes of McCormick agents. In November 1884, a local agent, J. R. Jordan, wrote from Stuart, Nebraska, to H. R. Gould, the Omaha agent, "in explanation of the Germans letter would say the haill destroyed his crops and he failled to get some funds from the oald country consequently he wants an extension of time on the first noat until Jan 86 at which time he will pay both noates he is *all right*."[56]

When Stewart did pursue payment, he followed fluctuations in the prices of commodities closely and adjusted his strategy accordingly. In September 1895, he wrote headquarters to advise patience for another month or so. The price of wheat had dropped below 50 cents per bushel in his territory and farmers were holding off selling for the time being. The agent observed, however, that all the wheat brought to town and placed in elevators had not been "stored awaiting an increase in price" but "actually sold." All this led him to speculate that the money would "come in in good shape" by early October, whether the price remained at the September level or improved. "You can look for something in the neighborhood of $100,000 in October," he predicted. "If I do not get that much I will surely miss my guess." But Stewart counted on the business and hired sixteen men to collect money in 113 townships of Minnesota and Wisconsin. He expected each collector to cash in about $7000 a month for the company, from which he substracted a 1 percent commission. The crop was good enough to expect such returns. Furthermore, he assured headquarters, "the men got after the parties early, and have tied up their crops so that the money must come. . . . You may rest assured that the paper taken this year will be collectible, if not all bankable."[57]

When forced to take action, McCormick agents displayed a complete knowledge of farming credit practices. Angus Stewart's activities in Minnesota reflect strategies necessitated by the financial arrangements which farmers resorted to. For instance, farmers routinely mortgaged their crops to secure a note. Creditors therefore had to take to locate crops of delinquent and recalcitrant farmers. In one case, McCormick and an elevator company competed for a customer's grain. The elevator company, which had sold the grain before the suit was decided, ended up having to reimburse McCormick both the value of the grain and legal fees. Sometimes, McCormick purchased the adjudication obtained from a farmer by other creditors or paid off a farmer's delinquent mortgage to the railroads or mortgage companies in order to acquire his land. It speculated on the land value to recover its losses.[58] In some instances, the company sued farmers directly.[59]

By the time of the formation of the International Harvester Company in 1903, the company readily acknowledged the special character of rural collecting and developed rules for its agents that conformed to the farmers' needs and aspirations. Good credit work was the key to sales and required extensive cooperation between the credit office at headquarters and agents in the field.[60] In other words, the corporations extended modern credit practices to their rural accounts. But the rules Harvester developed reflected the company's realization of the farmers' independent spirit and their readiness to contend with representatives of urban capital. Once again, the potential for conflict was a part of business as usual. Thus in collecting, the best results were not obtained by "the browbeating type who collect for loan and other sharks in cities, carrying the exempt household necessities from the homes of people too poor to defend themselves." Such men would "be jailed or mobbed before they finished one county."[61] Consequently, the company advised field men to understand the debtors' point of view, to measure his resources, and to help him devise a reasonable plan of repayment. Farmers perhaps paved the way for the great revolution in consumer credit in the cities that took place in the twenties. They practiced the installment plan long before analogous practices saddened the Lynds when they saw them flourishing in Middletown.[62] Although the large corporations developed modern credit practices, they did not revolutionize the rural world nearly as much as they transformed the habits of the urban working class.

SUPERIMPOSING NETWORKS

The McCormick agents spread over a vast territory and built a tight organization through which they could make their presence felt. Not surprisingly, the location and development of agencies paralleled those of rural towns. It is generally admitted that Chrystaller's central place theory, a descriptive account of settlement patterns in rural southern Germany in 1933, is equally relevant to the American Great Plains.[63] The theory holds that central places control overlapping sets of market areas. Central places of higher order dominate larger regions than those of lesser order, exercise more important functions and therefore have greater centrality. For all, however, "the sum of the distances which rural residents travel to the central place is the smallest conceivable sum."[64] Analogous principles applied to the creation of the corporate network of agencies. The location of agencies along the transportation lines was therefore an important decision, partly affected by existing conditions such as the presence of a market and service center and partly by the response to projected needs. Some of the towns where business representatives settled were state capitals or large regional centers. Others were barely more than railroad crossings where farmers brought their wheat and corn to store in silos. These small crossroad towns functioned as outposts of corporate America. From these towns, business representatives of all kinds reached out to the farming population.[65]

The representatives of big business spread across the countryside over three decades. Singer pioneered with a distribution network for sewing machines. All large firms selling technologically complex products followed suit, bypassing the wholesale jobber.[66] The network was at first quite loose as potential clients were scattered across large regions and manufacturers often relied on local lawyers for collections. In the 1870s, the average McCormick agent rarely made a trip of less than one month at a time. It was not rare for him to spend three months or more on the road and ride horseback alone for several weeks before returning to a railroad. That kind of travel, even on the railroads, was hard. "You will be surprised to learn that I have not yet left this place," reported H. C. Addis from Des Moines, Iowa, in March 1867 "but we had a very unfortunate journey." After a delay in Davenport, his party was held up "one day longer by Freight Train being off the track." Then "one of the Deep Cuts west of Iowa City was closed up by the embankments thawing out and closeing in." Other unforeseen adventures followed as the high waters had taken nearly all the bridges away and "the bottoms are so covered with water and Ice that it makes difficult crossing." If it was not the weather, it was the Indians "stealing Horses and committing all measures of depredation all along the line of road."[67]

From Omaha, Addis in 1874 opened agencies (with men on salaries), as well as dealerships. He reported that one man went "farthest west, with Hastings for headquarters. He takes all the Russian settlements/they speak German. he will have many Germans also." But not all sites required an agency.[68] While traveling through Colorado in 1874, Addis wrote the Chicago headquarters: "My reason for thinking it will not pay to employ a man [on salary] here is this. The settlements are scattered over so large a tract of country and a man would have to travel so much to make few sales that his expenses would be to great. . . . He would have to keep a team, and the expense of team and hotel bills would be enormous."[69]

After three decades of McCormick and Harvester agents crisscrossing the territory, the system of agencies had become dense. By 1910, International Harvester had consolidated its components' networks and had permanent representatives in thirty-one states. These were unevenly distributed. Most agencies were obviously concentrated in the areas of staple agriculture where mechanized implements had the greatest impact. Wheat and corn were the keys. Generally speaking, there was no need for a dense organization in those eastern states with few large farms or hilly terrains poorly suited to mechanization, in the southern states with their poor soil and cheap, black labor, or in the western states, which were mostly devoted to ranching. Fifteen states—Massachussets, Maryland, Virginia, West Virginia, Kentucky, Georgia, Louisiana, Alabama, Oklahoma, Colorado, Utah, Montana, Washington, Oregon, California—had only one agency. Only one southern state, Tennessee, had three agencies. Michigan, South Dakota, and Nebraska also had three. North Dakota, Minnesota, Wisconsin, Missouri, Ohio, and Pennsylvania had four each; New York State five, Indiana and Kansas six, the prairie states of Illinois and Iowa eight each. In 1910, there were eighty-five general agencies across the country. Harvester records only list the names of employees who reached the rank of general and assistant general agent in the sales department. Altogether, 622 men, recruited between 1876 and 1919, reached these ranks in the sales organization.[70]

The network established by Chicago representatives in the neighboring states of the Great Plains was particularly thick. By 1910, forty-eight employees who eventually became either general agents or assistant general agents worked directly for Harvester agencies in Iowa, Nebraska, South Dakota, and North Dakota. They helped dealers or marketed the equipment directly to farmers. The three agencies of Nebraska, situated at Lincoln (43,973 inhabitants), Crawford (1,323 inhabitants), and Omaha (124,096), counted seven employees who became general agents and assistant general agents. Twenty-four were distributed among the eight agencies of Iowa located in Cedar Falls (5,102), Council Bluffs (29,292), Sioux City (47,828), Des Moines (86,368), Davenport (43,028), Dubuque (38,494), Fort Dodge (15,543), and Mason City (11,230). There were seven general and assistant general agents in the three South Dakota agencies of Sioux Falls (14,094), Aberdeen (10,753), and Watertown (7,010); and ten in the four agencies of Minot (6,188), Fargo (14,331), Grand Forks (12,478), and Bismarck (5,443) in North Dakota.[71] These career people made between $2,500 and $3,600 in 1910 if they were general agents and between $2,000 and $2,500 as assistant general agents.[72]

These midwestern representatives coordinated the efforts of a substantial additional sales force whom they hired, some on salary and some on commission. Often a small agency employed seven or eight such salesmen—several blockmen (salesmen assigned to subregions), canvassers, and special salesmen—beyond the general agent and his assistant. All these agents and their hired help effectively established connections between those urban centers of industry and finance and their rural hinterland.

FROM LINCOLN TO CRAWFORD

To appreciate the agents' significant role in the process of change, it is important not only to see the density of the network of rural central places they helped establish but also to understand how agents integrated the communities in which they worked. Agents supported the dealers, trained them technically, and also established additional contact with the farmers. Their initial frame of reference was the organization to which they belonged, and their affiliation with big business established the boundaries of their intellectual horizon. Yet business agents also identified with local causes and took local responsibilities. In that sense, they became, like Du Pont representatives in Pennsylvania, true insiders while retaining outsiders' status. The agents' dual allegiance assisted the transmittal of corporate values to the rural world. The heads of the Harvester agencies in Lincoln, Nebraska's capital, and in Crawford, a small railroad crossing in the western part of the state, are good examples of how corporate personnel not only carried out their duties but also penetrated their new communities.

C. E. Haynie was the McCormick agent, then the Harvester agent, in Lincoln from 1898 to 1912. Lincoln, midway between Chicago and Denver on the main C. B. & Q. line, became the state capital when Nebraska was admitted to the Union in 1868. Three years later the state university opened its door. The town grew rapidly from a nucleus of 500 inhabitants in 1868 to 43,973 in 1910. Lincoln was a market center with its clusters of commercial establishments, banks, newspapers, saloons, and the jail. It also had light industries such as lumber yards and a few packing plants, although the Union stockyards were located in nearby Omaha, twenty miles away.[73]

By the 1890s, the town was diversified ethnically, as the presence of thirty-eight different churches indicates. Thirteen temperance societies joined in the struggle against the wets, an issue which dominated local politics in Lincoln as elsewhere. As corn prices dropped to low points in the 1890s, populists who waged their war on banks, tariffs, currency standards, railroad monopolies, pools, and big business found a sympathizer in William Jennings Bryan, who had settled in Lincoln as a young lawyer.[74]

Haynie's activities in Lincoln are highly instructive about the ways in which representatives of national firms took part in local life. Haynie supervised a staff of nine in the Lincoln agency. Several were men who had come off the farm and whose career, like that of their boss, now revolved around regional and national organizations rather than local businesses. One of Haynie's collaborators, for instance, had started with the C.B. & Q. and would leave Harvester for the insurance industry.[75]

Haynie joined the Union Commercial Club immediately after he arrived. The club became the Lincoln Commercial Club in 1904 and later the Chamber of Commerce. At the club, local merchants, local industrialists, and city officials mingled with a few railway managers, such as the C. B. & Q. city passenger and ticket agent, and a few agents of distant firms such as Haynie himself. The club had both a social and a commercial function. Members had access to a large pool room with four billiard tables and four pool tables surrounded by ten cuspidors, as well as a card room and a dining room. Members also made frequent use of the reading room supplied with reference books, a dictionary, magazines, and, in 1910, the year when Brandeis argued his famous rate case before the Interstate Commerce Commission (see chap. 1), fifteen volumes of ICC railway hearings. Seven volumes of *International Law Digest*, eleven volumes of census reports, and the publications of the Nebraska State Historical Society filled out the holdings.[76]

By 1904, the club had shifted its emphasis from social activities to promoting commercial development, and in 1910 Haynie was appointed to the important commercial committee. The businessmen who met at the club were involved in a miscellany of endeavors, some of national significance, others local. In May 1910, they endorsed a bill introduced by Senator Owen of Oklahoma to establish a department of public health.[77] They also requested that the local high school YWCA, which was raising money to send a delegate to the YWCA National Convention in Denver, discontinue selling sundry toilet articles produced by the distant Larkin Co. of Buffalo. The YWCA's response was to ask the club to provide the money for the trip.[78] The club also petitioned the ICC to make an exhaustive investigation of express rates but, perhaps due to the influence of railroad officers among them, the assembled businessmen shied away from a uniform condemnation of the railroad freight structure.[79] The club organized weekly luncheons, inviting authorities to lecture on dairying and milk supply or good roads.

Charles Bryan, William Jennings's brother, was an influential member of the Chamber of Commerce. Also a politician, he became reform mayor of Lincoln and led the movement to establish a commission form of government. The Bryan brothers were pillars of the church and teetotalers (Lincoln went dry in 1909). Within the Chamber of Commerce, C. E. Haynie worked several times with Charles Bryan. Together they prepared a motion to send the club's secretary to attend the fourth annual convention of commercial executives in Buffalo. The club also sent seven representatives to the mayoral committee to study a new city charter. When the club collected subscriptions for the construction of an auditorium, Haynie ranked among the substantial donors.[80]

Thus, in the state capital, the Harvester representative worked with local boosters and identified with local causes. Although Haynie clearly represented big business and not local merchants, the sharp cleavages and hatreds of history books faded at the door of the Chamber of Commerce. In the meetings of the Commercial Club, Haynie carried weight because he was the head of the Harvester Agency but he also came to be perceived as a fellow local developer. The interests of national and local organizations slowly merged.

The same was true in outlying places. Harvester set up its third Nebraska agency in its western railroad crossing of Crawford, a town of only 1,323 inhabitants in 1910.[81] In the 1880s, C. B. & Q. agents found Crawford a wild frontier community. The C. B. & Q. right-of-way agent Edgar Westervelt (see chap. 2) remembered that in his day Crawford was "a wide open town [with] enough saloons to supply the state of Nebraska adequately. . . . It was not very long until liquor, colored troops and hoboes made a bad combination. . . . The fight started in one of the saloons. . . . The shooting was fast and furious," and the young railroad agent headed for cover behind a bale of wool.[82]

The Harvester agency opened its door in 1909, the year the town—its streets still unpaved—was incorporated. As a junction, Crawford could be used to supply the routes of three separate railroads: the Union Pacific, the B. & M., and the Northwest. W. E. Acker, a sometime justice of the peace known as "Judge," headed the agency. Acker had learned the implement business in Iowa, had been a traveling salesman for McCormick for ten years, and was the assistant to the general agent in Omaha after 1905. He supervised a staff of eight traveling men.[83]

The activities of the Harvester agency were part of the daily concerns of the town. No news was too small in Crawford to escape the local press. When a farmer bought a new piece of equipment, when a resident entertained friends with a game of cards, when the owner of the local millinery shop went to Chicago to replenish her stock, the local reporters wrote it up. The local newspaper also took note when local businessmen met to create a commercial club, when the construction of the Harvester company building along the Northwestern RR tracks was delayed because of cold weather, when the itinerant eye, ear, nose, and throat doctor was available to see patients at the Gate City Hotel, or when the traveling opera company played *His Highness the Bay*.[84]

Politically, here as elsewhere, the town was divided between wets and drys—the latter arguing that only in dry counties and towns were taxes paid and improvements made. Like William Jennings and Charles Bryan in Lincoln, Acker belonged to the Knights of Pythias and was active in the temperance movement.[85] In his new town, Acker settled into politics and became president of the city council. In the 1910 election, as women were not yet voting in Nebraska, the wet candidate won the mayoralty by one vote (163 to 162). Shortly thereafter the mayor had to resign because of irregularities, and Acker was appointed to his office.[86]

Both in Lincoln and in out-of-the-way Crawford, representatives of the giant Chicago firms behaved just like other newcomers. They identified with local issues and became involved in the politics of local development. Although they did so initially with the purpose of promoting their companies' interests, they soon found themselves involved in the larger scheme of social development. In the process of doing so, they familiarized rural America with corporate values.

IMBRICATED ORDERS

Big business was quick to attribute to itself the credit for advances in the development of agriculture. An editorial of *The Harvester World* thus explained that "by the intelligent use of modern farm implements, the standard of the world's living is raised." And the representatives of big business were

> entitled to a large portion of the honor incidental to the
> upbuilding and the uplifting of the people who depend on
> the produce of the farms for sustenance. . . . By assisting
> in building up this prosperous country, we have not only
> helped ourselves, but we have helped everybody else. . . .
> Were it not for the modern way of tilling the soil and of har-
> vesting the crops, do you suppose that our farmer friends
> would be able to send their boys and girls to college, or to
> provide for their home use telephones, automobiles, electric
> lights plants, the daily paper, bathrooms, and all those other
> conveniences which make life worth while?[87]

To be sure, this enumeration was not followed by any hard statistics. These pronouncements actually betray the feeling of insecurity that often marked the relationship between corporations and farmers. Corporations liked to believe that they played a major role in educating farmers by providing them not only with new technology but also with new ways of doing business. The reality was less simple. Corporations did not so much impose a new order as they modified an existing one, sometimes in agreement and sometimes in opposition with government agencies and the farming population.

The hundreds of Harvester representatives spread across rural America contributed to changing the meaning of mobility in the countryside. The new order was no more wedded to place than the old but geographic mobility became more closely tied to status. Corporate employees worked within a large geographic framework. Thus Harvester agents operated not from one town but from a series of towns in the course of their careers. As managers and agents gained in experience they were promoted up the hierarchy of central places. Whereas many nineteenth-century Du Pont agents in eastern Pennsylvania were chosen from among the local mercantile establishment and were expected to remain there (see chap. 1), Harvester agents moved along the newly developed corporate-rural network. For example, Harvey A. Jetmore was general agent in Cedar Falls, Iowa, in 1910. He started with McCormick in 1897 as a salesman in Kansas City, Missouri, until 1902, spent a year in Mankato, Minnesota, as a general agent and two years in Concordia, Kansas, as an assistant general agent and an engine traveler. Then he took over the agency in Topeka, Kansas, from 1906 to 1908 before moving back to Cedar Falls, where he remained general agent until 1917. The company took advantage of his experience by sending him to New Orleans as a special salesman for two years, Minneapolis for three and to headquarters at Chicago for another two. He returned to Topeka in 1923 and retired in 1925. He had made eight moves during his tenure of twenty-eight years with the company.[88] Other agents were more stable, but the majority experienced several moves along an increasingly complex company network of offices and agencies.

In directing this geographic mobility, corporate headquarters, then, redefined traditional ideas about social mobility. Time after time, the company reminded its salesforce in the field that "the competent blockman will soon be wanted for more advanced work" and that every member of the organization would benefit from it.[89] "The openings are here for you—an assortment of them—every size to fit every calibre of ability."[90] The company could give plenty of evidence to support this claim. Thus when the general agent at Madison, Wisconsin, was promoted to headquarters to become a district manager, when the general agent at Milwaukee, Wisconsin, was asked to head the auto, spreader, and separator branches at the Chicago office, and when the general agent at Council Bluffs, Iowa, was called to headquarters to take charge of the gasoline engine department, the company commented, "the graduated development of these men runs parallel with the development of the farm machine business."[91]

This abstract notion of organizational and bureaucratic mobility—the influence of which Willa Cather had detected among railroad employees in Red Cloud, was exhibited again and again in the heart of rural America. Not only did farmers experience it by encountering the emissaries of big business but many a farmer's son could now move, not just farther west or to a distant anonymous great city as in the past, but into the large corporate workforces and could participate in the corporations' conquest of the rural market and the larger transformation of the countryside.

To penetrate a diversified rural world, corporations had to make their presence felt constantly and go beyond the strict business of selling. Educating farmers actually became a leitmotiv as corporate organizations realized that they had to capture the progressive goal of upgrading farm life. This was no easy task as farmers could not readily translate the productivity gains heralded by corporations into other tangible gains. Furthermore, education was subsumed under the larger category of corporate marketing, and funds were not spent where they could not be justified by a financial return to the company. Implement companies had invested in agricultural fairs for a long time. McCormick agents like E. C. Beardsley, for instance, made their presence felt in the early days of the business by setting up a "mower *in operation*" beside the fair grounds in small Illinois towns.[92] In 1880, Beardsley persuaded his company to build a separate building at a large fair in Minnesota. He made sure to have the company name on three sides of the building in letters big enough so "that 'he who run'—the ticket taker at the gate—might read."[93] By 1910, International Harvester exhibited its line of machines at thirty-seven different state and larger district fairs in addition to innumerable county fairs. "The state fair is the high school of agriculture," declared the implement company in its magazine, but it is also "the agricultural roundup of the year; the after-harvest business vacation. Agent meets agent, dealer meets dealer, farmer meets farmer, and all meet each other. And they mingle in a big week of talk, argument, comparison, and demonstration." Yet the fairs must pay. "So great indeed is the outlay in these enterprises each year that it is of vital importance that we get the largest possible return from the investment."[94]

The company experimented with other sorts of educational work—general and scientific. Harvester agents were instructed to cooperate "in every way" with the Department of Agriculture, the experiment stations, the state agricultural colleges, and other colleges. The company loaned machines to colleges for demonstration purposes and funded scholarships to agricultural schools.[95] As at least some of the graduates would stay on the farm, it was hoped they would remember their benefactors.

So intermixed were business marketing and educational efforts that representatives of USDA became adamant that only they, free as they were from the profit motive, were qualified to educate the farmers. USDA county agents, whose own agendas had more to do with soil conservation and public health than mechanization, were actually instructed to stay clear of business representatives.[96] Educators in agricultural colleges also felt uneasy about the quality of the educational advertising published by big business. Thus, the supervisor of the Farmer's Institute at Ohio State University wrote in 1916 to the Kelley Island Lime and Transport Company of Cleveland, Ohio, that the company had behaved irresponsibly in presenting a moving picture at the institute by

> 1st: Giving the young girls of the country the idea that washing dishes, etc. is drudgery, in the scene 'Mary Graham is reduced to drudgery.' 2nd: Giving the young men of the country a low standard of business methods in the scene in which the agent treats the prospective purchaser, Mr. Graham, to a cigar. 3rd: There seems to be some objection to the display of the mail order catalogs in the scene in which the purchase of a piano and automobile are contemplated.[97]

Actually, big business had little competition for the farmer's attention. International Harvester had representatives in numbers superior to all of the county agents involved nationwide in farm and home demonstration work and supported by USDA. Furthermore, most of the county agents concentrated their missionary work in the disaster areas of the South while representatives of new, technologically complex businesses, interacted routinely with farmers elsewhere.[98] Before 1911, there were no county agents in the North. By 1914, the year the Smith-Lever Act set up an elaborate system of agricultural extension work, there were only two hundred.[99]

The strength of Harvester and other corporate representatives was their ability to go beyond fairs and scattered agricultural colleges to school houses of the rural districts, local agents sample rooms, picnics and other public gatherings as well as isolated farmsteads. Harvester agents were well aware of their advantage in this respect over agricultural colleges and experimental stations. Even though corporate agents compounded advertising and education in a mixture uniquely their own, they had a direct effect on the farmer to whom they provided a whole range of services from credit to technical advice. While education hardly precluded self-promotion, the corporations encouraged the imposition of a technical culture across the rural landscape. Government programs had little effect until after the passage of the Smith-Lever Act, while the interaction between farmers and representatives of large corporations created new habits, and indirectly a different way of thinking, over the course of a generation.

The railroad, the reaper, the automobile, the sewing machine, and other corporate ventures profoundly and cumulatively transformed the agricultural world. Yet corporate organizations did not reshape the rural areas merely because of the superiority of the technology they produced and its ready acceptance by farmers in search of progress and profits. Their penetration required the dispatch of scores of men to live with farmers. These men served as intermediaries between their company and the farmers and were well aware that they had to do more than blindly represent their company's interests if they wanted to be successful. With the meeting of the farmers and the corporations, we witness not the decline of agrarian democracy but rather the coming to terms of several competing versions of agrarian democracy. One was based on the cooperative visions of farming communities, another on the farmers' entrepreneurial self-interest, and yet another on the new corporate way of producing and consuming. The corporations' goal was to impose more homogenization on the farm landscape so as to develop the new patterns of production and consumption. They did so by accommodating these other visions, but not before the corporations were influenced by them. That the corporations were thus far successful is a testimony to the ingenuity of their middle management and agents as well as the farmers themselves.

SEVEN

DRUMMERS
AND
SALESMEN

The man of system . . . is apt to be very wise in his own conceit, and is often so enamoured with the supposed beauty of his own plan of government, that he cannot suffer the smallest deviation from any part of it. He goes on to establish it completely and in all its parts, without any regard to the great interests or to the strong prejudices which may oppose it: he seems to imagine that he can arrange the different members of a great society with as much ease as the hand arranges the different pieces upon a chess-board; he does not consider that the pieces upon the chess-board have no other principle of motion besides that which the hand impresses upon them; but that, in the great chess-board of human society, every single piece has a principle of motion of its own.

Adam Smith, *The Theory of Moral Sentiments*, 1759

CHAPTER SEVEN

A lthough selling has always been a ubiquitous activity, it was changed radically by the rise of corporations. Those men and women who had acted as salesmen—owners and employees of large urban mercantile houses and modest country stores, long-distance drummers and door-to-door peddlers alike—saw their occupations transformed. With the development of marketing divisions, salesmanship and advertising became the two main components of a new "science of service." And they were now approached methodically, if not scientifically. Smaller industrial firms, even when they recruited their own salesmen, never had the resources to translate experience into a system of formal knowledge and formal knowledge into policy. They invested in product development, not in salesmanship, which was left to the inspired patter of the individual. And advertising, typified by the promotion of patent medicines, was little more than printed ballyhoo.[1] Large corporations transformed all this. They opened a national market by launching the legal battles that forced state legislatures to abandon disguised protectionism against out-of-state products and by creating new sales and advertising divisions to serve these newly opened territories.[2] The degree of penetration we have seen corporate salesmen achieving in the countryside (chap. 6) is an indication of the growing strength of corporate organizations.

DRUMMERS

The precursors of the corporate salesmen were the drummers who, in the 1880s and 1890s, crossed and recrossed the states as representatives of manufacturing concerns.[3] They were a common enough fixture of late-nineteenth-century life that novelists took special note of their rapid climb to success or fall from fortune, their appearance, their tactics, and their ambitions. Thus Theodore Dreiser opens *Sister Carrie* (1900) with Charles Drouet, the salesman who introduces himself to Carrie Meeber, the young country girl, on the Chicago train. Dreiser remarks:

> Here was a type of the travelling canvasser for a manufacturing house—a class which at that time was first being dubbed by the slang of the day "drummers." . . . His suit was of a striped and crossed pattern of brown wool, new at that time, but since become familiar as a business suit. The low crotch of the vest revealed a stiff shirt bosom of white and pink stripes. From his coat sleeves protruded a pair of linen cuffs

of the same pattern, fastened with large, gold plate buttons, set with the common yellow agates known as "cat's-eyes." His fingers bore several rings—one, the ever-enduring heavy seal—and from his vest dangled a neat gold watch chain, from which was suspended the secret insignia of the Order of Elks. The whole suit was rather tight-fitting, and was finished off with heavy-soled tan shoes, highly polished, and the grey fedora hat.[4]

In his appearance, Drouet epitomizes abundance of material wealth, and it is this abundance that sways Carrie's judgment.[5]

As the story of less fortunate drummers shows, the sort of unity Drouet achieves with the more luxurious products of the manufacturing age was not so easy to accomplish. In the summer of 1895, the Arlington Collar and Cuff Company, a subsidiary of the Arlington Company of New Jersey (which would become a part of the Du Pont empire some twenty years later), sent one of its new sales recruits, Louis Wiener, on a routine sales trip to the Midwest from its offices on Broadway. But Wiener had neither the know-how nor the salesmanship to make a success. He went as far as Kansas City before being ordered back to Buffalo, his hometown and dismissed.[6]

Wiener did not fail from want of effort. He took the train to Chicago and from there journeyed to small towns all across the Illinois prairie. He went first to Joliet, a large agricultural and industrial center of over 23,000 people and then to the surrounding towns of Ottawa, Streator, Pontiac, La Salle, and Bloomington, a busy manufacturing town of over 20,000 inhabitants and an important railway center for coal and agricultural products.[7] He then moved to the center of the state, traveling to Peoria, a river and railroad terminal; then down the Illinois River to Pekin, a small rail center for the surrounding agricultural and mining region; to Canton, in the heart of the Illinois corn belt; and finally to the quiet river town of Havana.

The longer he was on the road, the dimmer were his prospects. After a trip east to the university town of Urbana and the coal mining area of Danville near the Indiana border, he headed south to the corn land of Mattoon and then back north to Lincoln, the seat of Logan County. He resumed his southward trek to Springfield, the state capital, with almost 25,000 inhabitants. Then, swinging east and west across the state, he visited Jacksonville (13,000), the agricultural railroad center of Decatur, the coal-mining towns of Pana and Litchfield, and a few brief stops before moving on to Missouri: St. Louis first, then Jefferson City, Louisiana, Sedalia, Kansas City. But by this time, his trip was an irremediable failure.

What went wrong? Everything. In the larger towns, Wiener was the victim of unkept promises made by previous travelers: promises to provide merchants with special sample cases to display the waterproof collars in water, promises to take old stock of the competition's collars in exchange for orders, promises that should not have been made and on which he could not deliver. Wiener was also faced with competition from Chicago firms who sold waterproof collars at sixty cents apiece rather than the ninety his company charged. He had to contend with the traditional cotton collar, which was cheaper and more popular. In the small towns, people were not interested in the newer "police collar" or in the "bishop-pope Leo XII [sic] collar"; "You can't get in with the 'Yokels,'" he wrote his boss in New York. But Wiener was undone by his inexperience and his lack of knowledge about such essentials as discount practices and freight rates. He did not even keep an orderly list of jobbers. Not surprisingly, only a few orders came in. Wiener was desperate for business and so was his boss when he ordered Wiener off the road. The sales manager wrote Wiener that he did not care to train him or to hear his excuses and dismissed him as an "utter failure." The hapless salesman lasted only five weeks.[8]

As Wiener's case demonstrates, salesmen were not given much time to prove their ability. Arlington's formula was simple enough: salary and travel expenses should not exceed 12.5 percent of sales. The average salesman was paid $1,500 a year (Wiener, as a novice, would have made $780 if he had lasted the year) and had an expense allowance of $1,875. He would thus be expected to have annual sales of $27,000. Of the $1,875 in his expense allowance, about $1,000 would go for train fares. This left him roughly $3 a day during his forty weeks of travel for other expenses, less than the cost of a room in a good hotel. Additional pay could come in the form of commission, up to 10 percent once the targeted sales figure was reached. Salesmen could also expand their lines by selling fancy goods and specialties made by the Arlington Cuff and Collar Company. Altogether, it was hard work, and success brought in an annual income between $780 and $3,500. Employment contracts were valid for a year but could be terminated on sixty-day notice. In 1898, a successful salesman from Arlington Cuff and Collar Company visited no fewer than 182 towns in six states—New York, Pennsylvania, Ohio, Indiana, Michigan, and a small part of Kentucky—for which he received a compensation of

$1,200. The more fortunate salesmen graduated to the large cities, where the volume of sales allowed for higher salaries and less traveling. From the big cities, senior salesmen supervised their younger colleagues on the road.[9]

A New Marketing Structure

Wiener and other drummers were competing not only with Chicago jobbers but also with representatives of large corporations. Selling under the new corporate structures was but one part of a comprehensive marketing strategy, and salesmen were viewed differently by corporate management than they had been. Like International Harvester, Du Pont offered salesmen, as important participants in the marketing sector, the opportunity for professional growth as well as a job. Accordingly, Du Pont developed an elaborate sales organization. Du Pont's sales department as originally organized in 1904 had three geographical districts and four bureaus. Just as International Harvester combined the sales networks of its constituent companies, former Du Pont agencies and those of other chemical concerns that had joined the newly consolidated corporation were converted to branch offices. Salesmen and office staff were paid by salary rather than commission.[10]

By 1917, Du Pont's salesforce, stimulated by war production, comprised 344 men distributed over forty-six states as well as representatives in Mexico, Canada, and Australia. The sales department was organized into a complex hierarchy of sales managers, districts managers, assistant managers, traffic specialists, accountants, technicians, clerks, advertisers, specialized sales agents, and salesmen themselves, who accounted for 71 percent of the sales department personnel. The sales network grew rapidly. A year later, the sales organization had grown to 379, as 39 men departed and 74 new men joined the company.[11]

The sales machinery for Du Pont's primary product, explosives, alone consisted of 196 men in 1917. Selling explosives was a complex operation that depended on the assistance of employees in divisions throughout the organization—in the agricultural, contractors, advertising, export, trade record, traffic, statistical, storage, delivery, and technical divisions—and in the branch offices the company maintained in Birmingham, Chicago, Denver, Duluth, Huntington (West Virginia), Joplin, New York, Pittsburgh, San Francisco, Scranton, Seattle, St. Louis, and Mexico City. Of the 196 employees responsible for the sales of explosives, 134 were on the road; they consisted of 92 explosives men (some with specializations within the explosives trade), 23 shooter salesmen, 2 salesmen specializing in exports in the New York office, 4 agricultural representatives, 4 composite salesmen, and 9 technical representatives.

Du Pont's complex sales organization also included sales personnel working at several subsidiary companies carefully integrated into the Du Pont organization although operating under their own names. Thus Arlington, which specialized in pyralin articles, collars and cuffs, had its main office in New York and branch offices in Boston, Chicago, St. Louis, and San Francisco. In 1917, its salesforce comprised 27 men, no Louis Wieners among them. Eighteen salesmen and a sales manager worked for the Bridgeport Works from Du Pont offices in New York, Boston, Newark, and Philadelphia, all specializing in the sales of paints and stains. Chemical mixtures were put on the market by the Du Pont Chemical Works, which operated from offices in the Equitable Building in New York (the massive skyscraper Coleman du Pont had built for the insurance company), with a sales manager, a chief clerk, and 11 salesmen. Ten salespeople worked for the Dye Works in Wilmington (the main office), Chicago, Philadelphia, Providence, and Charlotte, North Carolina. Du Pont Fabrikoid had a sales staff of 20 people, 15 of whom were salesmen. Its home office was in Wilmington, and it maintained offices in Canada and Australia. Harrison Paint Products, with headquarters in Philadelphia and other offices in New York, Newark, Chicago, Minneapolis, and St. Louis, had a salesforce of 60 individuals, 47 of whom were salesmen. These associate companies, either created or bought by Du Pont, employed 148 sales people, of whom 111 salesmen were on the road all year, the rest serving as chief clerks, branch managers, or sales managers.

Altogether there were sales offices in thirty-three cities to which the various salesmen living in 123 towns reported. From this network of offices, the company covered a vast territory. For instance, the main company and its subsidiaries (Arlington, Harrison, and so on) had 51 employees in sales reporting to the Chicago office but 30 of them had territories covering two to five midwestern states. In fact 23 salesmen who reported to Chicago resided outside the midwestern metropolis. They lived in the cities of the Midwest, in Cleveland, Indianapolis, Detroit and Highland Park, Grand Rapids, Kansas City, Minneapolis and St. Paul, and St. Louis. They lived in railroad terminals, such as Aurora, and in towns in the heart of the coal country, such as Springfield. Others lived in small towns such as Terre Haute, Indiana, Hartford, Kentucky, Fond du Lac, Wisconsin, and Cedar Rapids, Iowa. The same organization prevailed in other regions.

The effect of this highly developed, highly diffused hierarchical structure was that it spread the new corporate culture through scores of employees, and through them to customers. In the new corporate order, exposing untrained and unorganized salesmen to the trials and tribulations of the road was no longer desirable and theoretically no longer possible.

THE NEW SCIENCE OF SALESMANSHIP

The formation of very large sales departments by corporations led to professionalized salesmen. The new science of salesmanship was distinguished by its recognition of ethical principles as well as its emphasis on carefully planned strategies. Because success in distribution depended on the coordinated efforts of a large number of people, employees not only should share the corporations' goal but should adhere to a single ideology. I do not mean by this word an overly systematized and simplified view of the world, but rather the sharing of a set of driving ideas. Only by focusing their efforts on these ideas could salesmen be influential enough to transform the prevailing culture.

These ethical ideals—compounded with the psychology of selling—were codified in business colleges throughout the country. These colleges, such as the Alexander Hamilton Institute in New York, gained in influence as they attracted well-known economists and successful publicists, like Bruce Barton, to their faculties.[12] In a series of copyrighted lectures for businessmen eager to advance in their line, the institute, in 1919, underscored "service" as the keynote of modern business and "true salesmanship" as "its most conspicuous embodiment." Salesmanship, in the institute's view, was no longer a collection of mere procedures and rehearsed spiels to get the customer's signature on the dotted line. It was a moral crusade that could be undertaken only by principled men. It involved a "constant endeavor to improve oneself." Salesmanship was no longer just "a garment to be taken off and put on when required" but instead "a part of a man's fiber and being." Only when the salesman was "confident and forceful," when he had "faith, faith in his product and faith in himself," could he induce other people to make decisions they would not necessarily make, although they might wish to make them in principle. "*Make* decisions—do not merely *expect* them," the advice went.[13] In this view, salesmanship became the means of realizing one's best inner qualities and inducing customers to realize theirs. Moral and ethical rigor were a prerequisite for financial success.

Furthermore, corporations strove to endow these jobs with socially useful functions.[14] In the corporations' view, salesmen served their communities by introducing high quality goods and by acting as conduits for advances in science and technology.

Pierre du Pont, who addressed the salesmen assembled at the General Sales Convention of the Du Pont Company in Atlantic City in 1918, reaffirmed the role of the corporation in society. In his address, du Pont carefully wove the motives that he felt should inspire his salesmen into a history of the company. His emphasis was on force of character, rather than profit. The Du Pont company went through two phases, he explained. First, it concentrated on acquiring the "force to face competition" in order to achieve "the right to live" as a company. Then, it used its "accumulated experience" to attain "the highest development of its powers, not only the power of the industry itself but the powers of the men whose strength and character alone limit accomplishment." These men are motivated by "the two great cornerstones of . . . business success": the "necessity of providing for home and family" and "ambition to accomplish."[15]

Things had gone wrong, however, just as the company had been about to achieve stage two—not through its own fault, du Pont insisted, but because the federal government had sought earlier in the century to limit growth in the explosives industry. Government intervention was the end of "opportunity," perhaps even "the starting point of retrogression and decay." "Men of enterprise" reacted strongly to this prospect. They found retrogression "intolerable" and struggled against it. As part of this struggle, the company diversified and underwent several reorganizations, which brought about an immediate boost in efficiency. While "purchasing and selling expenses and many other forms of outlay decreased in proportion to output, there was a tremendous increase in the number of men employed and in their individual and total compensation."

This increase in compensation was just one social good achieved by the corporation. This aggressive response in the face of adversity, du Pont contended, was also beneficial to society at large. Having reorganized, the company was able to meet the war demand and to progress in "four years to an extent that might have taken forty years under normal times." The reorganization enabled it to boost its capacity for producing smokeless powder from 8,400,000 pounds a year in

1914 to 440,000,000 pounds by the time of this sales convention. That the reorganizations had been prompted in part by the actions of the Justice Department went unacknowledged. According to du Pont, the search for efficiency helped secure lower costs and larger profits more readily than "all the effects of consolidation opposed by the Sherman Law."

When du Pont went on to consider the future of the company after its great achievement of the war years, he maintained his focus on its moral imperative. He felt assured that the future of the United States afforded "equal opportunity to energetic citizens" and that Du Pont American Industries would represent a source of this opportunity. But in the corporate setting, individual opportunity exists only as part of a larger, collective activity. "Material success of a group of persons cannot be dependent upon the advancement of some individuals at the expense of others," du Pont stressed. Instead, there must be "an uplift of the whole." "The rock of selfishness" must be avoided for the benefit of all the "believers."

Du Pont's message to his salesmen was both simple and powerful. Industry's contribution to society is to make available useful products that make for a better world. The profit it makes in the course of this undertaking is only its due. A large, integrated enterprise is better suited to this task than a smaller one because it can make the greatest number of products available in the most efficient manner. Furthermore, corporate endeavor leads to the material and moral betterment of those who participate in it.

The location of du Pont's talk was appropriate for the message the salesmen heard. Atlantic City was the physical embodiment of the benefits of consumption that du Pont stressed in his speech. By 1916, an estimated ten million people visited the resort annually, a greater number than at any other resort in the world. It was a popular place for conventions of manufacturing concerns and business and fraternal organizations. As if to make the connection explicit, the company had started a trap shooting school and opened a special store in Atlantic City to promote its products. To attract marksmen to the school, the company sent personal letters and pamphlets stressing the unusual opportunity of shooting over the ocean. All who enjoyed a stroll on the boardwalk could see the displays of Du Pont's new products, the new lines of "ivory" toiletware (pyralin), consumer products made of artificial leather, the paints and other goods that were being mass marketed. In addition, a special display of Du Pont products was highlighted on the Million Dollar Pier.[16]

SYSTEM

Salesmen were expected to develop expertise in their field and to act on this expertise. Thus selling became a discipline and required training. The largest companies, eager to instill the allegiance necessary to preserve their trade secrets, supplemented the generalized course of instruction found in business institutes with specialized formal training programs of their own. The basic purpose was to create a type of individual who could act creatively within the organization's stringent requirements. At Du Pont, new salesmen went through school at headquarters. They were taught the nuts and bolts of salesmanship as well as Du Pont's version of its role in the economic and political life of the nation. They were provided with textbooks and exercise sheets on how to keep records of one's expenses and how to file trade reports. They were taught how the "efficiency" plan worked, introduced to the advertising and other divisions, and took technical courses on the various product lines: blasting powders, high explosives, agricultural explosives, shotgun powders, fabrikoid, the paint and pyralin articles. They were also given a general education on the important economic issues of the day. Just as the Hamilton Institute had commissioned studies on "the ability of America's industries to serve the Government and care for the needs of private consumers during the war," Colonel Edmund Buckner, Du Pont's vice-president for military sales, wrote a pamphlet for the salesman course on Du Pont's role in the great war.[17]

Salesmen were instructed to read their texts through to get the main ideas, to read them again for specific analysis, to study them with the idea of retaining the information given, but not to memorize them unless absolutely necessary ("It is better to use your own words in your answer than the words of the text").[18] They took their examinations on the honor basis. High performance on the courses brought official recognition. Salesmen were expected to perform well anywhere in the Du Pont organization. William Coyne, the director of the sales department, impressed on the new recruits that the key to advancement was one's ability to prove both pliable and independent, that is, ready to accept directives while capable of personal judgment.[19]

The key to professional salesmanship in the age of corporations was system. Salesmen were expected to conform to a "system." "Don't forget you are a part of the organization just as much as the bass drum is part of the orchestra—likewise, don't forget that bass drum solos are rather monotonous," they were told at Du Pont.[20] The company expected salesmen to display just enough independence to improve the system while conforming to its main outlines. E. T. Wolf was one of the company's top salesmen. The notion of system, which allowed him to outsmart his rivals and stay ahead of his competition, is at the root of the methods he described to his peers at the sales convention. He explained the ways in which he built on the "block book" so that he could have before him "at all times complete data of the individual trade in the territory." He kept on hand at all times a "pocket trade record bureau" containing information on several hundred customers. The data was coded so that if the book were lost and happened to be found by a competitor, it would reveal no significant information except names and addresses. He kept several copies of each district's books. Those not in use were kept safely at home; on the road, the book was carried in a vest pocket so that it could not be overlooked. The small portable books could be updated in the evenings or on Sunday mornings and supplemented the larger trade reports required by the company.[21]

Wolf reminded his fellow salesmen, however, that system without determination was not enough to get ahead. "Take two men with same amount of personality, same selling powder [sic], and the fellow who gets [his reports] in promptly forges ahead" (powder for power is not an infrequent misspelling in Du Pont company papers).[22] Other sales representatives followed him on the convention podium. When they finished, George Kerr, manager of the trade records division, made a pitch for standardized reporting procedures, a standardization that would match current practice in the home and in the branch offices.[23] Kerr had already argued the point at the sales convention ten years before when he boasted that the trade record system he had set up at Du Pont had just been adopted by U.S. Steel.[24]

Vice President J. Amory Haskell, a member of the du Pont's inner circle, opened the second and third sales conventions in 1905 and 1906 by underscoring the need to exchange ideas.[25] Business, he insisted, requires technical knowledge. Accordingly, the company created a new technical division in 1905 within the sales department to provide the salesmen with the technological and scientific counsel they needed.[26] By organizing large sales conventions for them, the company conferred professional status on salesmen. In effect, the sales conventions told the men that their knowledge was important enough to be codified and transmitted in a systematic manner and their activities were important enough to benefit from criticism and suggestions of their peers. Accordingly, the conventions were largely technical, and a prominent role was given to those in the technical division who held a bachelor of science or an engineering degree.[27] But ordinary salesmen also presented the fruits of their research. Most papers were on the art of blasting. One salesman reported the conclusions of a detailed study he had conducted of coal mining in Illinois, which listed the number of employees at each mine, types of equipment, output, and other technical data. The corporation encouraged the exchange of information, data gathering, and compilation of expert reports at departmental conventions. Later the conventions were divided equally among technical, commercial, and organizational topics.

The meetings had social activities that also built corporate spirit. Salesmen enjoyed good food served at dinners with elaborate menus. They revelled in convention entertainment: A shotgun tournament (with a prize cup), music, professional theatre, comic magicians. Occasionally, they made fun of each other and punned on the names of company products.[28]

Corporations were careful to present their ideas within a generalized, secular code of ethics. Thus Pierre S. du Pont dismissed a suggestion from a technical representative from Pittsburgh that his company's sales convention begin with a prayer.[29] The attempt to reconcile Christianity with corporate ideals would have to await publicist Bruce Barton, who, in *The Man Nobody Knows*, depicted Jesus as a great executive who had picked twelve unknown men and with them successfully built an organization that had conquered the world.[30] Still, keeping in line with the larger corporate goal of service, the regular meetings stressed the commitment of the corporation to society. With the country's mobilization for war, patriotism and loyalty to the president of the United States were important themes of the conventions and strong reminders of the role the company played in the war economy. The Fabrikoid people sang:

> We're all with you Mr. Wilson, in everything you do.
> Waiting your call, you'll find us all,
> Steady and ready whate'er befall.
> Just like our fathers before us,
> We're here to dare and do
> For our country's cause and right
> If we must, then, we will fight,
> Mr. Wilson we're with you.[31]

In 1918, support for the war effort remained strong:

> What are you going to do for Uncle Sammy?
> What are you going to do to help the boys?

If you mean to stay at home
While they're fighting o'er the foam,
The least that you can do
Is buy a Liberty Bond or Two!
If you're going to be a sympathetic miser,
The kind that only lends a lot of noise,
You're no better than the one who loves the kaiser-
So what are you going to do to help the boys?[32]

The source of the corporate salesman's self-esteem was his sense that he was balancing material and idealistic goals. It is therefore not surprising that management carefully designed systems that emphasized this balance.

STANDARDS OF BEHAVIOR

The professionalization of salesmanship would lead to higher standards of behavior. Salesmen were to observe thrift and to follow a conservative dress code while preaching consumption. Dreiser's Drouet, quite the dandy, would have been forced to tone down his clothes as a corporate salesman (if he had not already been fired for keeping a mistress). The company recommended "every salesman should be equipped with a full length mirror with this suggestion hanging above it: 'Before you go out to tell people you represent this firm look yourself over and see whether you do or not.'" More specifically, salesmen were told: "You are well dressed when no one can remember anything you are wearing. You are not dressed for work until you put on a smile. Noisy dress has kept many a man from hearing a sales argument."[33] Quite conveniently, Du Pont synthetic products came handy for good grooming on the road. Drouet's high, white, cotton collars were replaced by those of the cleanable variety that Wiener could not sell when he was working for Arlington but that Du Pont's advertising manager, George Frank Lord, was now aggressively marketing.[34]

A carefully groomed appearance was not quite enough. Thrift was also a virtue. Much time was spent discussing cutting expenses on the road. At the 1916 convention, three explosives salesmen talked about how they economized. In 1921, C. W. Phellis, who had reached the position of general director of sales after starting as a salesman reminded his salesforce how he used to reduce costs:

Cut out taxi and livery fares when street cars are available, or the walk is not too great. Walking is healthful and pays good

constitutional dividends. When time is not a vital factor, a
few miles walk harms no man. In fact hiking along a few
miles of railroad tiles from one customer's location to another frequently afforded me an opportunity to construct my
best sales arguments, resulting in my most successful performance as a salesman . . . .

   An every night room with bath is not necessary to health
and happiness. I have taken many a sponge bath from wash
bowl and pitcher, with satisfactory results.[35]

Loyalty was also essential to the workings of the corporation and,
as we have seen, was a paramount goal of the corporate training programs. The acceptance of an oath of loyalty and a code of conduct
were prerequisites. A formal pledge of loyalty reinforced personal ties
to the organization and imbued the corporate salesman with a sense
of corporate identity that distinguished him from ordinary drummers.
Such an exacting commitment, however, had moral as well as business
implications and often placed the salesmen in an ambivalent position.
Nonetheless, Du Pont actively sought to enforce this loyalty. Thus the
director of sales asked the men assembled in convention in 1916 to
pass a resolution acknowledging the high quality of the Du Pont
products.[36]

   Such loyalty was important for the proper conduct of business
because the salesmen were entrusted with trade secrets and confidential information, including a carefully prepared and updated salesmen's handbook.[37] So careful was the Du Pont organization about this
book that new leaves were supplied for each new edition and old
leaves were collected and returned to the sales auditor in Wilmington.[38] The sales department kept a close tab on the number of sales-
books outstanding. Executives, even Pierre S. du Pont, were asked to
return them if they no longer needed them.[39] The company could
under no circumstances allow the handbooks to fall into the hands of
competitors.

   The salesmen's loyalty was also instrumental in keeping tabs on
Du Pont's competitors. Salesmen were responsible for intelligence
gathering in the field, collecting information on what competitors
were selling and the prices they were getting.[40]

   Salesmen internalized loyalty as a matter of principle. But management insistence upon absolute loyalty could turn into outright po-
licing of employees. Witness the fuss that William Coyne, then vice
president in charge of sales and consultant for Pierre S. Du Pont's

reorganization of General Motors, made in 1922 when Du Pont employees purchased cars from other makers. Coyne went as far as singling out three individuals, one from the accounting department, one from the purchasing department, and another from the order section of the explosives division, in a memorandum written to other vice-presidents. Working off his anger, Coyne wrote:

> No one questions the right of our people to spend their money where they please, but, when our men know that their Corporation is as heavily interested in the General Motors Corporation as the Du Pont company is, and that the Chairman of our board and Chairman of our Finance Committee is Chairman of the Board and President of the General Motors Corporation [Pierre S. du Pont], that our President [Irénée du Pont, P.S.'s brother] is a Director and member of the Finance Committee of the General Motors, that our Vice President in charge of Finance is Chairman of their Finance Committee, and another member of our Finance Committee and a Director of our Company is a member of the Finance Committee and a Director of the General Motors, and that our officials are keenly interested in General Motors' welfare and that its earnings mean considerable to Du Pont Company; a Du Pont man who buys a car competitive to General Motors line, certainly does not show the high degree of loyalty and support to his Corporation and its officials that it and they have a right to expect, nor should he look for consideration from it or them.[41]

MOBILITY AND OTHER INCENTIVES

The salesman represented the corporation, its power, its wealth, its prestige, and its products. But to win customers' confidence and trust and make sales, he needed to recognize their interests and attempt to form a partnership between them and the corporation, a difficult job. The company sought to stimulate him and provided him with both material and moral incentives. And it recognized his achievements through advancement. In the absence of payroll registers from which to compute employment statistics systematically, information on promotion at Du Pont is guesswork. We can, however, make a few inferences. As the company grew and diversified its products, it published a journal, the *Du Pont Magazine*, and some information may be surmised from it. Of the 344 people listed in the company's sales directory for 1917, 127 sales-affiliated people contributed almost 400 articles to the magazine at some time between 1913 and 1956.[42] A third of the contributors to the magazine who were salesmen in 1917 stayed with the company for a minimum of ten years and others remained considerably more. Among 69 such ordinary road salesmen who contributed to the *Du Pont Magazine*—their position was indicated in their byline—at least 17 earned a significant promotion during their tenure. They became technical representatives, district sales managers, or regional managers. In these higher level managerial positions, they gained equal footing with college-educated men who entered the managerial hierarchy. Long after their retirement, some of these men still corresponded with Pierre S. du Pont or John Raskob.[43]

There were other incentives and rewards, and the company believed it important that they be distributed on an objective basis. The system designed by Du Pont—characteristically called the efficiency system—itself epitomizes the corporate belief in controlled, rational, behavior that it was intended to reward. Each salesman received an efficiency rating every month. The efficiency grade was carefully worked out taking into account factors in productivity (disposal of slow-moving stocks, diversion of business from competitors, new business secured versus business lost), the human equation (effort, cooperation, deportment), satisfying the requirements of the home office (accuracy and promptness of trade and expense reports; economy in the handling of company funds), and visitation effort (proportion of trade visited measured against the extent of the territory). Productivity accounted for 50 percent of the final rating while the other three factors accounted each for 16.7 percent. At the end of each month, ratings were published internally and circulated: each salesman knew how he compared with his peers. In addition, individual salesmen received comments on how best to improve their performance.[44]

Needless to say, a system that played such an important role in their success was subject to careful scrutiny by salesmen. While the 1921 efficiency bulletin pointed to a variety of career opportunities within Du Pont and listed several executives who had started as junior clerks in branch offices, salesmen with experience in the field questioned the wisdom of categories devised by the home office that were used in the computations published in the bulletin. E. T. Wolf, for instance, complained that there was no real way to enter initiative in the efficiency report: "The right speed in mailing in reports, the correct addition of expense accounts are trifles . . . . The [individual] sales are not a real factor by any means. It is easier now for me to sell one customer $50,000 a year than it is to secure three orders for $40 a piece." Despite some flaws, the efficiency ratings caused salesmen to concentrate on the performance criteria computed by the home office and to weigh all aspects of their activity carefully. When E. T. Wolf became the second-most-successful salesman for the first half of 1917, F. C. Peters, the New York office manager wrote to him: "This should demonstrate to you that it certainly pays to play the game." Wolf received a bonus of three shares of common stock for 1918.[45]

Recognition came through other channels too. One was the suggestion plan that the sales department instituted in 1908. Salesmen's suggestions were subject to a blind evaluation by a committee. The first year's winner was one salesman who suggested demonstrating stump blasting to sell explosives. Demonstrations had not been used before, but they would expand the market for dynamite in a period when the land, formerly covered by forests, was being cultivated. By 1914, the suggestion plan became a company-wide institution. Once a suggestion was implemented, the employee was rewarded 20 percent of the estimated annual saving his suggestion brought to the company or, in some instances, by an award of preferred, A stock.[46]

Bonuses, consisting of common stock granted yearly to employees, who through their inventions, ability, industry, or loyalty contributed in an unusual degree to the welfare of the company, were another way to increase the efficiency and quality of salesmanship. Furthermore, large corporations, Du Pont among them, pioneered other programs such as pensions for employees who served a minimum of fifteen years. The board of pension had the authority to deny a pension to undeserving employees. The monthly pension was computed by taking 1.5 percent of the highest monthly salary during previous years and multiplying the resulting figure by the number of years in service. Thus a salesman whose highest monthly salary was $100 and who had twenty years of service was entitled to a pension of $30 per month (see chap. 3). The corporation was a pioneer in the pension scheme and encouraged its salesmen to explain the benefit to other concerns who were interested.[47] To be sure, such a program was beneficial to Du Pont in that it fostered needed employment stability and loyalty. It was nonetheless made possible only by the pooling of resources that the large corporation gradually acquired.

CONFLICT MANAGEMENT

Despite its impressive efforts to inculcate salesmen with uniform systems and standards, Du Pont was not entirely successful in eliminating conflict. Conflict resolution was part of middle management's daily responsibility. Interpreting Wilmington's guidelines, working out co-operation and lines of authority, and resolving disputes among sales-men were essential tasks. Deviations not only undermined shared values, they carried with them the potential of disrupting the entire organization. Indeed, what is striking is how sensitive company offi-cials were to conflict within the managerial hierarchy.

At the end of 1913, the Denver office was the scene of a revealing incident, pitting the branch manager, a Mr. Howard, who had twenty-six years of service with the company against one of his salesman, Horace Middleton, who had been with Du Pont for over ten years.[48] Middleton suddenly turned against his boss and wrote headquarters that the latter was drunk so often that he was unable to conduct busi-ness. This case attracted attention in high managerial circles at head-quarters, perhaps because Middleton was an employee of long service or because he was related to Hamilton Barksdale, part of the du Pont family executive circle, member of the executive committee, and gen-eral manager of the company.[49] Not only did the director and assistant director of sales become involved in the case but Barksdale and an-other vice-president did too. It also drew in Coleman du Pont, the company's president, who himself wrote no fewer than nine letters to the salesman and even loaned him some money from his private ac-count to allow him to come to Wilmington to present his case for reinstatement after having been fired, a loan on which Middleton ul-timately defaulted.

The Colorado mining district was an important territory for the Du Pont's interests, and the company executive officers were suffi-ciently concerned with Middleton's allegations that they put Howard, his boss, under detective's surveillance in December 1913. When it became clear early in 1914 that Middleton's accusations were un-founded, that Howard's drinking had been only occasional and some-times the result of entertaining drinking customers, the executives authorized Howard to fire his salesman if he wished to.

Middleton's firing did not close the incident but instead opened a year-long argument as the salesman fought for his reinstatement. Al-though Middleton's tactics led him nowhere, the large correspondence which this incident generated reveals much about branch office cul-ture. Both Howard and Middleton were adamant about their unfail-ing faithfulness to the company and their unswerving dedication; both provided evidence of their irreproachable behavior through af-fidavits of customers—a disquieting procedure in the executives' eyes

because it made internal company affairs a matter of common knowledge. Both men also claimed that they were so devoted to their jobs
that they cultivated after-hours friendships with such customers and
social contacts that furthered the business interests of the company.
Howard saw one in his club; Middleton's wife was supposedly a close
friend of an important customer's wife. When Middleton was finally
fired, he felt fully the effects of corporate displeasure. He did not find
another job and his wife, who had written on his behalf to the company president, left him when he became unable to support her.

The Middleton incident reveals the extent to which a large corporation controlled middle-level employees, that is, from training to
retirement. Although salesmen could change jobs as they wished
when the opportunity arose, they were actually more dependent on
the corporate career structure for their advancement and on corporate values for their judgments than were the executives to whom they
reported. The higher executives, by virtue of their background and
education, often had connections with independent professional organizations which salesmen lacked. A number of executives had gone
through college and graduate or professional programs. They met
their former classmates at college football games and other reunions
and could, at least theoretically, use these contacts to secure advancement through other jobs. Salesmen, however, had received their entire training within the company and knew only other salesmen.
Executives received larger bonuses, owned more company stock,
and could become, when needed—and this happened frequently—
financially independent of their managerial position.[50] This alternative was not open to the salesman, who amassed only modest amounts.
Failure left him penniless. Success hooked him for good.

But salesmen did not simply contribute to the success of corporate
marketing from fear of failure. Money alone was not a sufficient in-
ducement, for the income of salesmen was certainly not lavish, and
expense accounts were not unlimited. It was not job security, for there
was none. It was not benefits, for these programs had just begun. The
hope for a promotion and Du Pont's package of incentives were real,
but they are not enough to explain the salesmen's dedication. At least
as important as the system was the moment. Although selling became
rapidly systematized, there was still ample opportunity at this stage in
Du Pont's history for individual salesmen like Wolf to place their mark
on the system. Salesmen participated in the different aspects of the
company's activities, and they found there a forum for their ideas and
a source of respect. And the company understood the stimulus gained

by involving a large number of people in sharing knowledge. Men who worked for big business were given a chance not only to keep abreast of industrial innovation, but also to be part of and influence economic and social change. Salesmen shared the fundamental vision that senior management described at annual meetings. Salesmen believed they had access to some of the power of the large corporation, especially its ability to communicate with speed to all parts of the country, to act on a large geographic scale, and to create innovative industrial and consumer products. What brought all these people together was that they were consciously participating in a vast venture that was larger than their individual selling job.

This enthusiasm for their mission can be seen in the detail of the articles they submitted to the *Du Pont Magazine*. Over a fourth of the salesforce was sufficiently involved with company affairs to share their special knowledge of a product, of a technique, or of a region. Salesmen, technical representatives, middle-level executives, branch managers, and statistical clerks wrote creatively about a variety of products. The articles show the level of expertise salesmen aspired to. They reveal their detailed technical knowledge of their field, their interest in sales techniques, and their understanding of work organization. Salesmen matched their increasing sales of dynamite with pieces on the special skills needed to use explosives safely.[51] An article in 1918 argued that more cotton fields needed to be cleared (using explosives to remove stumps) to meet war-generated demand for more cotton, a component in the manufacture of explosives.[52] The piece showed a good understanding of soil types and crop cultivation. Another salesman conducted research on the many uses of cotton in Du Pont products.[53] A series of articles described the strategies sheepmen used to keep predators away in the West.[54] One technical piece, a collaboration between the manager and the technical representative of the Joplin, Missouri, sales district, described in detail the wartime use of zinc and lead.[55]

Others wrote on high explosives in bauxite mining in Arkansas, in road building in the Rockies, in the creation of artificial lakes for irrigation, in extracting stone from quarries, in digging tunnels, and in clearing land.[56] One article in 1913 went through a detailed description of engineering a dam in Iowa with discussions of the uses of dynamite. There were others on how to reclaim swamp land and others on road building.[57] Railroad work, one of the activities which accounted for so much of Du Pont's expansion in the nineteenth century, continued to be a regular feature until well into the 1920s.

Explosives were also used in densely populated areas, and an article related the difficulties of quarrying a canal in the heart of Rochester.[58]

Others specialized in still other lines of consumer durables such as paint and fabrikoid material and their many markets in the automobile and other industries.[59] A salesman reported on the San Francisco auto show in June 1920, as the California dream was on its way to becoming the American dream.[60] Articles on sales techniques focused on the value of specific demonstrations in attracting customers (like at International Harvester; see chap. 6); or on the effective use of photographs when describing the application of dynamite in demolition work.[61]

While some salesmen devoted themselves to the needs of heavy industry, others introduced their peers to the newly acquired pyralin line which comprised "all the toilet articles essential to a well-equipped boudoir."[62] These salesmen explained how they sold toiletware and "reducing girdles," the new wonder garment, to the growing department stores and advised store managers on styles of window displays—"putting the win in the windows." With the introduction of rayon in the mid-twenties, the magazine became partly a fashion publication.[63]

Many men who wrote for the company magazine clearly felt they had more than just a selling job. They were helping their fellow salesmen and influencing the course of the communities they served. Selling, as one Du Pont salesman put it, "requires the highest and most constructive type of business ability. It depends not only upon a thorough analysis of customs and conditions in the community, but often upon a complete understanding of the mind of the community, of the local sense of values, of preferences and prejudices."[64] The almost exclusive concentration by historians on the creation of a consumer society and its negative effects is clearly one-sided.[65] To men in the business of selling, the distinction between producing goods and services and consuming was not clear cut.

The salesmen especially derived satisfaction from being a part of a large organization that widened their knowledge. Practically, salesmen in big business could participate in innovation without years of investment in higher education. The various technical reports routinely routed to the salesforce kept them abreast of scientific, technological, and economic developments. Other marketing surveys led the sales department to advise salesmen to reorient their strategies toward different parts of society. Because their activities opened them to a variety of social strata, salesmen had constantly to sharpen their own vision of the corporate world in order to communicate it forcefully to the diverse groups they encountered. The salesmen were encouraged to use their social skills to equalize themselves "with the common laborer or with the man of letters" and make themselves "equally agreeable to either."[66] Appointed apostles of progress, the representatives of large corporations thought of themselves as specialists in rational, systematic innovation.

FROM SYSTEM TO SOCIETY

Upper-level executives could indulge themselves with the view of corporations as a complete, self-contained social unit at the service of the society at large. Yet the connection between the interests of the corporation, which were reflected in the system of selling, and the interests of society the corporation was supposed to serve was the source of much ambiguity. The science of corporate salesmanship actually lost much of its raison d'être when not propelled by genuine technological innovation or when not supported by those organizations large enough—or determined enough—to maintain a sustained commitment to society at large.

The discrepancy is clearly observed when corporate leaders and salesmen alike tried to generalize about the principles of salesmanship. Attempts to describe the composite qualities of a corporate salesman in the abstract, that is, independent of the system of required tasks and stated objectives of a company, soon turned into an exercise in self-delusion. At one Du Pont convention, a salesman used such adjectives as "energetic, industrious, observing, honest, diplomatic" to describe himself and his peers. He ventured into the concrete just briefly, noting "I trust I need not add sober, for the 'booze-hoister' is not admitted within our lines."[67] The "science of service" was defined in such all encompassing terms that it became meaningless. For instance, in 1911, the Du Pont employee committee, an organization in charge of organizing a club house that employees could join by paying membership dues, sponsored a series of lectures on the "science of service" and on how to take a leading role in it. The speaker gave his Du Pont audience the rules for the development of endurance (health), will power (action), reliability and ability.[68] Shortly before, the New York *World*, publishing the ten best health rules from a contest the newspaper had sponsored, advised its readers to "think healthy thoughts; breathe deep and always through the nose; drink plenty of water between meals; eat moderately—masticate thoroughly; work hard and bathe often; relax both mind and body one hour every noon; associate with healthy people; study the 'Law of Thought' and apply its teachings; relax every limb and muscle before dropping asleep, sleep in a cool, clean, well-ventilated room, eight hour at least out of every twenty-four."[69] The list published by the newspaper so closely resembled the kind of advice the lecturer had given Du Pont employees in promoting the science of service that the employee committee distributed copies of the article to all company employees. Other rules of the Du Pont course were designed to promote the development of sales ability with thirteen conditions to train the memory: "concentration," "health," "interest," "association of ideas," "recall," "repetition," "self-confidence," maintaining a "clear brain," "visualization," "attention," "writing what is to be remembered," "localization," and "thoroughly understand" the matter at hand. Employees were told that, as full participants in this new "science of service," they had as much an opportunity for education as if they had been in college, for "education is a thing that goes all through life."[70] Any attempt to reach an overall transformation of human beings through such vague programs served only to expose the underlying separation between system and society. And this disjunction widened with corporate success.

Here lay the paradox of the science of service. It is not a philosophy but a response to specific corporate opportunities. It worked only in a specific time frame and in a particular context within the corporation. And it worked when salesmen were propelled by genuine challenges in the market place. The balance that an organization like Du Pont seemed to have reached by the early teens was necessarily short-lived. Unless Du Pont and corporations like it found new challenges after markets were conquered or when growth slowed, it could not sustain the illusion of the congruence between system and society. The science of service which depended on that congruence would time and again reveal its shallow philosophical underpinnings.

CONCLUSION

In the summer of 1914, the editor of the *American Journal of Sociology* wrote to a select group of Americans from diverse callings—the judiciary, the labor movement, the learned professions, manufacturing, journalism, and philanthropy—and asked each one, "Upon what ideals, policies, programs, or specific purposes should Americans place most stress in the immediate future?" The editor, Albion Small, proposed to combine the answers into a "prospectus of impending American tasks," a document rendered all the more urgent by the outbreak of the great war.

Only forty-four of the 250 personalities who had been approached replied, and the prospectus consequently was never written. The *AJS*, instead, published all forty-four answers verbatim.[1] Not surprisingly, the respondents insisted on the primacy of their particular preoccupations. Eugene Debs declared that "privately owned industry and production for individual profit" were no longer compatible with "social progress." W. E. B. Du Bois answered that "Americans in the immediate future should place most stress upon the abolition of the color line." Edward A. Ross seized on the opportunity to champion eugenics and called for curtailing "the propagation of the proven subnormal." University presidents, however, uniformly asked to be excused from Small's poll. They wrote brief apologetic notes to explain that they were so deeply absorbed in administrative tasks and budget planning they could no longer afford to think. As one of them put it, "I am perfectly incapable of anything like sustained or continuous mental effort."[2] Businessmen were only slightly more forthcoming. Although some businessmen wrote back, most presidents of large corporations simply left Small's letter unanswered.

Cyrus McCormick, Jr. did draft an answer.[3] While his advice was to drop "impractical theorizing" and go for "common sense," he indulged in a little self-justifying theorizing of his own. "Civilization needs leaders," he asserted "but it is equally essential there should be followers. Nature has so provided that for one man capable of the larger tasks of brain or brawn, tens of thousands are unequal to it. In the frank recognition of this natural law, and the acceptance of it, and obedience to it, much depends." McCormick proceeded to argue that the most valuable Americans were men like himself who gave "remunerative employment to the largest number of his fellow men and under the most approved conditions of comfort and safety." Having thus reaffirmed the moral superiority of leaders, McCormick went on to argue that the most urgent task was for private enterprise, not the state, to provide for "remunerative and permanent" employment.

McCormick had inherited his fortune,[4] so he could hardly claim that he, like the early robber barons, had the special endowments that entitled him to own the means of production. He insisted, nonetheless, on the primacy of private enterprise and the natural superiority of men like himself. Like Pierre du Pont (chap. 7), he considered the rise of the corporation an issue to be judged on the basis of its moral efficacy, and moral efficacy he measured in material terms, by the increased levels of consumption ordinary Americans could enjoy. In other words, if McCormick, du Pont, and their counterparts could significantly raise the standard of living, thus accelerating a trend in increased consumption initiated almost two centuries before, they could justify their activities.

McCormick's position was not without its detractors. Thorstein Veblen, prominent among a variegated group of critics who challenged big business's position, returned to John Ruskin, William Morris, and the English Arts and Crafts movement to champion the good "instinct of workmanship." The Norwegian farmer's son turned economist and sociologist struck a sensitive chord when he denounced corporate organizational and financial schemes as a form of degeneration. For him, the separation of ownership and control only brought with it the reign of predatory finance and bureaucratization. Veblen concluded *The Engineers and the Price System* (1921) in a tone actually reminiscent of Max Weber. With corporation finance driving industry, industrialists had lost touch with the management of industrial processes, while the very "management of corporate business has, in effect, been shifting into the hands of a bureaucratic clerical staff," headed by a "chief of bureau." Veblen, influenced by disciples of F. W. Taylor but failing to take note of the entrepreneurial qualities shared by many engineers, hoped further that the growth of engineering science would make the "technological man" more independent of the "captain of finance."[5]

Both du Pont's and McCormick's optimistic equation of morality with production and consumerism and Veblen's equation of morality with workmanship set the initial terms of an enduring debate on the ethics of corporate capitalism. But proponents in this debate, standing as they were on the right or on the left of history, have missed much of the action. In this book, I have focused on vital, if forgotten, groups of corporate actors who did not subscribe fully to either McCormick's or Veblen's point of view: the new groups of middle-class Americans who filled hierarchical corporate structures and promoted new ways of working, living, and interacting with one another. To be sure, some actors of this book openly took part on behalf of their employers in the conflicts that dominated their time. They took stands in labor and regulatory conflicts that fitted into larger ideological categories. C. B. & Q. agents like trainmaster Oscar Stewart fought the labor movement, just as Ford tinkerers like Bill Klann did. Harry Bennett, Ford's "ultimate henchman," became a symbol of industrial violence, walking about the Rouge with a gun in his pocket.[6] But by and large, managers bypassed larger ideological debates. Instead, they worked to develop corporate systems and, in the process, invented the modern work culture.

Their contribution has gone largely unheralded because they were rapidly succeeded by changes in American society they had not foreseen: the stockmarket crash and the depression. Many historians have since recounted the emergence of a new social contract in the 1930s based on a compromise among corporate, state, and labor bureaucracies. To them, the story of the formative years of the American managerial class became a mere episode in the larger framework of the rise of "countervailing powers."[7] At stake in their vision was the extent to which corporations could impose their bigness on society, the time it would take for the regulatory principles articulated in the progressive era by such men as Herbert Croly and Louis Brandeis to be felt, and the degree to which the state would become a full partner in the task of allocating society's resources. When this partnership was finally implemented, big industrialists, who seemingly had reached some unity in their opposition to the progressives, broke ranks. Thus, McCormick would not join the American Liberty League, the organization Raskob promoted from his office in the Empire State Building. The du Pont-led American Liberty League was dedicated to doing "everything possible to root out the vicious radical element that threatens the destruction of our government."[8] But in the aftermath of the Great Depression, Franklin Delano Roosevelt had become too popular among farmers for the head of International Harvester to take such a public stand. How big business, labor, and government would cooperate became the major preoccupation of the day. And the story I have told faded in the face of this more pressing issue.

Managers received a fair amount of credit for the smooth functioning of the corporate commonwealth during the period of postwar prosperity, when the United States dominated the world markets. But

CONCLUSION

another kind of criticism set in as millions of Americans who worked in large corporations—many of them the sons and daughters of the men and women who created the corporate systems—came to view work in giant enterprises as an unhappy combination of boredom and stress. Americans also wrestled with the cult of efficiency. The concept of system that was the hallmark of the corporate middle-class in the progressive era—and that reformers, while denouncing excessive concentrations of power, sought to adopt for government and public service—also showed its negative effects. Many came to realize that although efficient business organizations contributed to an increase in the standard of living, they tended to sidestep moral issues. Time and again in the twentieth century, efficient systems, generated in large corporate organizations, have actually accommodated and sometimes served the unfolding of human tragedies.

This book thus is not about managerial capitalism as a panacea for the twentieth century's ills. Nor does it seek to trace the roots of bureaucratic anomie or of the managerial crisis that pervades our late-twentieth century global economy. I sought instead to explain why so many ordinary Americans were involved in the creation of the modern work culture and why their lives were historically significant. Not only did they derive individual rewards from their collective actions, they prompted change.

American corporate capitalism was largely the creation of a new middle class that assumed an influential place in American society. Managers were responsible for hiring and organizing the increasingly large number of white-collar workers who processed the reams of paper the corporations used. By recruiting heavily among large sections of the working class, they expanded middle-class boundaries considerably and redefined middle-class values. Their influence was such that by the 1920s, a larger part of the population could share them. The new middle-class came to encompass a whole gamut of occupations, ranging, as C. Wright Mills correctly understood it, from "Prima Donna Vice-Presidents of corporations who boast that they are merely salesmen" to "the five-and-ten-cent-store girls who work for half days several months before they leave the job market for marriage."[9] Nineteenth-century mercantile culture receded as a new, white-collar mindset became the hallmark of the twentieth century. Alfred P. Sloan, whom Pierre du Pont had handpicked to succeed him at the presidency of General Motors, was far more revealing than deceptive when he entitled his autobiography *Adventures of a White-Collar Man*.[10] Although vague definitions frustrate our yearning for certainty, the swelling of a loosely defined middle class left an enduring imprint on the twentieth century.

In the formative years of corporate capitalism, middle-level managers, engineers, white-collar employees, salesmen, and other representatives of growing corporations resolved conflicts arising from their multiple loyalties to employers, independent professional organizations, and community associations by searching for rational systems of work. Members of this new middle class collectively invented a way of doing business and interacting with one another that for the first time made full use of the economy's continental dimension and would eventually lead the country to world power. They advocated a practical consensus in the realm of work culture that partly compensated for both the segmentation of the society in which they had grown up and the increasing intricacy of communication channels. While the socialist project failed in the United States in part because the working class insisted on its heterogeneity,[11] they promoted a relative simplification of America's cultural system—a simplification directly linked to their position in the new corporate order. Their multifaceted effort to create and live with giant organizations ended in a more homogeneous society.

The motives and actions of those who participated in "the process of creative destruction," to borrow Joseph Schumpeter's definition of capitalist innovation,[12] were initially remarkably diverse. Only such a variety of talents and motives can account for the large number of middle-class Americans who identified with corporations. With personal goals but not, at least immediately, a common vision, they were guided by the requirements of the special task they engaged in. Once involved, however, the growing managerial groups embraced the corporate project of building a continental economy. And its diverse members invested their talent and aspirations in achieving the great economic and technological changes that marked their generation and touched all the generations that have succeeded them.

NOTES

INTRODUCTION

1. See for instance Matthew Josephson, *The Robber Barons: The Great American Capitalists, 1861–1901*. (New York: Harcourt, Brace & Co., 1934). On the shift in emphasis from Charles Francis Adams's *A Chapter of Erie* (1869) to Brandeis's writings, see Thomas K. McCraw, *Prophets of Regulation: Charles Francis Adams, Louis D. Brandeis, James M. Landis, Alfred E. Kahn* (Cambridge: Harvard University Press, Belknap Press, 1984).

2. M. A. Adelman, "The Measurement of Industrial Concentration," *Reviews of Economics and Statistics* 33 (November 1951): 276–77.

3. As Adolf A. Berle, Jr., and Gardiner Means had correctly predicted in *The Modern Corporation and Private Property* (Chicago: Commerce Clearing House, 1932), 24–26.

4. Robert Griffith, "Dwight D. Eisenhower and the Corporate Commonwealth," *American Historical Review* 87 (February 1982): 88, 91. See also Louis Galambos and Joseph Pratt, *The Rise of the Corporate Commonwealth: U.S. Business and Public Opinion in the Twentieth Century* (New York: Basic Books, 1988).

5. See David M. Potter, *People of Plenty: Economic Abundance and the American Character* (Chicago: University of Chicago Press, 1954); Olivier Zunz, "The Synthesis of Social Change: Reflections on American Social History," in *Reliving the Past: The Worlds of Social History*, ed. Olivier Zunz (Chapel Hill: University of North Carolina Press, 1985), 56.

6. Arthur Miller, *Death of a Salesman: Certain Private Conversations in Two Acts and a Requiem* (New York: Penguin Books, 1949), 5, 22.

7. C. Wright Mills, *White Collar: The American Middle Classes* (New York: Oxford University Press, 1953), xv, 9, 54, 11, 161, xvi.

8. Raymond Aron, Introduction to Thorstein Veblen, *Théorie de la classe de loisir*, trans. Louis Evrard (Paris: Gallimard, 1970), xix.

9. Quoted in Richard Wightman Fox, "Epitaph for Middletown: Robert S. Lynd and the Analysis of Consumer Culture," in *The Culture of Consumption: Critical Essays in American History, 1880–1980*, ed. Richard Wightman Fox and T. J. Jackson Lears (New York: Pantheon Books, 1983), 122. See also Robert S. Lynd and Helen Merrell Lynd, *Middletown: A Study in American Culture* (New York: Harcourt Brace, 1929), 73–89.

10. Quoted in Irving Louis Horowitz, *C. Wright Mills: An American Utopian* (New York: Free Press, 1983), 250–51.

11. James Weinstein suggested that "false consciousness of the nature of American liberalism has been one of the most powerful ideological weapons that American capitalism has had in maintaining its hegemony," in *The Corporate Ideal in the Liberal State, 1900–1918* (Boston: Beacon Press, 1968), xi; see also Gabriel Kolko, *Railroads and Regulation, 1877–1916* (Princeton: Princeton University Press, 1965); idem, *The Triumph of Conservatism: A Re-Interpretation of American History, 1900–1916* (New York: Free Press of Glencoe, 1963); and Martin J. Sklar, *The Corporate Reconstruction of American Capitalism, 1890–1916: The Market, the Law, and Politics* (Cambridge: Cambridge University Press, 1988).

12. Naomi R. Lamoreaux, *The Great Merger Movement in American Business, 1895–1904* (Cambridge: Cambridge University Press, 1985).

13. Thomas C. Cochran, *Railroad Leaders, 1845–1890: The Business Mind in Action* (Cambridge: Harvard University Press, 1953), 13, 2, 67; *The Education of Henry Adams: An Autobiography* (1907), Library of America Edition (New York: Viking Press, 1983), 940.

14. Harry Braverman, *Labor and Monopoly Capital: The Degradation of Work in the Twentieth Century* (New York: Monthly Review Press, 1974); see also Rosabeth Moss Kanter, *Men and Women of the Corporation* (New York: Basic Books, 1977).

15. Charles Tilly, "Retrieving European Lives," in Zunz, *Reliving the Past*, 11–52.

16. See Jackson Lears's review of Horowitz's *C. Wright Mills* in *Journal of American History* 71 (June 1984): 173–74.

17. Chandler broke ground in 1962 with *Strategy and Structure: Chapters in the History of Industrial Enterprise* (Cambridge: MIT Press, 1962).

18. Alfred D. Chandler, Jr., *The Visible Hand: The Managerial Revolution in American Business* (Cambridge: Harvard University Press, Belknap Press, 1977), 187.

19. See Zunz, "Synthesis of Social Change," in *Reliving the Past*, 53–114.

20. See Richard J. Oestreicher, *Solidarity and Fragmentation: Working People and Class Consciousness in Detroit* (Urbana: University of Illinois Press, 1986).

21. Daniel Horowitz, *The Morality of Spending: Attitudes Toward the Consumer Society in America, 1875–1940* (Baltimore: Johns Hopkins University Press, 1985).

22. Werner Sombart, *Why Is There No Socialism in the United States?* (1906), ed. C. T. Husbands, trans. C. T. Husbands and Patricia M. Hocking (White Plains, N.Y.: M. E. Sharpe, 1976), 110. The Sombart question still animated works as different as Stephan Thernstrom, *The Other Bostonians: Poverty and Progress in the American Metropolis, 1880–1970* (Cambridge: Harvard University Press, 1973); Alan Dawley, *Class and Community: The Industrial Revolution*

in Lynn (Cambridge: Harvard University Press, 1976); and Ira Katznelson, *City Trenches: Urban Politics and the Patterning of Class in the United States* (New York: Pantheon Books, 1981).

23. See Cindy Sondik Aron, *Ladies and Gentlemen of the Civil Service: Middle-Class Workers in Victorian America* (New York: Oxford University Press, 1987); and Susan Porter Benson, *Counter Cultures: Saleswomen, Managers, and Customers in American Department Stores, 1890–1940* (Urbana: University of Illinois Press, 1986). For the correspondence from Marie Louise Brodhead Smith to her aunt Sophie du Pont, see Boxes 161–163, Series E, Group 9, the Henry Francis du Pont Collection of Winterthur Manuscripts, Hagley Museum and Library.

24. Richard Hofstadter, *The Age of Reform: From Bryan to FDR* (New York: Alfred A. Knopf, 1955). Hofstadter also imbued his own analyses of "the age of reform" with the very sort of psychological projection he rejected in Mills's work; see Alan Brinkley, "Richard Hofstadter's *The Age of Reform*: A Reconsideration," *Reviews in American History* 13 (September 1985): 462–80.

25. Robert H. Wiebe, *The Search for Order, 1877–1920* (New York: Hill & Wang, 1967), 166. Important books on the middle class include Mary Ryan, *Cradle of the Middle Class: The Family in Oneida County, New York, 1790–1865* (Cambridge: Cambridge University Press, 1981); John S. Gilkeson, Jr., *Middle-Class Providence, 1820–1910* (Princeton: Princeton University Press, 1986); and Stuart Blumin, *The Emergence of the Middle Class: Social Experience in the American City, 1760–1900* (Cambridge: Cambridge University Press, 1989); these treatments tend to focus on the earlier period. Although it deals more specifically with the issue of professionalization, Burton J. Bledstein, *The Culture of Professionalism: The Middle Class and the Development of Higher Education in America* (New York: W. W. Norton, 1976) is also important. For a good discussion of the historiography on the middle class, see Stuart M. Blumin, "Hypothesis of Middle-Class Formation in Nineteenth-Century America: A Critique and Some Proposals," *American Historical Review* 90 (April 1985): 299–338.

26. See Olivier Zunz, "Genèse du pluralisme américain," *Annales: Economies, sociétés, civilisations* 42 (March–April 1987): 432; also available as "The Genesis of American Pluralism," *Tocqueville Review* 9 (1987/88): 201–19.

27. The archives of the C. B. & Q. Railroad are at the Newberry Library in Chicago; the E. I. Du Pont de Nemours Powder Company papers at the Hagley Museum and Library in Wilmington, Delaware; the Ford Motor Company archives at the Edison Institute, Henry Ford Museum and Greenfield Village in Dearborn, Michigan; the surviving personnel files still in the company's hands at the Ford Industrial Archives; the McCormick papers at the State Historical Society of Wisconsin in Madison; the International Har-

vester Company papers at the Chicago headquarters of Navistar International Transportation Corp.; and the Metropolitan Life Insurance Company archives at that company's headquarters in New York City.

CHAPTER ONE

1. See Naomi R. Lamoreaux, *The Great Merger Movement in American Business, 1895–1904* (Cambridge: Cambridge University Press, 1985); on the theme of autonomy, see Robert Wiebe's well-known discussion in *The Search for Order, 1877–1920* (New York: Hill & Wang, 1967).

2. See Stuart Blumin, *The Urban Threshold: Growth and Change in a Nineteenth-Century American Community* (Chicago: University of Chicago Press, 1976); Michael P. Conzen, "The American Urban System in the Nineteenth Century," in *Geography and the Urban Environment: Progress in Research and Applications*, ed. D. T. Herbert and R. J. Johnson (New York: John Wiley & Sons, 1981), 4:295–347; and idem, "The Maturing Urban System in the United States, 1840–1910," *Annals of the Association of American Geographers* 67 (March 1977): 88–108.

3. "The Fate of the Salaried Man," *Independent* 60 (August 20, 1903): 2002–3.

4. Quoted in David W. Levy, *Herbert Croly of the New Republic: The Life and Thought of an American Progressive* (Princeton: Princeton University Press, 1985), 105.

5. Glenn Porter and Harold C. Livesay, *Merchants and Manufacturers: Studies in the Changing Structure of Nineteenth-Century Marketing* (Baltimore: Johns Hopkins Press, 1971), 2, 3.

6. Ibid., 4; and David A. Hounshell, *From the American System to Mass Production, 1800–1932: The Development of Manufacturing Technology in the United States* (Baltimore: Johns Hopkins Press, 1984).

7. Porter and Livesay, *Merchants and Manufacturers*, 3; for the legal dimensions of this change, see Charles W. McCurdy, "American Law and the Marketing Structure of the Large Corporation, 1875–1890," *Journal of Economic History* 38 (September 1978): 631–49.

8. See James T. Lemon, "Colonial America in the Eighteenth Century," in *North America: The Historical Geography of a Changing Continent*, ed. Robert D. Mitchell and Paul A. Groves (Totawa, N.J.: Rowman & Littlefield, 1987), 121–46; and Stanley Lebergott, *The Americans: An Economic Record* (New York: W. W. Norton, 1984).

9. Thomas Childs Cochran, *Pennsylvania: A Bicentennial History* (New York: W. W. Norton, 1978), 131–35.

10. Between 1876 and 1885, Du Pont corresponded with 215 agents all over the country: in Alabama, California, Colorado, Washington, D.C., Delaware, Florida, Georgia, etc. See Accession 500, Series I, Hagley Museum and Library (hereafter HML); a list of these agents can also be found in John Beverly Riggs, *A Guide to the Manuscripts in the Eleutherian Mills Historical Library* (Greenville, Del.: Eleutherian Mills Historical Library, 1970), 584–665. Rather than study every distributor, I decided to focus on the state with the most agents, Pennsylvania. Du Pont corresponded with 56 different Pennsylvania agents and companies in 29 different counties. I traced these individuals in 102 local histories, found 37 of them, and constructed their biographies. The examples in the text are a representative sample of the most typical of those merchants; for the sake of readability, in the notes below I will cite only those local histories relevant to these examples. On country stores, see Lewis Eldon Atherton, *Main Street on the Middle Border* (Bloomington: Indiana University Press, 1954).

11. *The Education of Henry Adams: An Autobiography* (1907), Library of America Edition (New York: Viking Press, 1983), 940.

12. See François Crouzet, *The First Industrialists: The Problem of Origins* (Cambridge: Cambridge University Press, 1985); and the articles by Alvin H. Hansen, Edward S. Mason, and Wolfgang F. Stolper in the special issue on Schumpeter of *Review of Economics and Statistics* 33 (May 1951).

13. Norman B. Wilkinson, *Lammot du Pont and the American Explosives Industry, 1850–1884* (Charlottesville: University Press of Virginia, 1984), 231–47.

14. Ibid., 248–79, 290; and Alfred D. Chandler, Jr., and Stephen Salsbury, *Pierre S. du Pont and the Making of the Modern Corporation* (New York: Harper & Row, 1971), 3–120.

15. See note 10 above; see also Wilkinson, *Lammot du Pont*, 38–40, on the purchase of sodium nitrate or soda powder from Peru.

16. See JoAnne Yates, *Control through Communication: The Rise of System in American Management* (Baltimore: Johns Hopkins University Press, 1989), 205–6; and Richard J. Ruth, "F. L. Kneeland of New York: A Study of the Changing Role of the Company Agent, 1849–1884" (Master's thesis, University of Delaware, 1967).

17. For the agents active between 1876 and 1885, the median number of letters sent to the company per year was 19. Kneeland of New York sent the largest number (11,500) during his tenure or an average of 235 per year from 1851 to 1900. J. T. Jones of Philadelphia sent an average of 233 letters a year between 1867 and 1888. The agents mentioned in the text corresponded as follows: Alexander, 14 letters per year (1880–83); Belin, 263 (1870–1888); Fries, 29 (1873–77); Good, 7 (1879–88); Holliday, 12 (1858–77); Hyde, 2

(1877); Kraus, 6 (1868–87); Leisenring, 76 (1852–88); Shellenberger, 15 (1881–84); Small, 10 (1834–88); Steinman, 23 (1859–88); Stichter, 313 (1858–88); Wharton, 8 (1868–75).

18. See John S. Gilkeson, Jr., *Middle-Class Providence, 1820–1940* (Princeton: Princeton University Press, 1986), 12, 13.

19. See James T. Lemon, *The Best Poor Man's Country: A Geographical Study of Early Southeastern Pennsylvania* (New Haven: Yale University Press, 1986), 120–21; see also Lemon, "Colonial America in the Eighteenth Century," 134.

20. Cochran, *Pennsylvania*, 14.

21. Karl Baedeker, ed., *The United States, with an Excursion into Mexico: A Handbook for Travellers—1893* (New York: Da Capo Press, 1971), 229; see Donald William Meinig, *The Shaping of America: A Geographical Perspective on 500 Years of History* (New Haven: Yale University Press, 1986), 449, for Latrobe's drawing of the Lancaster courthouse built in 1799.

22. Baedeker, *United States*, 229; Morton L. Montgomery, *History of Berks County in Pennsylvania* (Philadelphia: Everts, Peck & Richards, 1886), 30, 102, 854.

23. The details of the Stichter family history were found in Montgomery, *History of Berks County*, 201–2, 473, 765, 820, 823, 839, 871, and in Cyrus T. Fox, ed., *Reading and Berks County Pennsylvania: A History* (New York: Lewis Historical Publishing Co., 1925), 3:358.

24. See Michael B. Katz, Michael M. Doucet, and Mark J. Stern, *The Social Organization of Early Industrial Capitalism* (Cambridge: Harvard University Press, 1982).

25. Other Keims were prominent locally. George de Benneville Keim, a lawyer who specialized in coal land titles, became an attorney for the Philadelphia and Reading Railroad and later president of that railroad's coal and iron company. In the 1870s, he was involved in the prosecution of the "Molly Maguires," the Irish miners whose murderous reprisals against mine bosses had sent a chill through the Pennsylvania coalfields. Although the Mollies may have sought "redistributive justice in a hostile world," to the mercantile, professional, and industrial elite, they were, in the words of Keim's local biographer, a "malicious and nefarious secret society"; see Anthony F. C. Wallace, *St. Clair: A Nineteenth-Century Coal Town's Experience with a Disaster-Prone Industry* (New York: Alfred A. Knopf, 1987), 358; and Morton L. Montgomery, *Historical and Biographical Annals of Berks County, Pennsylvania* (Chicago: J. H. Beers & Co., 1909), 2:496.

26. On Fourth of July celebrations, see Rush Welter, *The Mind of America, 1820–1860* (New York: Columbia University Press, 1975), 3–74 passim.

27. Lynn Dumenil, *Freemasonry and American Culture, 1880–1930* (Princeton: Princeton University Press, 1984), 72.

28. The information in the following paragraphs was gleaned from George R. Prowell, *History of York County, Pennsylvania* (Chicago: J. H. Beers & Co., 1907), 1:657, 669–74, 730–31, 734, 751.

29. See William R. Johnson, *Schooled Lawyers: A Study in the Clash of Professional Cultures* (New York: New York University Press, 1978), 49–50; Robert Stevens, "Two Cheers for 1870: The American Law School," *Perspectives in American History* 5 (1971): 416–41; and Robert W. Gordon, "Legal Thought and Legal Practice in the Age of Enterprise, 1870–1900," in *Professions and Professional Ideologies in America*, ed. Gerald L. Geison (Chapel Hill: University of North Carolina Press, 1983), 70–110, on specialization, tax law, patent law, and railroad law.

30. William Henry Egle, *History of the Counties of Dauphin and Lebanon in the Commonwealth of Pennsylvania: Biographical and Genealogical* (Philadelphia: Everts & Peck, 1883), 2:278.

31. Luther Reily Kelker, *History of Dauphin County, Pennsylvania* (New York: Lewis Publishing Co., 1907), 3:12–13.

32. Franklin Ellis and Samuel Evans, *History of Lancaster County, with Biographical Sketches of Many of Its Pioneers and Prominent Men* (Philadelphia: Everts & Peck, 1883), 527; Frederic Shriver Klein, *Lancaster County, 1841–1941* (Lancaster, Pa.: Lancaster County National Bank, 1941), 45.

33. *Commemorative Biographical Encyclopedia of Dauphin County, Pennsylvania, Containing Sketches of Prominent and Representative Citizens, and Many of the Early Scotch-Irish and German Settlers* (Chambersburg, Pa.: J. M. Runk & Co., 1896), 480–81; Alfred D. Chandler, Jr., *Henry Varnum Poor: Business Editor, Analyst, and Reformer* (Cambridge: Harvard University Press, 1956).

34. The information on the Leisenrings and the Packers was found in Alfred Mathews and Austin N. Hungerford, *History of the Counties of Lehigh and Carbon in the Commonwealth of Pennsylvania* (Philadelphia: Everts & Richards, 1884), 484–85, 667, 673–74, 677, 706–8; *Portrait and Biographical Record of Lehigh, Northampton and Carbon Counties, Pennsylvania, Containing Biographical Sketches of Prominent and Representative Citizens of the Counties, Together with Biographies and Portraits of All the Presidents of the United States* (Chicago: Chapman Publishing Co., 1894), 569–70; John W. Jordan, Edgar Morre Green, and George T. Ettinger, *Historic Homes and Institutions and Genealogical and Personal Memoirs of the Lehigh Valley, Pennsylvania* (New York: Lewis Publishing Co., 1905), 1:195–98; Burton W. Folsom, *Urban Capitalists: Entrepreneurs and City Growth in Pennsylvania's Lackawanna and Lehigh Regions, 1800–1920* (Baltimore: Johns Hopkins University Press, 1981), 117–19; Baedeker, *United States*, 227; for comparisons with New York canal towns, see Blumin, *Urban Threshold*.

35. Folsom, *Urban Capitalists*, 119.

36. A. W. Leisenring to Du Pont, May 9, 1885, and June 13, 1888, HML, Acc. 500, Series I, Box 245. One of his customers, located near the Schuylkill region, learned that powder there was cheaper than in the Lehigh region and complained about it. On warfare over prices, see Yates, *Control through Communication*, 219. Alexander had a cousin, W. A. Leisenring, who was also a Du Pont agent; in January 1891, he sold $3,250 worth of powder, over half of it to one big colliery and the rest to six other collieries and the Lehigh Valley Railroad; W. A. Leisenring to Du Pont, January 1891, HML, Acc. 500, Series I, Box 245; see also Charles Rhoads Roberts et al., *History of Lehigh County, Pennsylvania, and a Genealogical and Biographical Record of Its Families* (Allentown, Pa.: Lehigh Valley Publishing Co., 1914), 2:804–7.

37. The information on the Brecks and the Belins was found in Horace Edwin Hayden, Alfred Hand, and John W. Jordan, *Genealogical and Family History of the Wyoming and Lackawanna Valleys, Pennsylvania* (New York: Lewis Publishing Co., 1906), 2:214–15; Benjamin H. Throop, *A Half Century in Scranton* (Scranton, Pa.: n.p., 1895), 236–38; and Frederick L. Hitchcock, *History of Scranton and Its People* (New York: Lewis Publishing Co., 1914), 1:144, 216–17, 223, 406–7, 2:53–55, 272.

38. Baedeker, *United States*, 233; *Commemorative Biographical Encyclopedia of the Juniata Valley, Comprising the Counties of Huntingdon, Mifflin, Juniata, and Perry, Pennsylvania, Containing Sketches of Prominent and Representative Citizens and Many of the Early Settlers* (Chambersburg, Pa.: J. M. Runk & Co., 1897), 525.

39. John Blair Linn, *History of Centre and Clinton Counties, Pennsylvania* (Philadelphia: Louis H. Everts, 1883), 382.

40. Ibid., 396.

41. *Commemorative Biographical Record of Central Pennsylvania, Including the Counties of Centre, Clinton, Union and Snyder, Containing Biographical Sketches of Prominent and Representative Citizens, and Many of the Early Settlers* (Chicago: J. H. Beers & Co., 1898), 680–81.

42. The following information was found in J. H. Ewing and Harry Slep, *History of the City of Altoona and Blair County, Including Sketches of the Shops of the Pennsylvania Railroad Co.* (Altoona, Pa.: Harry Slep's Mirror Printing House, 1880), 203; Samuel T. Wiley and W. Scott Garner, ed., *Biographical and Portrait Cyclopedia of Blair County, Pennsylvania* (Philadelphia: Gresham Publishing Co., 1982), 121–23; George A. Wolf et al., *Blair County's First Hundred Years, 1846–1946* (Hollidaysburg, Pa.: Blair County Historical Society, 1945), 54–58, 99, 421; and Jesse C. Sell, *Twentieth Century History of Altoona and Blair County, Pennsylvania, and Representative Citizens* (Chicago: Richmond-Arnold Publishing Co., 1911), 401.

43. W. J. McKnight, *A Pioneer Outline History of Northwestern Pennsylvania*

Embracing the Counties of Tioga, Potter, McKean, Warren, Crawford, Venango, Forest, Clarion, Elk, Jefferson, Cameron, Butler, Lawrence, and Mercer, Also A Pioneer Sketch of the Cities of Allegheny, Beaver, Du Bois, and Towanda (Philadelphia: J. B. Lippincott Co., 1905), 507, 515–17; and *History of the Counties of McKean, Potter, Cameron and Elk, Pennsylvania, with Biographical Sections, Including Their Early Settlement and Development* (Chicago: J. H. Beers & Co., 1889), 577, 699–700; William Dean Howells, *The Rise of Silas Lapham* (New York, 1885).

44. *The City of Altoona, Pennsylvania, A.D. 1896* (n.p., n.d.), 125–26; Baedeker, *United States*, 234.

45. In the third quarter of 1883, Fries sold fourteen kegs of Du Pont sporting powder, eighty-seven kegs of Du Pont soda, and twenty-one kegs of Du Pont rifle powder for $350. He paid $16.20 for freight, retained $42.50 that he had overpaid to Du Pont the previous quarter, kept $35.00 for his commission and sent $256.30 to the company; Fries to Du Pont, October 1, 1883, HML, Acc. 500, Series I, Box 451.

46. Fries to Du Pont, September 22, 1876, HML, Acc. 500, Series I, Box 103.

47. Benjamin Whitman, *Nelson's Biographical Dictionary and Historical Reference Book of Erie County, Pennsylvania* (Erie, Pa.: S. B. Nelson, 1986), 590; and John Miller, *A Twentieth Century History of Erie County, Pennsylvania: A Narrative Account of Its Historical Progress, Its People, and Its Principal Interests* (Chicago: Lewis Publishing Co., 1909), 1:253, 2:43–45.

48. Rice to Du Pont, January 17, 1888, HML, Acc. 504, Series I, Box 16. Yates cites this same letter in a different context, see *Control through Communication*, 211. Du Pont was not especially advanced in its office technology; the Treasury Department had switched to the typewriter in 1884, four years before the Brandywine offices had their quill-pen updated; see Mary Louise Brodhead Smith to Sophie du Pont, August 24, 1884, HML, Acc. W, Group 9, Series E, Box 159.

49. Alfred D. Chandler, Jr., *The Visible Hand: The Managerial Revolution in American Business* (Cambridge: Harvard University Press, Belknap Press, 1977), 438.

50. Rice to Coleman du Pont, May 22, 1902, du Pont to Rice, May 24, 1902; Rice to du Pont, May 27, 1902, HML, Acc. 1075, Series II, Part 2, Box 805, File 8B; Chandler and Salsbury offer a slightly different interpretation in *Pierre S. du Pont and the Making of the Modern Corporation*, 72, 73.

51. Dunham to Rice, May 13, 1902; Rice to du Pont, May 21, 1902; du Pont to Rice, May 23, 1902; Rice to du Pont, May 31, 1902; du Pont to Rice, June 2, 1902; Rice to du Pont, June 18, 1902, HML, Acc. 1075, Series II, Part 2, Box 805, File 8A.

52. Rice to du Pont, June 18, June 21, June 26, 1902, HML, Acc. 1075,

Series II, Part 2, Box 805, File 8A; Rice to du Pont, August 25, 1902; HML, Acc. 472, Series II, Part 3, Box 123.

53. Du Pont to Haskell, January 24, 1905; Haskell to du Pont, January 25, 1905; Rice to Col. H. A. du Pont, June 15, 1905, HML, Acc. 472, Series II, Part 3, Box 123.

54. McCraw, *Prophets of Regulation*, 93–94.

55. Richard Hofstadter, *The Age of Reform: From Bryan to FDR* (New York: Alfred A. Knopf, 1955), 135.

56. On Brandeis, see Leonard Baker, *Brandeis and Frankfurter: A Dual Biography* (New York: Harper & Row, 1984), 19; and Samuel Haber, *Efficiency and Uplift: Scientific Management in the Progressive Era, 1890–1920* (Chicago: University of Chicago Press, 1964), 75.

57. On the curious relationship between Brandeis and Taylor, see Haber, *Efficiency and Uplift*, 54–80; McCraw, *Prophets of Regulation*, 92; Daniel Nelson, *Frederick W. Taylor and the Rise of Scientific Management* (Madison: University of Wisconsin Press, 1980), 174–75; and Keith D. Revell, "Professionalism and Public Service: The Brandeis-Taylor Alliance of 1910" (Master's thesis, University of Virginia, 1989).

58. Chandler, *Visible Hand*, 438; Chandler and Salsbury, *Pierre S. du Pont*, 32.

59. Thorstein Veblen, *The Engineers and the Price System* (New York: B. W. Huebsch, 1921).

60. Olivier Zunz, "Genèse du pluralisme américain," *Annales: Economies, sociétés, civilisations* 42 (March–April 1987): 436.

CHAPTER TWO

1. Frank Norris, *The Octopus: A Story of California* (1901), Library of America Edition (New York: Viking Press, 1986), 616–17. See also James A. Ward, *Railroads and the Character of America, 1820–1887* (Knoxville: University of Tennessee Press, 1986).

2. On Adams, see Thomas K. McCraw, *Prophets of Regulation: Charles Francis Adams, Louis D. Brandeis, James M. Landis, Alfred E. Kahn* (Cambridge: Harvard University Press, Belknap Press, 1984), 16.

3. Max Weber, *Economy and Society: An Outline of Interpretive Sociology* (1925), ed. Guenther Roth and Claus Wittich, trans. Ephraim Fischof et al., (2 vols., Berkeley: University of California Press, 1978); Emile Durkheim, *De la division du travail social* (Paris: F. Alcan, 1893); and Dominick LaCapra, *Emile Durkheim, Sociologist and Philosopher* (Ithaca, N.Y.: Cornell University Press, 1972), 85. On Weber's notion of charismatic leadership within democracy and

conflict within bureaucracy, see James T. Kloppenberg, *Uncertain Victory: Social Democracy and Progressivism in European and American Thought, 1870–1920* (New York: Oxford University Press, 1986), 381–94.

4. Max Weber, *Economy and Society*, 957.

5. Nathaniel Hawthorne, *The Scarlet Letter* (1850), Library of America Edition (New York: Viking Press, 1983), 121–57. In 1891 there were 39,492 soldiers, sailors, and marines in the United States armed services; the largest government employer, the Post Office, had 95,440 workers in 1891 in one of the 64,000 post offices; most of these positions were payment for political support. By contrast in 1891 the Pennsylvania Railroad employed over 110,000 workers. See Alfred D. Chandler, Jr., *The Visible Hand: The Managerial Revolution in American Business* (Cambridge: Harvard University Press, Belknap Press, 1977), 204–5. Cindy Sondik Aron, *Ladies and Gentlemen of the Civil Service: Middle-Class Workers in Victorian America* (New York: Oxford University Press, 1987), 5, gives the following figures for males and females employed in the executive departments in Washington, D.C.: 1,268 in 1859; 5,824 in 1870; 7,866 in 1880; 17,304 in 1893; 25,675 in 1903.

6. I wish to thank Jürgen Kocka for his helpful comments on a paper regarding this point I gave at the 1986 Organization of American Historians meeting.

7. Chandler, *Visible Hand*, 209–10.

8. Alfred D. Chandler, Jr., Foreword to *Bonds of Enterprise: John Murray Forbes and Western Development in America's Railway Age*, by John Lauritz Larson (Cambridge: Harvard University Press, 1984), x.

9. The Chicago Stock Exchange was permanently organized in 1887; Frederic Cople Jaher, *The Urban Establishment: Upper Strata in Boston, New York, Charleston, Chicago, and Los Angeles* (Urbana: University of Illinois Press, 1982), 486.

10. Ibid., 460.

11. Chandler, *Visible Hand*, 162; see the series of maps in Richard C. Overton, *Burlington West: A Colonization History of the Burlington Railroad* (Cambridge: Harvard University Press, 1941), 462; and idem, *Burlington Route: A History of the Burlington Lines* (New York: Alfred A. Knopf, 1965), 192–93.

12. JoAnne Yates, *Control through Communication: The Rise of System in American Management* (Baltimore: Johns Hopkins University Press, 1989), 24–25, 101–2.

13. Chandler, *Visible Hand*, 151, 137–43, 158. Thus, to make the northern road competitive, Perkins and the two chief executives of the Chicago, Burlington, and Northern (C. B. & N.), A. E. Touzalin and George B. Harris, effectively withdrew from the Northwestern Association in order to be free to cut its secretly agreed-upon rate schedule; see Donald L. McMurry, *The Great*

Burlington Strike of 1888: A Case History in Labor Relations (Cambridge: Harvard University Press, 1956), 6–8; on the withdrawal from the western states passenger association, see Harris to Forbes, December 30, 1889, C. B. & Q. archives, Newberry Library (hereafter, CBQ), 8 C 5.162. Maury Klein, *The Life and Legend of Jay Gould* (Baltimore: Johns Hopkins University Press, 1986), stresses Gould's role as a manager rather than a financial operator.

14. Chandler, *Visible Hand*, 155; see also Vincent P. Carosso, *Investment Banking in America: A History* (Cambridge: Harvard University Press, 1970), 1–50.

15. Chandler, *Visible Hand*, 107.

16. C. B. & Q. and affiliated roads' salary lists for executives paid above $1,500 for the year 1880 can be found under the following archival call numbers: eight salary lists in CBQ, 33 1880 3.2; one in 33 1880 3.21; one in 33 1880 3.23 ; one in 33 1880 8.11; and one in 33 1880 8.12. All lists give annual salary entries; another list in 33 1870 3.2 gives some monthly salary entries. I have compiled each executive's name, position, department, and location from these various lists. I then traced the executives in the manuscript schedules of the 1880 federal census for Chicago and its immediate suburbs as well as in local histories of Chicago, Omaha, Burlington, and other towns along the line. The manuscript census yielded thirty-four of the forty-nine executives I had located in Chicago and four of the five suburbanites. These various sources allowed me to draw a composite portrait of these men's lives, at work, at home, and in their larger community. Each file was computerized for easy retrieval of individual information and record linkages. See chap. 4 for another use of these computer files.

17. Who observed it firsthand in their respective countries; Charles Tilly, "Retrieving European Lives," in *Reliving the Past: The Worlds of Social History*, ed. Olivier Zunz (Chapel Hill: University of North Carolina Press, 1985), 17, 18.

18. Organizational charts and salary lists listed in note 16. See also Paul V. Black, "The Development of Management Personnel Policies on the Burlington Railroad, 1860–1900" (Ph.D. diss., University of Wisconsin, 1973), 35–101. As Yates shows in her study of the Illinois Central, railroad executives developed systems to keep managers of various divisions abreast of what was happening outside their divisions. She calls that process "compiling an organizational memory"; see *Control through Communication*, 150–53.

19. One hundred and forty-eight exclusive of affiliated roads; statistics on salary below include affiliated roads. See memo, CBQ, 33 1880 8.11, for number of employees. Black estimates the total number of employees for C. B. & Q. lines west of the Missouri River to be between 4,000 and 5,000 in 1880 (Black, "Development of Management Personnel Policies," 22, n. 6); it is

therefore reasonable to expect that the total number of employees in the C. B. & Q. system was around 15,000 in 1880.

20. Perkins to Ladd, July 2, 1880, CBQ, 33 1880 3.23; see note 16 above.

21. Since 1878; see the salary lists mentioned in note 16 above and Overton, *Burlington Route*, 161.

22. See Overton, *Burlington West*, 111–13.

23. Overton, *Burlington Route*, 110; idem, *Burlington West*, 276.

24. Hooper to Turner, May 11, 1931, *Dear Lady: The Letters of Frederick Jackson Turner and Alice Forbes Perkins Hooper, 1910–1932*, ed. Ray Allen Billington (San Marino, Calif.: Huntington Library, 1970), 453, and Billington's introduction, 16, 17.

25. Jaher, *The Urban Establishment*, 492, 496.

26. Ibid., 484, 479.

27. See Chandler, *Visible Hand*, 176; and Black, "Development of Management Personnel Policies," 71, 79, 81.

28. Those towns were, in Illinois: Aurora, Beardstown, Galesburg, Peoria, Quincy, Rock Island; in Iowa: Council Bluffs, Creston, Des Moines, Keokuk, Ottumwa; in Nebraska: Omaha, Plattsmouth; in Kansas: Atchinson, Leavenworth; in Missouri: Kansas City, St. Joseph, St. Louis; for freight agents in New York, see Walker to Perkins, July 9, 1880, CBQ, 33 1880 8.12.

29. A normal trend in a deflationary period; these salary figures are adjusted for deflation. On fluctuating salaries and belt-tightening in other categories of railroad employees, see Black, "Development of Management Personnel Policies," 263.

30. Robert W. Gordon, "Legal Thought and Legal Practice in the Age of Enterprise, 1870–1900," in *Professions and Professional Ideologies in America*, ed. Gerald L. Geison (Chapel Hill: University of North Carolina Press, 1983), 78–79. See also William R. Johnson, *Schooled Lawyers: A Study in the Clash of Professional Cultures* (New York: New York University Press, 1978); *In Memoriam: James M. Walker* (Chicago: 1881), in the collection of the Chicago Historical Society; and Thomas R. Navin and Marian V. Sears, "The Rise of a Market for Industrial Securities, 1887–1902," *Business History Review* 29 (June 1955): 105–38.

31. Perkins to Ladd, July 2, 1880, CBQ, 33 1880 3.23.

32. Ibid.

33. Stephen Skowronek, *Building a New American State: The Expansion of National Administrative Capacities, 1877–1920* (Cambridge: Cambridge University Press, 1982), 125–27.

34. McMurry, *Great Burlington Strike*, 18, 3, 155; [Lloyd Shaw?] *Prominent Democrats of Illinois* (Chicago: Democrat Publishing Co., 1899), 368; A. T. Andreas, *History of Chicago* (Chicago: A. T. Andreas, Publisher, 1885–86), 2:145;

The Biographical Directory of the Railway Officials of America for 1887 (Chicago: Railway Age Publishing Co., 1887), 312; see also Perkins to Harris, June 7, 1889, and Losey to Harris, November 15, 1889, CBQ, 8 C 5.162.

35. Some Features in the History of the Burlington Road, CBQ, 32.9. On the leading role of the Pennsylvania Railroad in administrative reform and career patterns, see Chandler, *Visible Hand*, 109–10.

36. *Encyclopedia of Biography of Illinois* (Chicago: Century Publishing & Engineering Co., 1902), 3:124–25; *Country Life in America* 15 (February 1909): 359–64, 408, 412, 414; Some Features, CBQ, 32.9; and *Biographical Directory*, 227; for the role of Joy, Forbes, Perkins, Holdredge, Morton, Olney, and Blythe, in politics after the Civil War, see Overton, *Burlington Route*, 81–85, 184, 240. On the common practice for wealthy young men to begin at the lower level of the hierarchy, see Walter Licht, *Working for the Railroad: The Organization of Work in the Nineteenth Century* (Princeton: Princeton University Press, 1983), 51, and Black, "Development of Management Personnel Policies," 44.

37. A point amply supported by Black, "Development of Management Personnel Policies," 124–89.

38. Newton Bateman and Paul Selby, eds., *Historical Encyclopedia of Illinois and Sangamon County* (Chicago: Munsell Publishing Co., 1912), 1:452; Edward F. Dunne, *Illinois: The Heart of the Nation* (Chicago: Lewis Publishing Co., 1933), 5:24; Andreas, *History of Chicago* 2:146; Overton, *Burlington Route*, 213.

39. Some Features, CBQ, 32.9. By 1885, the largest percentage of railway managers had begun their careers as station clerks; Licht, *Working for the Railroad*, 26. See also Stuart Morris, "Stalled Professionalism: The Recruitment of Railway Officials in the U.S., 1885–1940," *Business History Review* 47 (Autumn 1973): 317–34.

40. Andreas, *History of Chicago* 2:145, 3:210.

41. McMurry, *Great Burlington Strike*, 11; Overton, *Burlington Route*, 99, 207; Weston A. Goodspeed and Daniel D. Healy, eds., *History of Cook County, Illinois* (Chicago: Goodspeed Historical Society, n.d.), 1:749.

42. Larson, *Bonds of Enterprise*, 35–36; Franc Wilkie Bangs, *The Chicago Bar Illustrated* (Chicago: R. R. Donnelly, 1872), 22; *In Memoriam: James M. Walker*, 5–7; Andreas, *History of Chicago* 2:145–46; for the increasing recruitment of educated civil engineers, see Black, "Development of Management Personnel Policies," 179–80.

43. Andreas, *History of Chicago* 2:145, 146; Andreas, *History of Chicago* 3:210.

44. Perkins memo, August 15, 1885, CBQ, 33 1870 3.6; see also Black, "Development of Management Personnel Policies," 190–255; Shelton Strom-

quist, *A Generation of Boomers: The Pattern of Railroad Labor Conflict in Nineteenth-Century America* (Urbana: University of Illinois Press, 1987), 100–141; and Licht, *Working for the Railroad*, 31–78.

45. The takeover of hiring functions by middle-level managers culminated in the twentieth century with the creation of personnel departments that undercut unions by preempting their policies; see Sanford M. Jacoby, *Employing Bureaucracy: Managers, Unions, and the Transformation of Work in American Industry, 1900–1945* (New York: Columbia University Press, 1985), 7, 280–81; and Daniel Nelson, *Managers and Workers: Origins of the New Factory System in the United States, 1880–1920* (Madison: University of Wisconsin Press, 1975), 148–56. On welfare programs in railroads as attempts to preempt unions, and Debs's reaction to them, see Stromquist, *A Generation of Boomers*, 246; and more generally Richard Edwards, *Contested Terrain: The Transformation of the Workplace in the Twentieth Century* (New York: Basic Books, 1979).

46. Overton, *Burlington Route*, 99. On colonization work, see Roy V. Scott, *Railroad Development Programs in the Twentieth Century* (Ames: Iowa State University, 1985), 4–9, and Overton, *Burlington West*; on Touzalin replacing George S. Harris, see ibid., 412–13; on the making of rules and regulations, see Touzalin memos, 1874–76, CBQ, 759.9.

47. The following paragraphs were drawn from Touzalin memos, CBQ, 759.9. Such efforts were in line with the railroads' efforts to avoid public embarrassments; see Black, "Development of Management Personnel Policies," 325–26.

48. Peasley to Harris, June 9, 1890; Harris to Peasley, June 11, 1890, CBQ, 3 P 2.52.

49. Besler to Peasley, April 18, 1890; Peasley to Merrill, December 11, 1890; Besler to Merrill, December 13, 1890, CBQ, 3 P 2.5.

50. Harris to Peasley, September 22, 1897, CBQ, 3 P 2.52. Drinking was a major problem among blue-collar workers and a major cause for firing; see Black, "Employee Alcoholism on the Burlington Railroad, 1896–1902," *Journal of the West* 17 (October 1978): 5–11; for a different opinion, see Stromquist, *A Generation of Boomers*, 238.

51. Besler to Peasley, November 11, 1893, CBQ, 3 P 2.5. On bonding practices, Licht, *Working for the Railroad*, 44, and Black, "Development of Management Personnel Policies," 470.

52. Harris to Peasley, March 11, 1899, CBQ, 3 P 2.52.

53. Colville to Rhodes, May 6, 1889, CBQ, 3 P 2.5; on garnishment, see Black, "Development of Management Personnel Policies," 484.

54. Bartlett to Peasley, June 30, 1893, CBQ, 3 P 2.5.

55. Harris to Peasley, May 16, 1895, CBQ, 3 P 2.52.

56. Harris to Peasley, May 11, 1893, CBQ, 3 P 2.52.

57. Thomas C. Cochran, *Railroad Leaders, 1845–1890: The Business Mind in Action* (Cambridge: Harvard University Press, 1953), 152–59; McCraw, *Prophets of Regulation*, 51, 60–65. On forecasting, see John C. Hudson, *Plains Country Towns* (Minneapolis: University of Minnesota Press, 1985), 75. Yates has shown how the ICC reporting requirements led the Illinois Central, reluctantly at first, to improve dramatically its statistical reporting, hence its ability to forecast, set rates, and analyze data; *Control through Communication*, 133–58.

58. Besler to Peasley, May 20, 1889, CBQ, 3 P 2.5.

59. West to Harris, May 14, 1889, CBQ, 8 C 5.162.

60. He was George B. Harris's father.

61. Overton, *Burlington West*, 390; for another important work on colonization, see Albro Martin, *James J. Hill and the Opening of the Northwest* (New York: Oxford University Press, 1976).

62. See the pamphlet in the Chicago Historical Society, John S. Cooper and William J. Hynes, *In the Appellate Court of Illinois, First District. Chicago, Burlington and Quincy Railroad Company, Appellant vs. Charles S. Bartlett, John G. Shortall, Samuel B. Barker and William Chisolm, Appellees. Brief and Argument for Appellees* (Chicago, 1886), 5–7.

63. Overton, *Burlington West*, 286, 277–78.

64. John William Reps, *Cities of the American West: A History of Frontier Urban Planning* (Princeton: Princeton University Press, 1979), 527, 529. On the use of the T-plan to avoid dangerous crossings, see Hudson, *Plains Country Towns*, 89–90.

65. Reps, *Cities of the American West*, fig. 16.3.

66. Overton, *Burlington West*, 373–76.

67. Reps, *Cities of the American West*, 529.

68. Monte Calvert, *The Mechanical Engineer in America, 1830–1910* (Baltimore: Johns Hopkins University Press, 1967); see also idem, "The Search for Engineering Unity: The Professionalization of Special Interest," in *Building the Organizational Society: Essays on Associational Activities in Modern America*, ed. Jerry Israel (New York: Free Press, 1972), 42–54; Edwin T. Layton, Jr., *The Revolt of the Engineers: Social Responsibility and the American Engineering Profession* (Baltimore: Johns Hopkins University Press, 1986); and Daniel H. Calhoun, *The American Civil Engineer: Origins and Conflict* (Cambridge, Mass.: Technology Press, 1960).

69. Calvert, *Mechanical Engineer*, 17.

70. The information in the following paragraphs was found in Perry's *Reminiscences*, CBQ, 32.92.

71. On naming sites, see Hudson, *Plains Country Towns*, 80.

72. Carl W. Condit, *The Port of New York: A History of the Rail and Terminal*

System from the Beginnings to Pennsylvania Station (Chicago: University of Chicago Press, 1980), 151.

73. The following paragraphs are based on Memorial Service for Joel West and C. W. Eckerson, CBQ, 32.9.

74. See John H. White, Jr., *The American Railroad Passenger Car* (Baltimore: Johns Hopkins University Press, 1978); and Condit, *The Port of New York*.

75. See Overton, *Burlington West*, 286–88.

76. The following is based on E. M. Westervelt, Rambling Reminiscences, CBQ, 32.92

77. See John Kenneth Galbraith, *The Affluent Society* (Boston: Houghton Mifflin, 1958).

78. Norris, *The Octopus*.

79. See Cochran, *Railroad Leaders*, 181–83; Stromquist, *A Generation of Boomers*, 234. See also Paul V. Black, "Experiment in Bureaucratic Centralization: Employee Blacklisting on the Burlington Railroad," *Business History Review* 51 (Winter 1977): 444–59. In 1880 Perkins reacted angrily to an unsigned editorial in *The Nation* which suggested that Boston railroad owners should pay more attention to their employees' personal welfare. The editorial was the work of Charles Francis Adams, Jr., who had corresponded with none other than A. E. Touzalin, then general manager of the B. & M. in Nebraska. Perkins responded with several memos and his own editorial, emphasizing that paternalism was an inappropriate policy for large firms; it misled employees about "the true character of the business relation," and smacked of "the worst doctrines of communism"; see Black, "Development of Management Personnel Policies," 331–33.

80. Eventually, the development of welfare programs became a way to preempt unionism. But according to an ICC poll of 350 railroads in 1892, only 17 percent had any kind of company insurance; 85 percent had no eating or lodging facilities for trainmen; 78 percent had no reading rooms or recreational facilities; and 96 percent had no pension plan; see Black, "Development of Management Personnel Policies," 427–28.

81. W. D. Howells, "The Great Railroad Strike," *Harper's Weekly* 32 (April 21, 1888): 286; on Howells's temporary isolation, see Thomas Bender, *New York Intellect: A History of Intellectual Life in New York, from 1750 to the Beginnings of Our Own Time* (New York: Alfred A. Knopf, 1987), 194.

82. McMurry, *Great Burlington Strike*, 11, 3, 16.

83. Ibid., 15. It is only after the crushing of the Great Pullman Strike that the federal government moved slowly in the area of arbitration. See Stromquist's interpretation of Olney's role, *A Generation of Boomers*, 259–63. The labor troubles of 1885–86 inspired Cyrus McCormick to try to avoid future

strikes or to gain public favor by raising wages for common laborers in advance of worker agitation; see Robert Ozanne, *Wages in Theory and Practice: McCormick and International Harvester, 1860–1960* (Madison: University of Wisconsin Press, 1968), 32–33, 41.

84. O. E. Stewart, Strike Notes, 1888, CBQ, 33 1880 9.83.

85. Westervelt, Rambling Reminiscences, CBQ, 32.92. See also Reports of Pinkerton's National Detective Agency, 1888–89, CBQ, 33 1880 9.3.

86. Richard J. Oestreicher, *Solidarity and Fragmentation: Working People and Class Consciousness in Detroit* (Urbana: University of Illinois Press, 1986), 249–50.

87. John S. Gilkeson, Jr., *Middle-Class Providence, 1820–1940* (Princeton: Princeton University Press, 1986), 175.

88. McMurry, *Great Burlington Strike*, 178.

89. Herbert Gutman, "Workers' Search for Power: Labor in the Gilded Age," in *The Gilded Age: A Reappraisal*, ed. J. Wayne Morgan (Syracuse, N.Y.: Syracuse University Press, 1963), 215–35; and idem, "Trouble on the Railroads, 1873–74: Prelude to the 1877 Crisis?" *Labor History* 2 (Spring 1961): 215–35; Stromquist reports that middle-class support was more forthcoming in small railway towns than in larger cities; see *A Generation of Boomers*, 174; Licht, *Working for the Railroad*, 253.

90. Klein, *Life and Legend of Jay Gould*, 330.

91. See Gerald Berk, "Constituting Corporations and Markets: Railroads and Courts in American Politics, 1870–1900" (paper prepared for delivery at the Annual Meeting of the Social Science History Association, New Orleans, October 29–November 1, 1987), and Thomas F. Vandenburg, "Equity Receivership and the Wabash Case" (seminar paper, University of Virginia, 1988); Klein's *Life and Legend of Jay Gould* is misleading on p. 330; the supreme court did not reverse or condemn the lower court opinion; instead, as Berks points out, the "friendly receiverships" became standard procedure.

92. Harlow Stafford Person, "Professional Training for Business," *World's Work* 8 (May 1904): 4767.

93. See, for instance, Henry A. Stimpson, "The Need for Advanced Commercial Education," *Forum* 29 (April 1900): 240–44; James B. Dill, "The College Man and the Corporate Proposition," *Munsey's Magazine* 24 (October 1900): 148–52; Henry Harrison Lewis, "Are Young Men's Chances Less?" *World's Work* 1 (December 1900): 170–73; R. H. Thurston, "The College-Man as Leader in the World's Work," *Popular Science Monthly* 60 (February 1902): 346–59; J. Laurence Laughlin, "Higher Commercial Education," *Atlantic Monthly* 89 (May 1902): 677–86; Edwin Grant Dexter, "A Study of Twentieth Century Success," *Popular Science Monthly* 61 (July 1902): 241–51; David Starr Jordan, "The Higher Education of the Business Man," *Independent* 54

(August 7, 1902): 1867–69; Cheesman A. Herrick, "Higher Commercial Education," *Annals of the American Academy of Political and Social Science* 21 (May 1903): 511–13; E. D. Jones, "Preparing College Students for Business," *World's Work* 6 (July 1903): 3686–87; Charles F. Thwing, "College Training and the Business Man," *North American Review* 563 (October 1903): 587–600; and William R. Harper, "A University Training for a Business Career," *Harper's Weekly* 48 (September 10, 1904): 1393–94.

94. "The Need of Trained Men," *Outlook* 65 (May 5, 1900): 16.

95. Weber, *Economy and Society,* 957–58.

96. Martin J. Schiesl, *The Politics of Efficiency: Municipal Administration and Reform in America, 1880–1920* (Berkeley: University of California Press, 1977).

97. See John L. Thomas, "Utopia for an Urban Age: Henry George, Henry Demarest Lloyd, Edward Bellamy," *Perspectives in American History* 6 (1972): 135–63.

CHAPTER THREE

1. See Charles W. McCurdy, "The *Knight* Sugar Decision of 1895 and the Modernization of American Corporation Law, 1869–1903," *Business History Review* 53 (Autumn 1979): 304–12; for a broader overview but a less convincing argument, see Martin J. Sklar, *The Corporate Reconstruction of American Capitalism, 1890–1916: The Market, the Law, and Politics* (Cambridge: Cambridge University Press, 1988).

2. James Livingston, "The Social Analysis of Economic History and Theory: Conjectures on Late Nineteenth-Century American Development," *American Historical Review* 92 (February 1987): 69–95.

3. See W. Elliot Brownlee, *Dynamics of Ascent: A History of the American Economy*, 2d ed. (Chicago: Dorsey Press, 1988), 267–364; for the legal side of this story, see Charles W. McCurdy, "American Law and the Marketing Structure of the Large Corporation, 1875–1890," *Journal of Economic History* 38 (September 1978): 631–49.

4. The key books are, on the one hand, Matthew Josephson, *The Robber Barons: The Great American Capitalists, 1861–1901* (New York: Harcourt, Brace & Co., 1934) and, on the other, Alfred D. Chandler, Jr., *The Visible Hand: The Managerial Revolution in American Business* (Cambridge: Harvard University Press, Belknap Press, 1977).

5. Alfred D. Chandler, Jr., and Stephen Salsbury, *Pierre S. du Pont and the Making of the Modern Corporation* (New York: Harper & Row, 1971), xxi.

6. Ibid.

7. These figure were derived from the following sources in the Hagley

Museum and Library (hereafter, HML): E. I. Du Pont de Nemours Co., 1902–1913, Longwood Manuscripts, Group 10, Series A, File 418, Box 1; Mooar, Iowa, plant material, Accession 439; Du Pont Centennial Resolutions, list of Brandywine Yards employees and office staff, 1902, Acc. 504; Du Pont employee Pierre Gentieu's essay, "The First Fifty Years at Carney's Point," Acc. 717; Du Pont accounting, sales and clerical staff housed in fourteen offices in and around Wilmington, Delaware, in 1902, Acc. 1410, Box 56; Repauno, New Jersey, pay ledger, 1884, Acc. 500, Series I, Part 1, Volume 1626, and Eastern Laboratory in New Jersey, miscellany, 1902–1920, Acc. 500, Series II, Part 2, Box 392; number of people shown on salary roll and wage rolls as of October 31, 1914, and December 31, 1915, Acc. 1662, Box 8, Folder "balance sheets."

8. David A. Hounshell and John Kenly Smith, Jr., *Science and Corporate Strategy: Du Pont R & D, 1902–1980* (Cambridge: Cambridge University Press, 1988).

9. *A History of the Du Pont Company's Relations with the United States Government, 1802–1927* (Wilmington, Del.: Smokeless Powder Department, E. I. Du Pont de Nemours & Co., n.d.), 66–72, HML; Chandler and Salsbury, *Pierre S. du Pont*, 248. On other antitrust cases, see Robert H. Wiebe, *Businessmen and Reform: A Study of the Progressive Movement* (Chicago: Quadrangle Books, 1962), 68–100.

10. Du Pont to Buckner, February 20, 1914, HML, Acc. 472, Series II, Part 3, Box 123, File 3L. Hounshell and Smith, *Science and Corporate Strategy*, 54, note that the Justice Department allowed Du Pont to retain all of its smokeless powder capacity in 1913.

11. See Chandler and Salsbury, *Pierre S. du Pont*, 384; and Hounshell and Smith, *Science and Corporate Strategy*, 76–97.

12. The information in this paragraph was gleaned from the product histories in the anniversary number "125 Years of Usefulness, 1802–1927" of the *Du Pont Magazine* (1927), HML.

13. Hounshell and Smith, *Science and Corporate Strategy*, 83.

14. Ibid., 138–40.

15. On the details of these reorganizations, see Chandler and Salsbury, *Pierre S. du Pont*, 303–21; Hounshell and Smith, *Science and Corporate Strategy*, 56–75; JoAnne Yates, *Control through Communication: The Rise of System in American Management* (Baltimore: Johns Hopkins University Press, 1989), 229–70.

16. Chandler and Salsbury, *Pierre S. du Pont*, 129; and David F. Noble, *America by Design: Science, Technology, and the Rise of Corporate Capitalism* (New York: Oxford University Press, 1977), 280–82.

17. Such as General Electric or Republic Steel and Iron Co.; see du Pont to Barksdale, February 12, 1914, and organization memo, n.d., HML, Acc. 472, Series II, Part 3, Box 131.

18. Ibid., and HML, Acc. 1662, boxes 8 and 26.

19. Chandler and Salsbury, *Pierre S. du Pont*, 227–55. For most chemical products, integration at Du Pont was never complete because the company sold technologically advanced products not to consumers but to other manufacturers; see Hounshell and Smith, *Science and Corporate Strategy*, 120.

20. At 34th and Broadway, the construction of which cousin Coleman had partly funded in 1910 with Charles Taft, President Taft's brother; see Chandler and Salsbury, *Pierre S. du Pont*, 311; see the hotel organization chart, HML, Longwood Manuscripts, Group 10, Series A, File 418, Box 4.

21. Alfred D. Chandler, Jr., *Strategy and Structure: Chapters in the History of Industrial Enterprise* (Cambridge: MIT Press, 1962), 112.

22. Chandler and Salsbury, *Pierre S. du Pont*, 505–10.

23. See Vincent P. Carosso, *Investment Banking in America: A History* (Cambridge: Harvard University Press, 1970), 1–50; Thomas R. Navin and Marian V. Sears, "The Rise of a Market for Industrial Securities, 1887–1902," *Business History Review* 29 (June 1955): 105–38; Robert W. Garnet, *The Telephone Enterprise: The Evolution of the Bell System's Horizontal Structure, 1876–1909* (Baltimore: Johns Hopkins University Press, 1985); Neil H. Wasserman, *From Invention to Innovation: Long-Distance Telephone Transmission at the Turn of the Century* (Baltimore: Johns Hopkins University Press, 1985), and George David Smith, *The Anatomy of a Business Strategy: Bell, Western Electric, and the Origins of the American Telephone Industry* (Baltimore: Johns Hopkins University Press, 1985).

24. Chandler, *Strategy and Structure*, 415, n. 11.

25. See Leonard S. Reich, *The Making of American Industrial Research: Science and Business at GE and Bell, 1876–1926* (Cambridge: Cambridge University Press, 1985); and W. Bernard Carlson, "Academic Entrepreneurship and Engineering Education: Dugald C. Jackson and the MIT-GE Cooperative Engineering Course, 1907–1932," *Technology and Culture* 29 (July 1988): 536–67.

26. See Hounshell and Smith, *Science and Corporate Strategy*, 54–55.

27. See Noble, *America by Design*, 281–82.

28. I am indebted to David Hounshell for his help on this point; for additional information see Hounshell and Smith, *Science and Corporate Strategy*, 21–24, 35–37; in 1919, the research staff, including administrators and service workers, exceeded 550 persons; for figures after 1921, see ibid., 288–90.

29. Reich, *Making of American Industrial Research*, 252–54; Hounshell and

Smith, *Science and Corporate Strategy*, 290; and Roger L. Geiger, *To Advance Knowledge: The Growth of American Research Universities, 1900–1940* (New York: Oxford University Press, 1986), 96, 97.

30. See Stuart W. Leslie, *Boss Kettering, Wizard of General Motors* (New York: Columbia University Press, 1983).

31. E. I. Du Pont de Nemours Powder Co., Annual Report, 1907, and Annual Report, 1912, HML, Acc. 472, Series II, Part 3, Box 131.

32. Du Pont to Perkins, January 29, 1914; du Pont to Tatnall, January 29, 1914; du Pont to Gary, April 15, 1914; du Pont to Vail, April 15, 1914; du Pont to Coffin, April 17, 1914, HML, Acc. 472, Series II, Part 3, Box 123, File 3L. See also Haskell to du Pont, January 14 and February 2, 1914, HML, Acc. 472, Series II, Part 3, Box 123, File 3L.

33. Perkins to du Pont, February 2, 1914, HML, Acc. 472, Series II, Part 3, Box 123, File 3L. On Perkins's views of benefits and more generally those of the National Civic Federation, see James Weinstein, *The Corporate Ideal in the Liberal State, 1900–1918* (Boston: Beacon Press, 1968), 3–39.

34. Pierre du Pont to S. H. du Pont, December 28, 1922, HML, Longwood Manuscripts 10, File 909.

35. Gone were the days when the du Ponts were flirting with reform. On their connection with Cleveland reform mayor Tom Johnson and with Arthur Moxham, see Chandler and Salsbury, *Pierre S. du Pont*, 25–28.

36. Du Pont to Seaver, February 27, 1950, HML, Longwood Manuscripts 10, File 384.

37. Chandler and Salsbury, *Pierre S. du Pont*, 270–71.

38. "Facts about the American Liberty League," 6, State Historical Society of Wisconsin, McCormick Collection, 1C, Part 9, Box 280, File 27.

39. See Robert T. Averitt, *The Dual Economy: The Dynamics of American Industry Structure* (New York: W. W. Norton, 1968); Thomas K. McCraw, ed., *The Essential Alfred Chandler: Essays toward a Historical Theory of Big Business* (Boston: Harvard Business School Press, 1988); and idem, "Rethinking the Trust Question," in *Regulation in Perspective: Historical Essays*, ed. Thomas K. McCraw (Cambridge: Harvard University Press, 1981), 1–55, on the terminology that has shaped much of our understanding of large business organizations.

40. See McCraw, "Rethinking the Trust Question," 17–18.

41. See Hounshell and Smith, *Science and Corporate Strategy*; Reich, *Making of American Industrial Research*; and Noble, *America by Design*.

42. Quoted in David Hounshell, *From the American System to Mass Production, 1800–1932: The Development of Manufacturing Technology in the United States* (Baltimore: Johns Hopkins University Press, 1984), 217.

43. As David Hounshell shows, ibid., 217–61.

44. David Montgomery, *Workers' Control in America: Studies in the History of Work, Technology, and Labor Struggles* (Cambridge: Cambridge University Press, 1979), 9–47.

45. The Reminiscences of Mr. W. C. Klann, Ford Motor Company Archives (hereafter, FMCA), Oral History Section, September 1955, vol. 1, p. 86.

46. Antonio Gramsci, *Selections from the Prison Notebooks*, ed. and trans. Quintin Hoare and Geoffrey Nowell Smith (New York: International Publishers, 1971), 296–97, 304.

47. Payroll information was taken from the Pay Check Rolls and Salary Check Registers in the FMCA, Acc. 707, Boxes 1 and 2. There were 1,224 individuals listed on the salary books for the years 1908 to 1912, 446 in 1910. I found 248 of these 446 salaried workers in the manuscript schedules of the federal census of 1910 for the city of Detroit. The information for each Ford employee was linked to the census information for the employee and his or her family. The census file thus comprises 1,343 records. Each file was computerized for easy retrieval and record linkages. See chap. 5 for a more intensive use of these computer files.

48. On Couzens, see Allan Nevins (with the collaboration of Frank Ernest Hill), *Ford* (New York: Charles Scribner's Sons, 1954), 1:241–45.

49. Noble, *America by Design*, 283, and Hounshell, *From American System to Mass Production*, 220, 251–52.

50. Interview with Mr. Joseph Galamb, FMCA, Oral History Section, January–February 1952, pp. 120, 145.

51. Nevins, *Ford* 2:111, and Hounshell, *From American System to Mass Production*, 220.

52. Donald F. Davis, *Conspicuous Production: Automobiles and Elites in Detroit, 1899–1933* (Philadelphia: Temple University Press, 1988).

53. Memorandum of conference . . . with Horace H. Rackham . . . , in Re: Additional 1919 Income Tax Case, FMCA, Acc. 96, Box 19.

54. Even the conservative business magazine *System* ran such articles as T. J. Zimmerman, "How the Stock Yards Strike Was Managed," 6 (September 1904): 181–96, and Samuel Gompers (AFL) vs. C. W. Post (Citizens Industrial Association of America), "Organization against Organization," 8 (November 1905): 420–29, to stress the convergence of methods used by management and labor.

55. Robert Lacey has provided a convenient summary of this period in *Ford: The Men and the Machine* (Boston: Little, Brown & Co., 1986): 87–179.

56. "Ford Thanksgiving Proclamation," *Ford Times* 5 (November 1911).

57. Hounshell, *From American System to Mass Production*, 224, and Alfred D.

Chandler, Jr., comp. and ed., *Giant Enterprise: Ford, General Motors, and the Automobile Industry: Sources and Readings* (New York: Harcourt Brace & World, 1964), 33.

58. Alfred P. Sloan, Jr., in collaboration with Boyden Sparks, *Adventures of a White-Collar Man* (New York: Doubleday, Doran, 1941), 25.

59. On this point, see Peter L. Berger, *The Capitalist Revolution: Fifty Propositions about Prosperity, Equality, and Liberty* (New York: Basic Books, 1986), 37.

60. Nevins, *Ford* 1:214, 391; Reminiscences of Mr. John Wandersee, FMCA, Oral History Section, September, 1952, pp. 1, 22; and computerized file, see note 47.

61. Wandersee Reminiscences, p. 4, and computerized file.

62. Wandersee Reminiscences, pp. 9–10; "Frank Kulick," *Ford Times* 1 (May 1, 1908): 1, and "Kulick at Chicago," *Ford Times* 3 (September 15, 1910): 554.

63. Klann Reminiscences, vol. 1, pp. 1–5.

64. Nevins, *Ford* 1:472; Klann Reminiscences, vol 1, p. 7.

65. Reminiscences of Mr. Ernest A. Pederson, Sr., FMCA, Oral History Section, October 1956, pp. 1–20.

66. Galamb Interview, pp. 1–5; Reminiscences of Mr. Walter Wagner, FMCA, Oral History Section, November 1956, p. 7; Nevins, *Ford* 1:268, 367, 456; Reminiscences of Mr. Richard Kroll, FMCA, Oral History Section, October 1953, pp. iii, 1–2.

67. Charles E. Sorensen, Organization and Administration, FMCA, n.p.; Avery, Edsel Ford's former teacher, was highly influenced by Taylor and is credited with the idea of putting the whole car on the production line; Nevins, *Ford* 1:474–75.

68. Sorensen, Organization and Administration, n.p.; Fred Allison, who made advances in solving electrical problems, was only twenty-seven in 1910. Charles B. Hartner was only twenty-five in 1910, when he presided over machine operations; Wandersee Reminiscences, 12; Nevins, *Ford* 2:16.

69. Nevins, *Ford* 2:465.

70. Klann Reminiscences, vol. 1, pp. 39–40.

71. Pederson Reminiscences, pp. 19–20.

72. See A. Russell Bond, "Going through the Shops—I: The Scientific American's Associate Editor Sees How a Factory Turns out a Thousand Cars a Day," *Scientific American* 110 (January 3, 1914): 8–10; idem, "Going through the Shops—II: Our Associate Editor Sees How the Automobile Industry Has Stimulated Machine Tool Manufacturing," *Scientific American* 110 (January 10, 1914): 50–51, 56; idem, "Going through the Shops—III: The Associate Editor of the Scientific American Witnesses Some of the Methods Used in Obtaining Extreme Accuracy in High Grade Motor Cars," *Scientific American* 110

(January 17, 1914): 66–67; and Horace L. Arnold and Fay L. Faurote, *Ford Methods and Ford Shops* (1915; reprint, New York: Arno Press, 1972).

73. Nevins, *Ford* 1:245, 365, 369.

74. Ibid., 1:267, 335, 353, 365, 470.

75. Reminiscences of Miss Georgia E. Boyer, FMCA, Oral History Section, January 1954, p. 9.

76. Computerized file, and Nevins, *Ford* 1:227, 214, 241–42, 269, 401–2, 2:24, 464.

77. Ibid., 1:342.

78. Ibid., 1:340, 342; Boyer Reminiscences, p. 10.

79. Nevins, *Ford* 1:342–44.

80. Ibid., 1:458, 532, 551, 2:161, 168; *Who's Who in Detroit* (Detroit: Walter Romig & Co., 1935), 188; C. M. Burton, *City of Detroit* (Detroit: S. J. Clarke Publishing Co., 1922), 5:84.

81. See also Stephen Meyer, *The Five Dollar Day: Labor, Management, and Social Control in the Ford Motor Company, 1908–1921* (Albany: State University of New York, 1981), and Olivier Zunz, *The Changing Face of Inequality: Urbanization, Industrial Development, and Immigrants in Detroit, 1880–1920* (Chicago: University of Chicago Press, 1982), 309–13.

82. Chandler and Salsbury, *Pierre S. du Pont*, 311.

83. Paul Morton, "The Executive as an Expert," *System* 6 (July 1904): 4; Morton Keller, *The Life Insurance Enterprise, 1885–1910: A Study in the Limits of Corporate Power* (Cambridge: Harvard University Press, Belknap Press, 1963), 249; and Marquis James, *The Metropolitan Life: A Study in Business Growth* (New York: Viking Press, 1947), 140.

84. Thomas W. Lawson, "Lawson and His Critics," in *The Muckrakers*, ed. Arthur and Lila Weinberg (New York: Capricorn Books, 1961), 290–91; see also ibid., 261–63. "Frenzied Finance" was the title of Lawson's exposé on Amalgamated Copper in 1904.

85. Keller, *Life Insurance Enterprise*, 245. See also Viviana A. Rotman Zelizer, *Morals and Markets: The Development of Life Insurance in the United States* (New York: Columbia University Press, 1979).

86. Quoted in Keller, *Life Insurance Enterprise*, 268; see also the pictures following p. 178.

87. Ibid., 10–11.

88. Louis I. Dublin, *A Family of Thirty Million: The Story of the Metropolitan Life Insurance Company* (New York: Metropolitan Life Insurance Co., 1943), 31.

89. See Stuart D. Brandes, *American Welfare Capitalism, 1880–1940* (Chicago: University of Chicago Press, 1970); and Zunz, *The Changing Face of Inequality*, 309–18.

90. Dublin, *A Family of Thirty Million*, 62, 63; James, *Metropolitan Life*, 176, 183–86.

91. Joseph Gollomb, "Profiles: Friend of the Average Man: Louis I. Dublin," *New Yorker*, May 22, 1942, 20–22.

92. I would like to thank my friend Thomas Dublin, grandson of Louis Dublin, for providing me with this information.

93. Annual Minutes, Greenwich House Series, Greenwich House Collection, Robert F. Wagner Labor Archives of the Tamiment Institute Library, New York University, Box 1, File 1; and *Who's Who in New York: A Biographical Dictionary of Prominent Citizens of New York City and State*, ed. Herman W. Knox, 7th ed. (New York: Who's Who Publishing Co., 1918), 141, 293, 607, 958.

94. Dublin, *A Family of Thirty Million*, 16, 424–25; Susan M. Reverby, *Ordered to Care: The Dilemma of American Nursing, 1850–1945* (Cambridge: Cambridge University Press, 1987), 72; and Diane B. Hamilton, "Metropolitan Life Insurance Company Visiting Nurse Service, 1909–1953" (Department of Nursing, diss., University of Virginia, 1987), 46, n. 86.

95. Dublin, *A Family of Thirty Million*, 16.

96. *The Metropolitan Life Insurance Company: Its History, Its Present Position in the Insurance World—Its Home Office Building and Its Work Carried on Therein* (New York: Metropolitan Life Insurance Co., 1914), 172.

97. Ibid., 184, and Roy Rosenzweig, *Eight Hours for What We Will: Workers and Leisure in an Industrial City, 1870–1920* (Cambridge: Cambridge University Press, 1983), 190, 193–94.

98. *The Metropolitan Life Insurance Company* (1914), 178–80; see also Paul Boyer, *Urban Masses and Moral Order in America, 1820–1920* (Cambridge: Harvard University Press, 1978), 359, n. 61 on the Boy Scouts; and Joseph F. Kett, *Rites of Passage: Adolescence in America, 1790 to the Present* (New York: Basic Books, 1977), 223–24.

99. See Robert W. DeForest and Lawrence Veiller, *The Tenement House Problem*, (2 vols., New York: Macmillan Co., 1903).

100. *The Metropolitan Life Insurance Company* (1914), 175–76, 185–86.

101. Ibid., 183; *The Metropolitan Life Insurance Company: Its History, Its Present Position in the Insurance World—Its Home Office Building and Its Work Carried on Therein* (New York: Metropolitan Life Insurance Co., 1908), 47; and Samuel Gompers, Introduction to *Health of the Worker: How to Safeguard It*, by Lee K. Frankel (New York: Funk & Wagnalls, 1924).

102. On the complex background of mutualization at Metropolitan and Prudential, see Keller's penetrating analysis in *Life Insurance Enterprise*, 271–74.

103. Dublin, *A Family of Thirty Million*, 41; see the sample policies following page 196 in *The Metropolitan Life Insurance Company* (1914); and James J. Far-

rell, *Inventing the American Way of Death, 1830–1920* (Philadelphia: Temple University Press, 1980), 165, 73.

104. Farrell, *Inventing the American Way of Death*, 73; Dublin, *A Family of Thirty Million*, 41.

105. This profile of the Metropolitan agents and executives is based on information gleaned from the biographical portraits in the *Souvenir Number of the Weekly Bulletin* (Metropolitan Life Insurance Company of New York, 1897), 47, 69–113, Metropolitan Life archives (hereafter, MLA).

106. Paul Johnson, *Saving and Spending: The Working-Class Economy in Britain, 1870–1939* (Oxford: Clarendon Press, 1985), 37–39.

107. See John Higham's Introduction to Abraham Cahan, *The Rise of David Levinsky* (New York: Harper & Row, 1960); and *Grandma Never Lived in America: The New Journalism of Abraham Cahan*, ed. Moses Rischin (Bloomington: Indiana University Press, 1985).

108. *To an Invisible Million*, Metropolitan Banquet Speeches Broadcasted by Radio to a Record Audience (pamphlet in MLA, n.d.), 11, 4, 5.

109. *To an Invisible Million*, 5.

110. Robert S. Lynd and Helen Merrell Lynd, *Middletown: A Study in American Culture* (New York: Harcourt Brace, 1929), 452–53, 457.

111. Adolf A. Berle, Jr., *Power without Property: A New Development in American Political Economy* (New York: Harcourt, Brace & Co., 1959), 94, 161, and Keller, *Life Insurance Enterprise*, 291.

112. Some sought to limit outside control by "capturing" regulation, as many historians have argued; see Thomas K. McCraw, "Regulation in America: A Review Article," *Business History Review* 49 (Summer 1975): 162–64. Others continued to entertain the belief that true social justice existed without such a partnership, and each side pretended to hold the single democratic formula for social change. For an interesting attempt to classify big business along political lines, see Thomas Ferguson, "From Normalcy to New Deal: Industrial Structure, Party Competition, and American Public Policy in the Great Depression," *International Organization* 38 (Winter 1984): 41–94.

CHAPTER FOUR

1. See Homer Hoyt, *One Hundred Years of Land Values in Chicago* (New York: Arno Press, 1970), 150–51, on the economic and noneconomic considerations of skyscrapers; and Thomas S. Hines, *Burnham of Chicago: Architect and Planner* (Chicago: University of Chicago Press, 1979), 44–49.

2. Hoyt, *One Hundred Years of Land Values*, 152–53, 337.

3. Robert Higgs, *The Transformation of the American Economy, 1865–1914:*

An Essay in Interpretation (New York: John Wiley & Sons, 1971), 74; Allan R. Pred, *The Spatial Dynamics of U.S. Urban-Industrial Growth, 1800–1914* (Cambridge: MIT Press, 1966), 90–98.

4. As Charles Dickens labeled it in *Hard Times* (1854); see also Lewis Mumford, *The City in History: It Origins, Its Transformations, and Its Prospects* (New York: Harcourt, Brace & World, 1961), 446–78.

5. Daniel Bluestone, "Landscape and Culture in Nineteenth-Century Chicago" (Ph.D. diss., University of Chicago, 1984), 245, 246, 248.

6. Ibid., 249–51.

7. Poe lived in England with his foster parents as a child in the 1810s.

8. See Jürgen Kocka, *White Collar Workers in America, 1890–1940: A Social-Political History in International Perspective*, trans. Maura Kealey (London: Sage Publications, 1980), 86–89.

9. Edgar Allan Poe, "The Man of the Crowd," in *Tales* (1845), Library of America Edition (New York: Viking Press, 1986), 389–90.

10. Historians have generally concluded that, politically, clerical workers drifted toward Toryism; see Geoffrey Crossick, "The Emergence of the Lower Middle Class in Britain: A Discussion," in *The Lower Middle Class in Britain*, ed. Geoffrey Crossick (London: Croom Helm, 1977), 40; and David Lockwood, *The Blackcoated Worker: A Study in Class Consciousness* (London: Allen & Unwin, 1966).

11. For example, see Edwin T. Freedley, *A Practical Treatise on Business: Or How to Get, Save, Spend, Give, Lend, and Bequeath Money with an Inquiry into the Chances of Success and Causes of Failure in Business* (Philadelphia: n.p., 1853), 119–20.

12. This testimony is cited in Margery W. Davis, *Woman's Place Is at the Typewriter: Office Work and Office Workers, 1870–1930* (Philadelphia: Temple University Press, 1982), 21.

13. See chap. 1, and Michael B. Katz, Michael J. Doucet, and Mark J. Stern, *The Social Organization of Early Industrial Capitalism* (Cambridge: Harvard University Press, 1982), 44–45, 192–93.

14. John D. Randall, *A Guide to Significant Chicago Architecture from 1872 to 1922* (Chicago: Privately published, 1958), 15; on Burnham and Root, see Carl W. Condit, *The Chicago School of Architecture: A History of Commercial and Public Building in the Chicago Area, 1875–1925* (Chicago: University of Chicago Press, 1964).

15. See the description of the building's interior in John S. Cooper and William J. Hynes, *In the Appellate Court of Illinois, First District. Chicago, Burlington and Quincy Railroad Company, Appellant vs. Charles S. Bartlett, John G. Shortall, Samuel B. Barker and William Chisolm, Appellees. Brief and Argument for*

Appellees (Chicago, 1886), 8–12, 14–15 (in the holdings of the Chicago Historical Society); and Hines, *Burnham of Chicago*, 54.

16. Uncataloged volumes of Pay Rolls for General Office (employees), June 1880, C. B. & Q. archives, Newberry Library (hereafter, CBQ).

17. See Alfred Sorenson, *History of Omaha from the Pioneer Days to the Present Time* (Omaha: Gibson, Miller & Richardson, 1889), 297; and the National Register of Historic Places, Inventory-Nomination Form at the Nebraska State Historical Society.

18. Hines, *Burnham of Chicago*, 48.

19. Jack Quinan, *Frank Lloyd Wright's Larkin Building: Myth and Fact* (Cambridge: MIT Press, 1987), 12–13, 21–84, 112.

20. See generally JoAnne Yates, *Control through Communication: The Rise of System in American Management* (Baltimore: Johns Hopkins University Press, 1989).

21. The following description was pieced together from Barlett to Board of Directors, April 14, 1884; letter to Forbes, April 21, 1884, CBQ, 33 1880 3.3; and Cooper and Hynes, *Chicago, Burlington and Quincy Railroad Company, Appellant vs. Charles S. Bartlett, John G. Shortall, Samuel B. Barker and William Chisolm, Appellees*.

22. "Battlefields of Business," *System* 6 (December 1904): 485; and David Lay, "A Desk System for the Executive," ibid., 525–28.

23. Montgomery Schuyler, "Architecture in Chicago: Adler and Sullivan," in *American Architecture and Other Writings*, ed. William H. Jordy and Ralph Coe (Cambridge: Harvard University Press, Belknap Press, 1961), 2:377.

24. See Harold M. Mayer and Richard C. Wade, *Chicago: Growth of a Metropolis* (Chicago: University of Chicago Press, 1969), 215, photograph 4.

25. On pass policy for employees, see Paul V. Black, "The Development of Management Personnel Policies on the Burlington Railroad, 1860–1900" (Ph.D. diss., University of Wisconsin, 1973), 338.

26. I obtained residential information by matching C. B. & Q. salary lists (see note 16 of chap. 2) with the manuscript schedules of the 1880 Census for Chicago and its immediate suburbs; of 49 executives located with certainty in Chicago from railroad sources and the City Directory, 10 were upper-level executives (making more than $4,000 a year) and the others middle-level executives (making between $1,500 and $4,000). I traced 7 upper-level executives in the city and 1 in Riverside; 31 middle-level executives but only 3 of them in the suburbs. I also tracked down clerks found in the volumes of Pay Rolls for General Office (note 16 above). Of 271 eligible clerks, I located 117 of them in the city, only 41 heads of households, with 18 in the suburbs. All these files were computerized for easy information retrieval and record link-

age. I treat the clerks in greater detail in the next chapter (see note 15 in chap. 5).

27. See *Riverside in 1871 with a Description of Its Improvements Together with Some Engravings of Views and Buildings* (Chicago: D. & C. H. Blakely, Printers, n.d.); see also Theodore Turak, *William Le Baron Jenney: A Pioneer of Modern Architecture* (Ann Arbor: UMI Research Press, 1986), 100; and for a discussion of the controversy surrounding Jenney's contribution to skeleton construction, ibid., 237–63.

28. David Hounshell, *From the American System to Mass Production, 1800–1932: The Development of Manufacturing Technology in the United States* (Baltimore: Johns Hopkins University Press, 1984), 226–27.

29. On the shift from Fordism to "Sloanism," see ibid., 267.

30. Hines, *Burnham of Chicago*, 80, 83, 86–87; Sigfried Giedion lamented the emergence of "mercantile classicism," signalled by the 1893 exposition, in *Space, Time, and Architecture: The Growth of a New Tradition* (Cambridge: Harvard University Press, 1967), 393–96; see Thomas Bender and William R. Taylor, "Culture and Architecture: Some Aesthetic Tensions in the Shaping of Modern New York City," in *Visions of the Modern City: Essays in History, Art, and Literature*, ed. William Sharpe and Leonard Wallock (New York: Heyman Center for the Humanities, 1983), 189–92. Bluestone, "Landscape and Culture," 277–78, notes that Chicago architecture was not so geometric either.

31. Bender and Taylor, "Culture and Architecture," 197–208.

32. Mardges Bacon, *Ernest Flagg, Beaux Arts Architect and Reformer* (Cambridge: MIT Press, 1986), 209; and Bender and Taylor, "Culture and Architecture," 208, 203–4.

33. See Edwin A. Cochran, *The Cathedral of Commerce* (New York: Broadway Park Place Co., 1917), 5, 7.

34. As Gail Fenske has clearly shown in "'The Skyscraper Problem' and the City Beautiful: The Woolworth Building" (Ph.D. diss, MIT, 1988), 8–57.

35. Description of the Tower Extension of the Home Office Building of the Metropolitan Life Insurance Company and General Date of Construction, n.d., Metropolitan Life archives (hereafter, MLA).

36. Photographic Section, MLA.

37. "The Great Tower of the Metropolitan Life," *Remington Notes* 1 (no. 7): 8, Hagley Museum and Library.

38. *Souvenir Number of the Weekly Bulletin* (Metropolitan Life Insurance Company of New York, 1897), 47, 48, 57, MLA.

39. Ibid., 57.

40. *The Metropolitan Life Insurance Company: Its History, Its Present Position in the Insurance World—Its Home Office Building and Its Work Carried on Therein*

(New York: Metropolitan Life Insurance Co., 1914), 71; see also Geoffrey D. Austrian, *Herman Hollerith: Forgotten Giant of Information Processing* (New York: Columbia University Press, 1982).

41. *Weekly Bulletin*, 25–27, 30.

42. Ibid., 27, 57.

43. *The Metropolitan Life Insurance Company* (1914), 49, 52, 66.

44. William H. Whyte, Jr., *The Organization Man* (New York: Simon & Schuster, 1956).

45. The Metropolitan was ahead of its time, for other large insurance companies only began to hire large numbers of women significantly later, in the 1920s; see Sharon Hartman Strom, "'Machines Instead of Clerks': Technology and the Feminization of Bookkeeping, 1910–1950," in *Computer Chips and Paper Clips: Technology and Women's Employment, Case Studies and Policy Perspectives*, ed. Heidi I. Hartmann (Washington, D.C.: National Academy Press, 1987), 73–83.

46. Edith Wharton, *The House of Mirth* (1905), Library of America Edition (New York: Viking Press, 1986), 116–17.

47. Cindy Sondik Aron, *Ladies and Gentlemen of the Civil Service: Middle-Class Workers in Victorian America* (New York: Oxford University Press, 1987), 162–83.

48. The dress code was gleaned from the Photographic Section, MLA, the photographs in the Byron Collection of the Museum of the City of New York, and *Rules Governing Home Office Clerical Employees* (Metropolitan Life Insurance Co., 1915), 13.

49. Thomas Dublin, *Women at Work: The Transformation of Work and Community in Lowell, Massachusetts, 1826–1860* (New York: Columbia University Press, 1979).

50. Aron, *Ladies and Gentlemen of the Civil Service*, 116–20.

51. *Weekly Bulletin* (1897), 32, 34, 36, 37, 51; *The Metropolitan Life Insurance Company* (1914), 93; and Photographic Section, MLA.

52. *The Metropolitan Life Insurance Company* (1914), 66.

53. Aron, *Ladies and Gentlemen of the Civil Service*, 89–90; *Weekly Bulletin* (1897), 53.

54. *The Metropolitan Life Insurance Company* (1914), 74, 75, 78, 79.

55. *Rules Governing Home Office Clerical Employees*, 5, 20.

56. Ibid., 13; see memos from Third Vice President, May 24, May 26, 1906, and May 27, 1908, MLA; and H. E. Coffin, "The Housekeeping of a Skyscraper," *The Bookkeeping Magazine* (June 1909), MLA.

57. *Rules Governing Home Office Clerical Employees*, 13; *The Metropolitan Life Insurance Company* (1914), 64; *Weekly Bulletin* (1897), 31, 32.

58. *The Metropolitan Life Insurance Company* (1914), 69.

59. *The Metropolitan Life Insurance Company* (1914), 47; *Weekly Bulletin* (1897), 25, 52. The same was true of the Woolworth Building; see Gilbert, office memoranda, March 3, 1913, Cass Gilbert Collection, New York Historical Society; I am indebted to Holly Wagner for this reference.

60. *Rules Governing Home Office Clerical Employees*, 17; *Rules and Regulations Governing the Office Employés of the Metropolitan Life Insurance Company of New York* (1895), 4, MLA; *Weekly Bulletin* (1897), 42.

61. See the Filing Section photographs in the Photographic Section, MLA; and *The Metropolitan Life Insurance Company* (1914), 86 (photograph).

62. Kathy Peiss, *Cheap Amusements: Working Women and Leisure in Turn-of-the-Century New York* (Philadelphia: Temple University Press, 1986), 88.

63. *Rules Governing Home Office Clerical Employees*, 20. And while at Coney Island, a variety of other amusements such as the scenic rides through tunnels and "caves" away from onlookers offered repeated occasions for "spooning" and "petting"; see John F. Kasson, *Amusing the Million: Coney Island at the Turn of the Century* (New York: Hill & Wang, 1978), 42, 43.

64. Aron, *Ladies and Gentlemen of the Civil Service*, 162–63.

65. Roy Rosenzweig, *Eight Hours for What We Will: Workers and Leisure in an Industrial City, 1870–1920* (Cambridge: Cambridge University Press, 1983), 191–221.

66. M. Christine Boyer, *Manhattan Manners: Architecture and Style, 1850–1900* (New York: Rizzoli International Publications, 1985), 120–29.

67. *Report of the Heights of Buildings Commission to the Committee on the Height, Size and Arrangement of Buildings of the Board of Estimate and Apportionment of the City of New York* (December 23, 1913), 52–53.

68. *New York Times*, November 28, 1912.

69. Alfred D. Chandler, Jr., and Stephen Salsbury, *Pierre S. du Pont and the Making of the Modern Corporation* (New York: Harper & Row, 1971), 311.

70. Bacon, *Ernest Flagg*, xiii, 222; see also *New York Times*, January 24, 1915, sec. 8.

71. Bacon, *Ernest Flagg*, 222–23.

72. See Carol Willis, "Zoning and *Zeitgeist*: The Skyscraper City in the 1920s," *Journal of the Society of Architectural Historians* 45 (March 1986): 47–59, on the architectural consequences of the 1916 setback law.

73. See Samuel Haber, *Efficiency and Uplift: Scientific Management in the Progressive Era, 1890–1920* (Chicago: University of Chicago Press, 1964), ix–x, on the multiple uses of the concept of efficiency.

74. "Skyscrapers Hurt Real Estate Values," *New York Times*, November 16, 1913, sec. 8

75. Ibid.

76. See the clipping "Election Returns 658 Feet in the Air," *New York Herald*, October 28, 1908, MLA; and Some Items about the Tower, n.d., MLA.

77. Description of the Tower Extension of the Home Office Building of the Metropolitan Life Insurance Company and General Date of Construction, n.d., MLA; see the advertisements for Coca-Cola, the E-M-F Company, and the Robert C. Fisher Company among others in the MLA clipping files; see also Kenneth Turney Gibbs, *Business Architectural Imagery, 1870–1930* (Ann Arbor: UMI Research Press, 1984), 143–44.

78. Estimate from the figures given in clipping "Visitors to the Tower," Intelligencer (March 9, 1912), MLA.

79. On Woolworth's desire to rent the building and anxiety about it, see Woolworth to Gilbert, December 27, 1911, Cass Gilbert Collection, New York Historical Society. On Woolworth's planning for the tallest building in New York, see Cass Gilbert's memoranda of September 16, 1910, and December 13, 1910, Cass Gilbert Collection. I am indebted to Holly Wagner for these references.

80. See Gunter Gad and Deryck Holdsworth, "Corporate Capitalism and the Emergence of the High-Rise Office Building," *Urban Geography* 8 (May–June 1987): 212–31.

81. Chandler and Salsbury, *Pierre S. du Pont*, 589.

82. "Skyscrapers Hurt Real Estate Values," *New York Times*, November 16, 1913, sec. 9. I am indebted to Keith Revell for his help on this section; see also his "Professionalism and Public Service: The Brandeis-Taylor Alliance of 1910" (Master's thesis, University of Virginia, 1989).

83. Henry A. Stimson, "The Small Business as a School of Manhood," *Atlantic Monthly* 93 (March 1904): 337, 339, 340.

CHAPTER FIVE

1. C. Wright Mills, *White Collar: The American Middle Classes* (New York: Oxford University Press, 1953), 69; Heidi I. Hartmann, Robert E. Kraut, and Louise A. Tilly, eds., *Computer Chips and Paper Clips: Technology and Women's Employment* (Washington, D.C.: National Academy Press, 1986), 3–5, 15; Simon Kuznets, Ann Ratner Miller, and Richard A. Easterlin, *Analyses of Economic Change*, vol. 2 of *Population Redistribution and Economic Growth, United States, 1870–1950* (Philadelphia: American Philosophical Society, 1960), 82; David L. Kaplan and M. Claire Casey, *Occupational Trends in the United States, 1900 to 1950*, Department of Commerce, Bureau of the Census Working Pa-

per No. 5 (Washington, D.C., 1958), 6, 8; *Handbook of Labor Statistics*, U.S. Department of Labor, Bureau of Labor Statistics Bulletin no. 2175 (Washington, D.C., 1983), 44, 46, 50–51; *Historical Statistics of the United States: Colonial Times to 1970 (Part 1)* (Washington, D.C., 1975), 1:139–40, 168; see also William Chafe, *The American Woman: Her Changing Social, Economic, and Political Roles, 1920–1970* (New York: Oxford University Press, 1972), 55. The number of clerks had reached 17 percent by 1980, and women made up 77 percent of them. By contrast, agricultural employment dropped from 52 percent in 1870 to 39 percent in 1900 to 18 percent in 1940 to a mere 3 percent in 1980.

2. Morton Keller, *Affairs of State: Public Life in Late Nineteenth Century America* (Cambridge: Harvard University Press, Belknap Press, 1977), 272–75, 313–14. The influence that well-entrenched political machines had on local governments also remained strong in most cities well into the twentieth century.

3. See, for example, William H. Whyte, Jr., *The Organization Man* (New York: Simon & Schuster, 1956), and David Riesman, with Nathan Glazer and Reuel Denney, *The Lonely Crowd: A Study in the Changing American Character* (1950; reprint, New Haven: Yale University Press, 1969).

4. See Richard Herbert Howe, "Early Office Proletariat? A Reconstruction of Sears' Order Processing—1910," *Studies in Symbolic Interaction* 5 (1984): 155–70.

5. See, for instance, Jürgen Kocka, *White Collar Workers in America, 1890–1940: A Social-Political History in International Perspective*, trans. Maura Kealey (London: Sage Publications, 1980), 124–25; Susan Porter Benson, *Counter Cultures: Saleswomen, Managers, and Customers in American Department Stores, 1890–1940* (Urbana: University of Illinois Press, 1986), 5. For a good overview of the expansion of the clerical workforce as well as a review of the recent historiography, see Stuart M. Blumin, *The Emergence of the Middle Class: Social Experience in the American City, 1760–1900* (Cambridge: Cambridge University Press, 1989), 258–97.

6. Kocka, *White Collar Workers in America*, 116.

7. Joseph F. Kett, "The Adolescence of Vocational Education," in *Work, Youth, and Schooling: Historical Perspectives on Vocationalism in American Education*, ed. Harvey Kantor and David B. Tyack (Stanford: Stanford University Press, 1982), 90–91.

8. Walter Licht, *Working for the Railroad: The Organization of Work in the Nineteenth Century* (Princeton: Princeton University Press, 1983), 34.

9. The elite railroad workers, the conductors and engineers, could not reasonably be bound by all the rules designed for them because the everyday contingencies of railroading forced them to improvise; clerical workers, on

the other hand, were controlled by a new breed of executives and had to go by the book; see Licht, *Working for the Railroad*, 89. See also the Joel West story, chap. 2.

10. This calculation is based on an analysis of 359 letters of application to the C. B. & Q., 1898–1903, C. B. & Q. archives (hereafter, CBQ), 33 1890 3.4; this information was linked with census data to create a collective biography of the applicants.

11. Olin to C. B. & Q., May 3, 1899; Jago to C. B. & Q., December 5, 1902; both letters found in CBQ, 33 1890 3.4.

12. Taylor to C. B. & Q., November 25, 1898; Handrath to Peasley, November 19, 1897; Felthouse to C. B. & Q., May 19, 1902; Willoughby to C. B. & Q., October 10, 1899; Pendleton to Peasley, March 16, 1898; all letters found in CBQ, 33 1880 3.4.

13. Lathrop to Peasley, January 22, 1902; Leavitt to Peasley, January 7, 1898; Kick to C. B. & Q., October 22, 1898; Doherty to C. B. & Q., April 18, 1900; Van Wanroy to Peasley, n.d.; Shorstall to Peasley, November 29, 1898; Sturgis to C. B. & Q., December 13, 1898; all letters found in CBQ, 33 1880 3.4.

14. Ebersold to Peasley, September 4, 1900, CBQ, 33 1880 3.4.

15. CBQ, uncataloged volumes of Pay Rolls for General Office (employees), June 1880, (see note 26 in chap. 4). This payroll recorded 307 clerks distributed as follows: Aurora 2, Burlington 9, Chicago 271, Galesburg 8, Quincy 2, and St. Louis 15. I located 147 of the Chicago clerks in the 1880 city directory and other sources, and identified 117 of this group, together with the other members of their households, in the manuscript schedules of the U.S. census taken the same month as the payroll. Taken together these sources provide an understanding of the clerks' social status and demographic strategies within the context of the family economy. Studying these people in the context of their living environment involved analyzing the socioeconomic characteristics of a total of 824 residents of the city and its immediate suburbs. This included other family members, fellow boarders in boardinghouses, and other non-kin-related members of their households.

16. There were 38 older clerks. See also the salary figures in Cindy Sondik Aron, *Ladies and Gentlemen of the Civil Service: Middle-Class Workers in Victorian America* (New York: Oxford University Press, 1987), 81–86.

17. On the Chicago suburbs see *Suburban Homes along the C. B. & Q.*, in the collection of the Chicago Historical Society; *History of Du Page County, Illinois* (Aurora, Ill.: Knickerbocker & Hodder, 1877), 156–61; Rufus Blanchard, *History of Du Page County, Illinois* (Chicago: O. L. Baskin & Co., 1882), 152, 155, 196–97; A. T. Andreas, *History of Cook County, Illinois* (Chicago: A. T. Andreas, 1884), 187–88, 708–9, 817–19, 876–77.

18. I could locate with certainty in the 1880 census manuscript 26 of these clerks. Eight families had servants. Four families had more than one member working for the C. B. & Q.

19. Six of the twenty-six sons clerking at C. B. & Q. came from blue-collar families.

20. There were forty-one boarders and lodgers.

21. Thomas Butler Gunn, *The Physiology of New York Boarding Houses* (New York: Mason Bros., 1857).

22. Kocka, *White Collar Workers in America*, 52–53, 136–41. When George Bernard Shaw was a clerical worker in the 1870s, he refused even to contemplate joining a trade union, for joining would "have been considered a most ungentlemanly thing to do—almost as outrageous as coming to the office in corduroy trousers, with a belcher handkerchief round my neck—but snobbery apart, it would have been stupid, because I should not have intended to remain a clerk. I should have taken the employer's point of view from the first"; quoted in Geoffrey Crossick, "The Emergence of the Lower Middle Class in Britain: A Discussion," in *The Lower Middle Class in Britain, 1870–1914*, ed. Geoffrey Crossick (London: Croom Helm, 1977), 24.

23. Eric Hobsbawm, *Workers: Worlds of Labor* (New York: Pantheon Books, 1984), 229–30.

24. On "craft control" and "workers' control," see Steve Jefferys, *Management and Managed: Fifty Years of Crisis at Chrysler* (Cambridge: Cambridge University Press, 1986), 14. See also Ileen A. DeVault, "Sons and Daughters of Labor: Class and Clerical Work in Pittsburgh, 1870s–1910s" (Ph.D. diss., Yale University, 1985), 342.

25. Olivier Zunz, *The Changing Face of Inequality: Urbanization, Industrial Development, and Immigrants in Detroit, 1880–1920* (Chicago: University of Chicago Press, 1982), 326–71.

26. Pay Check Rolls and Salary Check Registers in the Ford Motor Company archives (hereafter, FMCA), Accession 707, Boxes 1 and 2 (see note 47 in chap. 3). Finding 248 clerks in the 1910 census out of 446 names in the Ford payroll is high considering the many common names and the fact that many clerks were not heads of households. Among the 248, there were 178 men and 70 women; 82 were heads of households or singles living by themselves, 57 sons and 46 daughters were still living at home with their parents, and 43 were boarders.

27. I was authorized to consult old personnel jackets transferred from the Highland Park factory to the Ford Industrial Archives (hereafter, FIA), still in possession of the Ford Motor Company. Although there were no jackets for any known executive, these files yielded much biographical information

on people listed in the salaried payrolls. For instance, Clarence M. Brown, a stock clerk in 1912, became an investigator. In 1919, after he had become superintendent of the education department, he left to take a Ford dealership in Indiana. Robert Simpson, who was working for Auburn Motor Car Company in Detroit when he was hired in 1913 to travel as a retail salesman, also became an investigator and was rewarded with a Ford agency in Oregon. But not all were so successful, nor were they all educated enough to meet the requirements of their new positions. Joseph W. Grant, for instance, whose reports reveal a dubious knowledge of spelling, was originally hired in 1912 in accounting after having been employed by E-M-F (the car manufacturing company later acquired by Studebaker). After a stint in investigating, he returned to accounting in 1918, where he was demoted to timekeeper in the office.

28. The Reminiscences of Mr. George Brown, FMCA, Oral History Section, May 1953, pp. 94–95.

29. The Reminiscences of Mr. Charles R. Smith, Jr., FMCA, Oral History Section, September 1953, p. 3.

30. Brown Reminiscences, 1, 2, 5, 6, 13–14.

31. Ibid., 15, 16, 13, 18.

32. Ibid., 19, 20.

33. The Reminiscences of Mr. W. C. Klann, FMCA, Oral History Section, September 1955, vol. 1, pp. 106–8. For an interesting essay on the ways in which automobile factory foremen were part of a "supervisory culture" (reinforced by Freemasonry in the 1920s) yet often felt on the "wrong side" of the collar line, see Nelson Lichtenstein, "'The Man in the Middle': A Social History of Automobile Industry Foremen," in *On the Line: Essays in the History of Auto Work*, ed. Nelson Lichtenstein and Stephen Meyer (Urbana: University of Illinois Press, 1989), 153–89.

34. Klann Reminiscenses, vol. 1, pp. 108–9.

35. Ibid., vol. 1, pp. 109–10.

36. Pay Check Rolls and Salary Check Registers in the FMCA, Acc. 707, Boxes 1 and 2; and Klann Reminiscences, vol. 1, p. 13.

37. Personnel jackets in FIA.

38. Klann Reminiscenses, vol. 1, pp. 134–35; see also Sidney Fine, *Sit-Down: The General Motors Strike of 1936–1937* (Ann Arbor: University of Michigan Press, 1970).

39. Reminiscences of Mr. W. Ernest Grimshaw, FMCA, Oral History Section, August 1956, pp. iii, 1, 6, 8–13, 24, 26.

40. Information from the Ford Payroll matched with Manuscript Census for 1910.

41. Zunz, *The Changing Face of Inequality*, 153, 155.

42. First Interview with Mr. Joseph Galamb, FMCA, Oral History Section, January 30, 1952, p. 116.

43. Brown Reminiscences, p. 177.

44. Ibid., pp. 178–81.

45. While it is often difficult to determine the origins of female employees who had left home, most unmarried young women at Ford still lived at home. We are, therefore, in an excellent position to assess the sociocultural composition of this new class of workers through an analysis of the 1910 census. Furthermore some of these young women left memoirs. The personnel jackets at FIA also cast light on these women's origins and lives.

46. Reminiscences of Miss Georgia E. Boyer, FMCA, Oral History Section, January 1954, pp. iii, 1, 3; see also Allan Nevins, with the collaboration of Frank Ernest Hill, *Ford* (New York: Charles Scribner's Sons, 1954), 1:180, 192.

47. Boyer Reminiscences, pp. 1, 3–4.

48. Information taken from individual personnel jackets in the FIA.

49. There were more than fifty stenographers. Other female workers— the filing clerks, the parts clerks, and the telephone operators—tended to come from the same sort of families.

50. Of the lower-middle-class households of the stenographers found in the census, there were twenty working fathers and one working mother.

51. There were 63 working brothers, 15 with blue collar jobs; 72 working sisters, 10 of them dressmakers.

52. Eleven of the stenographers lived by themselves, three boarded with families, eight lived in boardinghouses.

53. There were six boardinghouses ranging in size from 4 to 31 people.

54. Lynn Y. Weiner, *From Working Girl to Working Mother: The Female Labor Force in the United States, 1820–1980* (Chapel Hill: University of North Carolina Press, 1985), 55; see also Lisa Michelle Fine, "'The Record Keepers of Property': The Making of the Female Clerical Labor Force in Chicago, 1870–1930" (Ph.D. diss., University of Wisconsin–Madison, 1985), 277–95; and Mary Catherine Creekmore, "Forging Their Own Identity: Female Clerical Workers in Twentieth Century America" (Master's thesis, University of Virginia, 1988), 27–32.

55. Investigator's report in personnel jacket for Elsie Bruggeman, FIA.

56. Investigator's report in personnel jacket for Bessie Smith, FIA.

57. By then the Sociology Department had been renamed the Investigation Department.

58. Investigator's report in personnel jacket for Florence Cunningham, FIA.

59. See personnel jackets for Mildred Baxter and Fern Chadwick, FIA.

60. See Janice Weiss, "The Advent of Education for Clerical Work in the High School: A Reconsideration of the Historiography of Vocationalism," *Teachers College Record* 83 (Summer 1982): 613–36; Reed Ueda, "The High School and Social Mobility in a Streetcar Suburb: Somerville, Massachusetts, 1870–1910," *Journal of Interdisciplinary History* 14 (Spring 1984): 751–71; and idem, "Suburban Social Change and Education Reform: The Case of Somerville, Massachusetts, 1912–1924," *Social Science History* 3 (1979): 167–203.

61. *Do You Object to Doubling Your Salary?* Pierce Collection, Pierce Junior College, Philadelphia, Pennsylvania; I am indebted to Alyson Brant for this reference. See also Janice Weiss, "Educating for Clerical Work: A History of Commercial Education in the United States Since 1850" (Ed. diss., Harvard University, 1978).

62. *Twenty-Third Annual Catalogue of Goldey College*, 3, 12, 18, 21–23, 25, Hagley Museum and Library.

63. Ibid., 42, 44–45, 15.

64. Carol E. Hoffecker, *Corporate Capital Wilmington in the Twentieth Century* (Philadelphia: Temple University Press, 1983), 40; Marjorie McNinch, "The Changing Face of Rodney Square," *Delaware History* 21 (Spring–Summer 1985): 139–63.

65. Twelve had households of their own.

66. I traced 65 of the Dupont employees (22 men and 43 women) listed in the *Catalogue of Goldey College*, 15, in the manuscript schedules of the 1910 census for Wilmington to construct this collective portrait.

67. See Marianne Morris, "Selling Perfume Suits Some Girls Better Than Cutting Chunks of Pork: Department Store Saleswomen in Wilmington, Delaware, 1910" (Master's thesis, University of Virginia, 1988).

68. According to Kocka, *White Collar Workers in America*, 75, the American sales clerks' union "allied [itself] with organized labor and shared the fundamental positions of the labor movement." But its membership was too small to have much impact.

69. Benson, *Counter Cultures*, 77.

70. *Remington Notes* 4 (no. 11): 8.

71. *Remington Notes* 2 (no. 8): 1.

72. Harry Braverman, *Labor and Monopoly Capital: The Degradation of Work in the Twentieth Century* (New York: Monthly Review Press, 1974).

73. Although many progressive thinkers, Walter Lippmann prominent among them, would have welcomed powerful mass unionism long before it actually acquired power, the expansion of middle-class boundaries into the traditional working class—not only through individual mobility but also through the corporate redefinition of class boundaries—was undoubtedly a

significant factor in delaying mass unionism until after the large corporation had come of age; see Sanford M. Jacoby, *Employing Bureaucracy: Managers, Unions, and the Transformation of Work in American Industry, 1900–1945* (New York: Columbia University Press, 1985), 281.

CHAPTER SIX

1. Arthur M. Schlesinger, Jr., ed., *The Almanac of American History* (New York: Bramhall House, 1983), 446.

2. Quoted in George M. Marsden, *Fundamentalism and American Culture: The Shaping of Twentieth Century Evangelicalism, 1870–1925* (New York: Oxford University Press, 1980), 186.

3. David B. Danbom, *The Resisted Revolution: Urban America and the Industrialization of Agriculture, 1900–1930* (Ames: Iowa State University Press, 1979), 26, 27; see also U.S. Congress, Senate, *Report of the Country Life Commission*, 60th Cong., 2d sess., 1909, S. Doc. 705 (Serial 5408).

4. See Bruce M. Stave, "A Conversation with Bayrd Still," *Journal of Urban History* 3 (May 1977): 332.

5. Arthur M. Schlesinger, *The Rise of the City, 1878–1898* (1933; reprint Chicago: Quadrangle Books, 1971), 79, 80.

6. Stuart Bruchey, *The Wealth of the Nation: An Economic History of the United States* (New York: Harper & Row, 1988), 81, 83–88.

7. Robert Higgs, *The Transformation of the American Economy, 1865–1914: An Essay in Interpretation* (New York: John Wiley & Sons, 1971), 82.

8. See Kathleen Neils Conzen, "Immigrants in Nineteenth Century Agricultural History," in *Agricultural and National Development: Views of the Nineteenth Century*, ed. Louis Ferleger (Ames: Iowa State University Press, 1990); see also Robert C. Ostergren, *A Community Transplanted: The Trans-Atlantic Experience of a Swedish Immigrant Settlement in the Upper Middle West, 1835–1915* (Madison: University of Wisconsin Press, 1988); Jon Gjerde, *From Peasants to Farmers: The Migration from Balestrand, Norway, to the Upper Middle West* (Cambridge: Cambridge University Press, 1985).

9. Mildred R. Bennett, *The World of Willa Cather* (Lincoln: University of Nebraska Press, 1951), 1–2; see also James Woodress, "Willa Cather," in *American Novelists, 1910–1945*, ed. James J. Martine, vol. 9, part I of *Dictionary of Literary Biography* (Detroit: Gale Research Co., 1981), 142.

10. See Elton Perkey, *Perkey's Nebraska Place-Names* (Lincoln, 1982), in the holdings of the Nebraska State Historical Society (hereafter, NSHS); on central places, see Edward Ullman, "A Theory of Location for Cities," *American Journal of Sociology* 46 (May 1941): 853–64.

11. See John T. Hiers and Floyd C. Watkins, "A Chat with Willa Cather," *Resources for American Literary Study* 9 (Spring 1979): 37.

12. Willa Cather, *My Ántonia* (1918), Library of America Edition (New York: Viking Press, 1987), 805.

13. See also John C. Hudson, *Plains Country Towns* (Minneapolis: University of Minnesota Press, 1985), 86–103.

14. Cather, *My Ántonia*, 898, 899, 878.

15. Ibid., 900, 901.

16. On Rural Free Delivery, see Boris Emmet and John E. Jeuck, *Catalogues and Counters: A History of Sears, Roebuck and Company* (Chicago: University of Chicago Press, 1950), 13–14; and Higgs, *The Transformation of the American Economy*, 101.

17. Cather, *My Ántonia*, 821.

18. Alfred D. Chandler, Jr., *The Visible Hand: The Managerial Revolution in American Business* (Cambridge: Harvard University Press, Belknap Press, 1977), 229.

19. Cather, *My Ántonia*, 927.

20. Norval A. Hawkins, "The Individual Transportation Line—Ford Model T," *Ford Times* 5 (1912): 111; Department of Commerce, Bureau of the Census, *Agriculture*, vol. 5 of *Fourteenth Census (1920)* (Washington: GPO, 1922), 513, 514.

21. Cyrus McCormick, *The Century of the Reaper* (Cambridge, Mass.: Riverside Press, 1931), 226.

22. The five companies that merged to form International Harvester Company were McCormick, Deering, Plano, Champion, and Milwaukee; see Helen M. Kramer, "Harvesters and High Finance: Formation of the International Harvester Company," *Business History Review* 38 (Autumn 1964): 290–91, 297.

23. Swift to McCormick, October 15, 1886, State Historical Society of Wisconsin, McCormick Collection (hereafter, SHSW), Series 2X, Box 216; see also, David Hounshell, *From the American System to Mass Production, 1800–1932: The Development of Manufacturing Technology in the United States* (Baltimore: Johns Hopkins University Press, 1984), 159.

24. Lamuth to McCormick, March 10, 1892, SHSW, Series 2X, Box 216.

25. Stevens to Swift, October 27, 1892, SHSW, Series 2X, Box 216.

26. Beardsley to McCormick, August 15, 1874, SHSW, Series 1A, Box 52.

27. Van Histyne to Swift, October 5, 1892, SHSW, Series 2X, Box 216; I have respected the original spelling.

28. Karvan to McCormick, n.d. (filed in 1888), SHSW, Series 2X, Box 216.

29. Ostergren, *A Community Transplanted*, 236–43, 205.

30. Grant McConnell, *The Decline of Agrarian Democracy* (Berkeley: University of California Press, 1953), 6.

31. For most farmers, the debt-to-asset ratio was 13 percent; Higgs, *The Transformation of the American Economy*, 99; for an excellent summary of the economic historians's perspective, see Bruchey, *The Wealth of the Nation*, 89–91.

32. Stephen Skowronek, *Building a New American State: The Expansion of National Administrative Capacities, 1877–1920* (Cambridge: Cambridge University Press, 1982), 126; see also George Miller, *Railroads and the Granger Laws* (Madison: University of Wisconsin Press, 1971), 94, 170.

33. Montgomery Ward and Sears offered advantages over country stores forced to charge high prices because of slow turnover, low volume, uncertain supply, and jobbers' markup; Emmet and Jeuck, *Catalogues and Counters*, 16–19.

34. Beardsley to McCormick, April 14, 1868, SHSW, Series 1A, Box 27.

35. Beardsley to McCormick, January 13, 1874, SHSW, Series 1A, Box 52.

36. Ibid.

37. Status of Harvesting Machines Received and Disposed of . . . during 1874, by E. C. Beardsley, SHSW, Series 1A, Box 31.

38. Preliminary Report of E. C. Beardsley, 1874, SHSW, Series 1A, Box 52.

39. Addis to McCormick, January 17, 1874, SHSW, Series 1A, Box 52.

40. Addis to McCormick, January 30, 1874, SHSW, Series 1A, Box 52.

41. Addis to McCormick, March 2, 1874, SHSW, Series 1A, Box 52.

42. Addis to McCormick, April 11, 1874, SHSW, Series 1A, Box 52.

43. Addis to McCormick, May 9, 1873, SHSW, Series 1A, Box 48.

44. Addis to McCormick, May 27, 1873, SHSW, Series 1A, Box 48.

45. Addis to McCormick, May 28, 1873, SHSW, Series 1A, Box 48; Addis to McCormick, June 12, 1874, SHSW, Series 1A, Box 52; Gould to McCormick, August 18, 1876, SHSW, Series 1A, Box 62.

46. Addis to McCormick, April 26, 1868, SHSW, Series 1A, Box 26.

47. Speech Concluding Debate on the Chicago Platform, in William J. Bryan, *The First Battle: A Story of the Campaign of 1896* (Chicago: W. B. Conkey Co., 1896), 206.

48. Stewart to McCormick, September 5, 1896, SHSW, Series 1A, Box 111.

49. See James Turner, "Understanding the Populists," *Journal of American History* 67 (September 1980): 354–73.

50. Stewart to McCormick, September 5, 1896, SHSW, Series 1A, Box 111.

51. See, for instance, Stanley Lebergott, *The Americans: An Economic Record* (New York: W. W. Norton, 1984), 297–310; and Milton Friedman and Anna

Jacobson Schwartz, *A Monetary History of the United States, 1867–1960* (Princeton: Princeton University Press, 1963), 89–134.

52. Stewart to McCormick, November 16, 1896, SHSW, Series 1A, Box 111.

53. Allan G. Bogue, *From Prairie to Corn Belt: Farming on the Illinois and Iowa Prairies in the Nineteenth Century* (Chicago: Quadrangle Books, 1968), 32–38, 172–80; Robert P. Swierenga, *Pioneers and Profits: Land Speculation on the Iowa Frontier* (Ames: Iowa State University Press, 1968), 15–17, 99, 212, 215; and Susan E. Gray, "Family, Land, and Credit: Yankee Communities of the Michigan Frontier, 1830–1860" (Ph.D. diss., University of Chicago, 1985), 257–319.

54. See Agnes Larson, *John A. Johnson: An Uncommon Man* (Northfield, Minn.: Norwegian-American Historical Association, 1969), 142, 155–56, 164–65.

55. Addis to McCormick, February 15, 1869, SHSW, Series 1A, Box 31.

56. Jordan to Gould, November 27, 1884, SHSW, Series 1A, Box 93; I have retained the original spelling.

57. Stewart to McCormick, September 10, 1895, SHSW, Series 1A, Box 111.

58. Stewart to McCormick, July 17, 1896, SHSW, Series 1A, Box 111; see also Stewart to McCormick, June 7, October 31, November 30, 1895; July 8, and August 18, 1896; all letters from SHSW, Series 1A, Box 111.

59. Between 1857 and 1880, 2,339 civil cases were filed with the district court of Stearns County, Minnesota. In a 5 percent sample of these cases (kept in the Minnesota State Archives), Kathleen Conzen found eight instances of litigation involving McCormick or other implement manufacturers; in some instances, the companies sued dealers; in other cases, they sued farmers. I am indebted to Kathleen Conzen for this information.

60. "The Credit Man," *Harvester World* 1 (October 1909): 14.

61. "On Collecting," *Harvester World* 1 (May 1910): 14.

62. Daniel Horowitz, *The Morality of Spending: Attitudes toward the Consumer Society in America, 1875–1940* (Baltimore: Johns Hopkins University Press, 1985), 148–49.

63. As E. L. Ullman posited in "A Theory of Location for Cities," *American Journal of Sociology* 46 (May 1941): 853–64.

64. Quoted in Brian J. L. Berry and Frank E. Horton, *Geographic Perspectives on Urban Systems* (Englewood Cliffs, N.J.: Prentice-Hall, 1970), 171.

65. Like Bonneville in Frank Norris, *The Octopus: A Story of California* (1901), Library of America Edition (New York: Viking Press, 1986).

66. See Charles W. McCurdy, "American Law and the Marketing Structure

of the Large Corporation, 1875–1890," *Journal of Economic History* 38 (September 1978): 631–49, on Singer; Wayne G. Broehl, Jr., *John Deere's Company: A History of Deere and Company and Its Times* (New York: Doubleday, 1984), 174–75, on Deere; and for a general treatment of distribution see Chandler, *Visible Hand*, 287–314.

67. Addis to McCormick, March 6, 1867, SHSW, Series 1A, Box 21; and Addis to McCormick, n.d., 1867, SHSW, Series 1A, Box 21.

68. Addis to McCormick, November 14, 1874, SHSW, Series 1A, Box 52.

69. Addis to McCormick, January 30, 1874, SHSW, Series 1A, Box 52.

70. Information on International Harvester Agents' careers at Harvester or at one of the five companies prior to the merger (see note 22 above) was gathered from card files on individual agents kept at the historical archive of the International Harvester Company (now Navistar International Transportation Corp.; hereafter IHC).

71. See the map of the location of the agencies in *Harvester World* 2 (January 1911): 16–17; population figures were found in Department of Commerce, Bureau of the Census, *Population, Thirteenth Census (1910)* (Washington: GPO, 1913), 2:605–9, 3:39–40, 338–39, 690–91; the composition of the agencies was derived from information in the IHC card files mentioned in note 70 and from multiple references to agents found in *Harvester World*.

72. Salary information from IHC card files.

73. Bureau of the Census, *Population, Thirteenth Census (1910)* 3:40; Federal Writers' Project, Works Progress Administration, State of Nebraska, *Lincoln City Guide* (Lincoln: Woodruff Printing, 1937), 10–11; Arthur B. Hayes and Sam D. Cox, *History of the City of Lincoln, Nebraska* (Lincoln: State Journal Co., 1889), 204.

74. *Lincoln City Guide*, 13–14. Lawrence Goodwyn sees Bryan as the leader of only a "shadow movement"; see *The Populist Movement: A Short History of the Agrarian Revolt in America* (New York: Oxford University Press, 1978), 143.

75. "Guy M. Davison Taken by Death," *Lincoln Star*, June 1, 1931.

76. Lincoln Commercial Club, Minutes, Membership in 1898, NSHS), MS 612.S1, vol. 4; Lincoln Commercial Club, Minutes, Inventory, May 1, 1910, NSHS, MS 612.S1, Vol. 5.

77. Minutes, February 14 and May 9, 1910, NSHS, MS 612.S1, vol. 5.

78. Minutes, June 13, 1910, NSHS, MS 612.S1, vol. 5.

79. They noted that the Rochester Chamber of Commerce had passed a motion not against a reasonable advance in freight rates; Minutes, June 13, 1910, NSHS, MS 612.S1, vol. 5.

80. Minutes, October 18 and February 22, 1909, NSHS, MS 612.S1, vol. 5; and *Crawford Tribune*, May 7, 1909.

81. Bureau of the Census, *Population, Thirteenth Census (1910)* 3:39.

82. E. M. Westervelt, Rambling Reminiscences, C. B. & Q. archives, New-berry Library, 32.92, 10.

83. *Crawford, Nebraska, 1886–1961*, 12, 21–22, in the holdings of the NSHS; IHC card file and *Harvester World*.

84. *Crawford Tribune*, January 1, January 22, February 12, February 29, and March 16, 1909.

85. Obituary, *Nebraska State Journal*, December 6, 1911.

86. *Crawford Tribune*, April 8, April 22, and May 29, 1910. Women were not yet voting in Nebraska.

87. "Be Proud That You Are a Salesman," *Harvester World* 3 (May 1912): 1.

88. IHC card file; and "Reward for Faithful Service," *Harvester World* 16 (April 1925): 21.

89. "The General Agent's Desk: The Blockman That Gets the Business," *Harvester World* 1 (November 1909): 4; for a broader perspective on occupa-tional mobility, see Stephan Thernstrom, *The Other Bostonians: Poverty and Progress in the American Metropolis, 1880–1970* (Cambridge: Harvard Univer-sity Press, 1973).

90. "Your Predecessors Had a Poorer Chance," *Harvester World* 1 (Novem-ber 1909): 15.

91. "The IHC Merit System," *Harvester World* 1 (March 1910): 2–3.

92. Beardsley to McCormick, June 30, 1867, NSHS, Series 1A, Box 21.

93. Beardsley to McCormick, September 18, 1880, NSHS, Series 1A, Box 75.

94. "The Trade Value of State Fairs," *Harvester World* 2 (November 1910): 2–3; and "Educational Value to the Farmer of State Fairs," *Harvester World* 2 (November 1910): 6–8.

95. "The IHC Service Bureau," *Harvester World* 3 (July 1912): 27–28.

96. Summary of the More Important Suggestions of the Conference of State Leaders in County Agent Work Held at Chicago, Ill., December 7–10, 1914, Records of President William O. Thompson, Ohio State University Ar-chives; I would like to thank William H. Harbaugh for providing me with this and the next reference.

97. F. L. Allen to Kelley Island Lime and Transport Co., November 21, 1916, Records of President William O. Thompson, Ohio State University Archives.

98. There were 639 men and 159 women county agents in 1912; see Dan-bom, *The Resisted Revolution*, 71.

99. Gladys Baker, *The County Agent* (Chicago: University of Chicago Press, 1939), 33, 35; see also William H. Harbaugh, "The Limits of Voluntarism: The County Agent System and the Conservation Movement," paper given at a symposium in honor of Arthur S. Link at Princeton University in May 1989.

CHAPTER SEVEN

1. Roland Marchand, *Advertising the American Dream: Making Way for Modernity, 1920–1940* (Berkeley: University of California Press, 1985), 8.

2. See Charles W. McCurdy, "American Law and the Marketing Structure of the Large Corporation, 1875–1890," *Journal of Economic History* 38 (September 1978): 631–49.

3. See ibid., 637, on the origins of the word "drummer."

4. Theodore Dreiser, *Sister Carrie* (1900) Library of America Edition (New York: Viking Press, 1987), 5.

5. See Neil Harris, "The Drama of Consumer Desire," in *Yankee Enterprise: The Rise of the American System of Manufactures*, ed. Otto Mayr and Robert C. Post (Washington, D.C.: Smithsonian Institution Press, 1981), 196.

6. The correspondence between Wiener and Arlington is in Hagley Museum and Library (hereafter, HML), Accession 472, Series II, Part 1, Box 125.

7. Karl Baedeker, ed., *The United States, with an Excursion into Mexico: A Handbook for Travellers—1893* (New York: Da Capo Press, 1971), 302, 290.

8. Wiener to Sickels, July 8, July 10, July 12, July 17, August 5, 1895; Sickels to Wiener, July 1, July 19, September 6, 1895; all letters from HML, Acc. 472, Series II, Part 1, Box 125.

9. France to Cahen, November 5, 1892; Sickels to Palmer, November 16, 1892; Sickels to Davis, December 30, 1892; France to Creasey, June 1, 1893; Sickels to McManus, July 14, 1894; Crane to Sickels, December 2, 1895; Crane to Blancjour, December 10, 1895; Crane to Fuller, December 12, 1895; Crane to Palmer, December 18, 1895; Crane to Fuller, December 26, 1895; Crane to Sickels, November 17, 1896; Crane to Fuller, January 22, 1897; Crane to Blancjour, January 22, 1897; Crane to Armstrong, January 29, 1897; and Crane to Armstrong, January 10, 1899; all letters from HML, Acc. 472, Series 2, Part 1, Box 99.

10. Alfred D. Chandler, Jr., and Stephen Salsbury, *Pierre S. du Pont and the Making of the Modern Corporation* (New York: Harper & Row, 1971), 140; and Alfred D. Chandler, Jr., *The Visible Hand: The Managerial Revolution in American Business* (Cambridge: Harvard University Press, Belknap Press, 1977), 442.

11. This data was compiled and computerized from the lists of salesmen in *Du Pont Sales Directory* (1917), 6–27, and *Sales Directory* (June 1918), 6–36; both directories at HML.

12. See the *Modern Business Talk* collection (48 lectures), HML.

13. "The Dominance of Salesmanship," *Modern Business Talk*, no. 11 (Revision 1923; New York: Alexander Hamilton Institute, 1919), 8, 12.

14. On the widespread ideology of service, see Jeffrey Charles, "Service Clubs in Twentieth Century America" (Ph.D. diss., Johns Hopkins University, 1987).

15. The following paragraphs are based upon Address by Pierre S. du Pont, Atlantic City, General Sales Convention, Garden Pier, June 17, 1918, 1–4, 7, 8, 10, 13, 14, 16, 17, 20, HML, Acc. 1662, Series II, Part 2, Box 69; figures for powder production from anniversary number "125 Years of Usefulness, 1802–1927" of the *Du Pont Magazine* (1927): 27, HML.

16. *Report of Proceedings at the Fourth Convention of the Sales Department of E. I. Du Pont de Nemours & Company Held at Wilmington, Del., February 21st to 25th, 1916*, 183–85, HML.

17. See *Salesmen's Instruction* (40 booklets, Wilmington: E. I. Du Pont de Nemours & Co., 1918–20); *Business and the War* (New York: Alexander Hamilton Institute, 1917); and Col. E. G. Buckner, "The Relation of Du Pont American Industries to the War," in *Salesmen's Instruction: History of the Du Pont Company* (Wilmington: E. I. Du Pont de Nemours & Co., 1920), 40–53, HML.

18. See *Salesmen's Instruction: History*, 2.

19. *Report of Proceedings at the Fourth Convention*, 350–51.

20. *Program of the Ninth Annual Banquet, Sales Convention and Dinner, E. I. Du Pont de Nemours & Company, January 5, 1922*, HML.

21. E. T. Wolf, "Don't Abuse It, Use It: System," HML, Acc. 641, Series II, Part 2, Box 352.

22. Ibid.; see also Pierre du Pont to Seaver, February 27, 1950, HML Longwood Manuscripts 10, File 384.

23. *Report of Proceedings at the Fourth Convention*, 69–77.

24. *Report of the Proceedings at the Third Convention of the Sales Department of E. I. Du Pont de Nemours Powder Company Held at Washington, D.C., October 15, 16, 17, 18, 19, and 20, 1906*, 27, HML.

25. *Report of Proceedings at Second Convention of the Sales Department of E. I. Du Pont de Nemours Powder Company, Indianapolis, Ind., November 20th–25th, 1905*, 3–9, HML; and *Report of the Proceedings at the Third Convention*, 17.

26. See Chandler, *Visible Hand*, 442, on engineers at Du Pont.

27. See, for instance, the paper by Arthur La Motte of the Technical Division, *Report of the Proceedings at the Third Convention*, 140ff.; and the discussion of quarrying by S. R. Russell, Technical Representative of the Wilmington Office, *Report of Proceedings at the Fourth Convention*, 219ff.

28. See, for instance, *Programme, Second Convention, Sales Department, E. I. Du Pont Company* (1905, Claypool Hotel, November 20 to 25, Indianapolis, Ind.) HML; and *Banquet, Sales Convention, Harrison's Inc.* (August 16, 1917) HML.

29. Memo from President to Director of Sales, February 17, 1916, HML, Acc. 1661, Series II, Part 2, Box 69; the du Ponts supported the Episcopal Church but even there never showed religious zeal.

30. This apparent deviation from neutrality by a well-known advertising executive reflected the ambivalence many an advocate of consumption felt toward unlimited consumerism and a strong attachment to those proven Christian virtues of moderation and thrift; see T. J. Jackson Lears, "From Salvation to Self-Realization: Advertising and the Therapeutic Roots of the Consumer Culture, 1880–1930," in *The Culture of Consumption: Critical Essays in American History, 1880–1920*, ed. Richard Wightman Fox and T. J. Jackson Lears (New York: Pantheon Books, 1983), 33; Warren I. Susman, *Culture as History: The Transformation of American Society in the Twentieth Century* (New York: Pantheon Books, 1973), 122–31; and Marchand, *Advertising the American Dream*, 159.

31. *Fifth Annual Round Table Dinner of the Du Pont Fabrikoid Knockers' Club, Joint Sales & Operating Forces, at Elks Club, Newburgh, New York* (Tuesday, December 28, 1915), HML.

32. First Annual Banquet Songs, Du Pont American Industries, HML, Acc. 641, Series II, Part 2, Box 352.

33. *Program of the Ninth Annual Banquet, Sales Convention and Dinner.*

34. On Lord's marketing efforts, see memos in HML, Acc. 473, Box 1384.

35. Bulletin No. 172 (Gen.), HML, Acc. 641, Series II, Part 2, Box 352.

36. *Report of Proceedings at the Fourth Convention*, 342.

37. See Irénée du Pont to Wishart, January 19, 1911; Wishart memo, October 16, 1911; and Coyne to Barksdale, November 22, 1911; all in HML, Acc. 518, Series II, Part 2, Box 1011.

38. *Personal and Confidential Information for the Use of Salesmen of Du Pont Chemical Works* (Wilmington: E. I. Du Pont de Nemours & Co., 1916), 7, HML.

39. Du Pont to Director of Sales, September 17, 1918, HML, Acc. 1662, Series II, Part 2, Box 69.

40. *Report of the Proceedings at the Third Convention*, 7–8.

41. Memo to Carpenter, Egle, and Patterson from Coyne, January 9, 1922, HML, Acc. 473, File 505.

42. I arrived at this figure by searching the lists of salesmen in the *Du Pont Sales Directory* (1917) and *Sales Directory* (1918) in the *Du Pont Magazine* from 1913 to 1955.

43. See the letters to du Pont from Wishart, HML, Longwood Manuscripts, Acc. 10, File 418; and from Phellis, HML, Longwood Manuscripts, Acc. 10, File 733; and the letters to Raskob from Calderon, HML, Acc. 473, File 325; from Wishart, HML, Acc. 473, File 2499; from Phellis, HML, Acc.

473, File 1816; from Orr, HML, Acc. 473, File 1748; and from Coyne, HML, Acc. 473, File 505.

44. See the material on the Efficiency System, HML, Acc. 641, Series II, Part 2, Box 352; and *Salesmen's Instruction: The Du Pont Efficiency Plan*, HML.

45. Undated memo from Wolf's Den; Peters to Wolf, July 24, 1917; and Peters to Wolf, February 24, 1919; all from HML, Acc. 641, Series II, Part 2, Box 352.

46. *Information for and Advice to All Members of the Sales Department of E. I. Du Pont de Nemours Powder Company Based upon Suggestions Submitted for the Quarter Ending June 30, 1908* [Suggestions; Pamphlet No. 2] (Baltimore: Lord Baltimore Press, n.d.), 7, HML; and President to Heads of Departments, April 15, 1914, HML, Acc. 472, Series II, Part 3, Box 123, File 5.

47. *Personal and Confidential Information for the Use of Salesmen*, 23, 37; see also William Graebner, *A History of Retirement: The Meaning and Function of an American Institution, 1885–1978* (New Haven: Yale University Press, 1980), 120–49; and David Hackett Fischer, *Growing Old in America* (New York: Oxford University Press, 1977), 157–95. There were 143 people on pensions in 1914, and 149 in 1915; Number of People Shown on Salary Roll and Wage Rolls as of October 31, 1914 and December 31, 1915, HML, Acc. 1662, Box 8, Folder "Salary Sheets."

48. The Howard-Middleton affair can be traced in the correspondence in HML, Acc. 518, Box 1003A and Acc. 473, Box 123, File 62.

49. Barksdale was married to one of Charles I. du Pont's sisters; see Chandler and Salsbury, *Pierre S. du Pont*, 49, and charts II and III facing 306.

50. For instance, Harry Austin, former vice-president and general manager of the General Motors Building Corporation, was able to live off his stock dividends after he left the company; see Austin to Raskob, October 3, 1934, HML, Acc. 473, File 108.

51. See S. R. Russell, "Springing Holes: Enlarging the Bottom of a Bore Hole for Blasting," *Du Pont Magazine* 11 (November 1919): 22–23.

52. F. W. Wilson, "Increasing Cotton Production," *Du Pont Magazine* 8 (April 1918): 8–9.

53. E. R. Galvin, "Speaking of Cotton Consumption," *Du Pont Magazine* 18 (May 1924): 13.

54. A. E. Anderson, "Protecting the Lambs," *Du Pont Magazine* 10 (February 1919): 20–21.

55. E. T. Lednum and R. H. Summer, "Zinc and Lead," *Du Pont Magazine* 8 (June 1918): 5–7, 19; and *Sales Directory* (1918), 9, 25.

56. L. A. Allen, "Bauxite Mining in Arkansas," *Du Pont Magazine* 19 (July 1925): 6–7, 15; A. E. Anderson, "Road Building in the Rockies," *Du Pont*

Magazine 12 (May 1920): 4–5; G. A. Kynaston, "Ditch-Blasting in Southeast Missouri," *Du Pont Magazine* 13 (October 1920): 3–4; John E. Miller, "The Virginian Railroad Improvement," *Du Pont Magazine* 13 (October 1920): 6–7; Guy G. Means, "Minnesota Land Clearing Special," *Du Pont Magazine* 13 (September 1920): 4–5.

57. E. T. Lednum, "The World's Greatest Hydro-Electric Power Plant," *Du Pont Magazine* 1 (October 1913): 2–7; E. M. McCarney, "Reclaiming Swamp Land," *Du Pont Magazine* 2 (January 1914): 6–7; A. E. Anderson, "Pike's Peak Automobile Highway," *Du Pont Magazine* 7 (November–December 1916): 5–7.

58. H. G. Horton, "Opening a New Railroad in Kentucky," *Du Pont Magazine* 18 (June 1924): 8–9; B. H. Nelson, "Quarrying a Canal in the Heart of a City," *Du Pont Magazine* 18 (June 1924): 4–5.

59. "The Australians Also Like Fabrikoid-finished Cars," *Du Pont Magazine* 17 (October 1923): 12; Henry Ferris, Jr., "Refinishing the Old Car," *Du Pont Magazine* 10 (January 1919): 12–13; G. M. Breinig, "Selling Service with Paint," *Du Pont Magazine* 11 (September 1919): 23–24.

60. R. H. Matthey, "Where California Leads the World," *Du Pont Magazine* 12 (June 1920): 6; on California, see Kevin Starr, *Inventing the Dream: California through the Progressive Era* (New York: Oxford University Press, 1985).

61. "Demonstrations and What They Accomplish," *Du Pont Magazine* 1 (November 1913): 11; Garrett M. Stack, "Getting Blasting with Photography," *Du Pont Magazine* 7 (October 1916): 17.

62. W. A. Holt, "The Merchandising of Toilet-ware," *Du Pont Magazine* 11 (September 1919): 12–13.

63. James A. Gwyn, "The Manufacture and Use of Pyralin," *Du Pont Magazine* 10 (March 1919): 12–13; L. B. Steele, "Putting the 'Win' in Windows," *Du Pont Magazine* 16 (September–October 1922): 6; idem, "Rayon on Dress Parade," *Du Pont Magazine* 20 (December 1926): 6.

64. A. H. Berwald, "The Country Dealer's Opportunity," *Du Pont Magazine* 10 (March 1919): 14–15.

65. Thomas Haskell, "Capitalism and the Origins of the Humanitarian Sensibility, Part 1," *American Historical Review* 90 (April 1985): 339–61, and "Capitalism and the Origins of the Humanitarian Sensibility, Part 2," *American Historical Review* 90 (June 1985): 547–66, stresses the civilizing influence of the market; T. J. Jackson Lears, "The Concept of Cultural Hegemony: Problems and Possibilities," *American Historical Review* 90 (June 1985): 567–93, stresses the more common opposite view. See also Albert O. Hirschman, *Rival Views of Market Society and Other Recent Essays* (New York: Elisabeth Sifton Books/Viking, 1986).

66. *Report of the Proceedings at the Third Convention*, 13.

67. Ibid., 11.

68. To the Students of "The Science of Service Course" (multipart memo), June 2, 1911, HML, Acc. 473, Box 777, File 690.

69. Ibid., Rules for the Development of Endurance or Health.

70. Ibid., Rules for the Development of Ability; and "Science of Service," Letter no. 6.

CONCLUSION

1. *American Journal of Sociology* 20 (January 1915): 433–86 and 20 (March 1915): 613–28.

2. Ibid., 461, 463, 471, 478.

3. McCormick to Small, February 3, 1915, State Historical Society of Wisconsin, McCormick Collection (hereafter, SHSW), 1C, Part 5, Box 122, File 26. Small's circular reached McCormick's desk only on November 20, 1914. The *AJS* claims to have published all answers. McCormick's letter was either not sent or sent too late to be included in the published symposium.

4. And his brother Harold had married John D. Rockefeller's daughter.

5. Thorstein Veblen, *The Engineers and the Price System* (New York: Viking Press, 1921), 41, 74.

6. On conflicts at the Rouge plant, see Robert Lacey, *Ford: The Men and the Machine* (Boston: Little, Brown & Co., 1986): 360, 362.

7. John Kenneth Galbraith, *American Capitalism: The Concept of Countervailing Power* (Boston: Houghton Mifflin, 1952).

8. Raskob to McCormick, January 30, 1936, SHSW, 1C, Part 9, Box 280, File 27. Irénée du Pont also tried to recruit McCormick, but to no avail.

9. C. Wright Mills, *White Collar: The American Middle Classes* (New York: Oxford University Press, 1953), 164.

10. Alfred P. Sloan, Jr., in collaboration with Boyden Sparkes, *Adventures of a White-Collar Man* (New York: Doubleday, Doran, 1941).

11. Amidst an abundant literature, the latest restatement of this point is John Bodnar's *The Transplanted, A History of Immigrants in Urban America* (Bloomington: Indiana University Press, 1985). Immigrants to urban America relied on their particular ethnic traditions to cushion the effects of industrial capitalism.

12. Joseph A. Schumpeter, *Capitalism, Socialism, and Democracy* (New York: Harper & Bros., 1942), 81.

INDEX

71; as protoexecutives, 24,
26–27, 30. *See also* Hardware
store owners; International
Harvester Company; McCor-
mick Harvesting Machinery
Company; Merchants; Pennsylvania; Salesmen
Corporations: and antitrust movement, 33; diversity of, 101; and
efficiency, 35–36, 68; and
farming, 151–54, 163–65,
169–70, 173; growth of, 1,
68–69; and merchants, 18,
25–26, 31–32; and the middle
class, 8, 12, 39; and the national market, 68, 176; and
regulation, 34–35; and specialization, 13. *See also* Bureaucracy; Managers; Middle class;
Railroads; Statistics; White-
collar workers; *and individual
corporations*
Country Life Commission, 150
County agents, 150, 172
Couzens, James, 81, 88–89, 133,
135, 138
Cox, D. W., 24
Coyne, William, 184, 188–89
Croly, Herbert, 13, 201
Curtze, Charles, 30
Curtze, Hermann, 30

Darwinism, 61, 63, 77
Datesman, Charles, 28
Debs, Eugene V., 199
DeForest, Robert, 95
Degener, August, 84–85
Dembitz, Lewis, 34
Devine, Edward T., 94
Diehl, F. H., 90, 138
Doane, Thomas, 54–55

Dodge, Grenville M., 55
Dodge, Horace E., 82
Dodge, James M., 35
Dodge, John F., 82
Dreiser, Theodore, 176, 187
Drew, Daniel, 38
Du Bois, W. E. B., 199
Dun & Bradstreet, 139
du Pont, Alfred, 17
du Pont, Coleman: and antitrust
movement, 71, 78; and conflict
management, 192; and organizational matters, 17, 69, 72, 76;
real estate ventures of, 90, 122,
180, 225n.20; and E. S. Rice,
31–33; and F. W. Taylor, 35
du Pont, Henry, 17
du Pont, Irénée, 72–73, 78, 189
du Pont, Lammot, 17, 26
du Pont, Mary, 26
du Pont, Pierre, 26, 90, 122; and
antitrust movement, 77–78;
and corporate ideology, 182–
83, 186, 200; and education,
78; and executives, 190; and
General Motors Corporation,
83, 188–90, 202; and organizational matters, 17, 69–70,
72–74; real estate ventures of,
123; and E. S. Rice, 31
du Pont, Samuel Hallock, 26, 77
du Pont, Sophie, 8
du Pont, Victor, 26
Du Pont de Nemours (E. I.) Powder
Company: agents of, 17; and
antitrust movement, 33, 77–
78, 183; conflict management
at, 191–92; diversification of,
70–71; and employee loyalty,
188–89; employee programs
at, 76–78; and expertise,

138, 147–48, 202–3, 243n.68,
243n.73; as depicted, 2–3,
105–6; and the family economy, 116–17, 130, 140; and
foremen, 135–36; growth
of, 124–26; and manual labor, 127; and salesgirls, 126,
146–47; as subordinates,
41, 43, 45, 49–53, 108, 117
120, 129, 141–44; training of,
144–46; women among, 8,
117, 119, 126, 138. *See also*
Goldey College; Remington;
Skycrapers; Stenographers;
and individual corporations
Wiebe, Robert, 9
Wills, C. Harold, 84, 86, 88
Wilson, Woodrow, 113, 186
Wolf, E. T., 185, 190–91, 193
Woolworth, Frank W., 113–14, 123

Women's history, 8
Women: as business agents, 32;
in department stores, 145–
46; and marriage, 121, 133,
142–43; in the workforce, 116,
124, 126, 147–48. *See also-*
White-collar workers; *and individual corporations*
World War I, 70, 76, 78, 89, 92,
104, 112, 186–87, 199
World's Columbian Exposition, 53,
112, 155
Wright, Frank Lloyd, 108

Yale University, 26, 48, 56
Young Men's Christian Association, 95

Zionism, 36